THE RIGHT TO A DECENT HOUSE

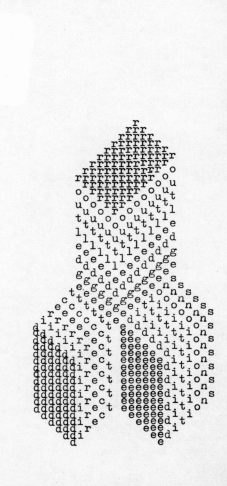

THE RIGHT TO A DECENT HOUSE

SIDNEY JACOBS

ROUTLEDGE DIRECT EDITIONS

ROUTLEDGE & KEGAN PAUL
London and Boston

First published in 1976
by Routledge & Kegan Paul Ltd
Broadway House, 68-74 Carter Lane
London EC4V 5EL and
9 Park Street,
Boston, Mass. 02108, USA
Manuscript typed by May Ling Wee
Printed and bound in Great Britain
by Unwin Brothers Limited,
The Gresham Press, Old Woking, Surrey
A member of the Staples Printing Group
© Sidney Jacobs 1976

ISBN 0 7100 8305 X

CONTENTS

v

PREFACE

Only the working class know what it is to be rehoused by a local
authority but their viewpoint is seldom recorded. The history of
local working-class militancy is frequently forgotten and my
account of one community's struggle was written in the belief that
the working class must preserve its heritage. This book is based
on my experiences as a community worker in the Gairbraid housing
clearance area of Maryhill, Glasgow, and I have attempted to
describe events from the community's perspective with the local
leaders being quoted throughout.

   The Gairbraid story is about community action, about a working-
class community under stress and about local authority rehousing.
In providing a detailed, blow for blow guide to the campaign, the
book is aimed at community workers, local activists, sociologists
and others interested in the working class and the ordeal they must
endure to attain decent living standards. Glasgow's rehousing
policy and practice is analysed throughout: by understanding the
rationale behind rehousing, local communities may best protect
their own interests. Little appears to have changed in Glasgow
since Gairbraid and in spite of new housing legislation and local
government reorganization, the conclusions drawn from the campaign
seem as valid now in late 1975 as they seemed then, between 1971
and 1973. Glasgow is an extreme among British cities, but rehousing there seems basically no different from that practised
anywhere else. The book thus attempts to explain local authority
rehousing, not merely in Glasgow but as practised throughout urban
Britain.

   The view taken here is that it is mistaken to blame individuals
for housing policy rather than the social, political and economic
structures of society. Although I am highly critical of Glasgow
Corporation's performance in Gairbraid, this is directed at the
system and is not intended to reflect on any individual. No one
is singled out for criticism; indeed, many council tenants have
reason to be grateful to a number of dedicated but anonymous
officials and councillors without whose effort rehousing would
have been a great deal more painful.

   Gairbraid's experience was of rehousing in a highly developed
capitalist democracy. While the alternative of a socialist

solution to our housing problems is not posed in this book, implicit in the arguments presented is that socialism offers the only possible way out of the present mess. In this sense, the book does not merely criticize without suggesting solutions: by demonstrating the solidarity, ability, commitment and potential that exists in local communities, Gairbraid glimpses a future where the working class have the power to control their own destinies.

For being permitted to share in Gairbraid's experience, I gratefully thank the people of the area. It is not possible to name all of those whose many acts of kindness and lavish hospitality I warmly remember. I cherish the friendship of the local activists and feel privileged to have been associated with their organization, the Gairbraid Housing Committee, and thank in particular its chairman, John Moir; its vice-chairman, Jimmy Gallagher; its secretary, Annie Mallon; and the other members: Georgina Atkinson, Davey and Jeannette Bouse, Ella Donnelly, Isa Hanlon, Adam and Margaret Hobson, Eileen Kelly, Jackie Moir, John Smith and Hugh and Eileen Thompson.

I was particularly fortunate in the assistance I received from Jane Skinner and Joan Shannon who, at different times, worked with me in Gairbraid. When Jane Skinner began work rehousing had only just started in Gairbraid. In addition to being responsible for organizing the local pre-school playgroup and mothers' group, she was actively involved in all aspects of the rehousing campaign. For instance, it was she who first drew local attention to Glasgow's housing visitor's report. Local people are perhaps in the best position to judge the contributions made by community workers: Jane Skinner was greatly missed when she left Glasgow and the fondness with which she is remembered is a tribute to her skill. Gairbraid, however, was extremely fortunate in her replacement. Less than thirty families remained in Gairbraid when Joan Shannon began work. She 'was appalled that people still lived in such conditions', and on climbing the stairs of deserted tenements admits to being 'terrified'. With much resourcefulness, initiative, energy and dedication she worked virtually single-handed, with the last families until the area was finally cleared. There can be no doubt that the pace of rehousing from Gairbraid was greatly accelerated by her efforts, attested to by the lasting relationships she formed with many of the people which continued long after they had been rehoused. Joan Shannon also conducted interviews and helped with transcribing the material and her ideas and enthusiasm were a continual source of encouragement throughout the writing of this book.

Community workers, operating in unstructured situations, often need constant support and encouragement. Richard Bryant performed this role for me in Gairbraid. Whenever I needed it, I was able to draw upon his considerable experience, knowledge and advice. It was he who first introduced me to Alinsky and helped shape my ideas about community action. I recall with great pleasure the long hours we spent together, heatedly discussing Gairbraid and never, or almost never, allowing the beer we consumed to distract us from the issues - if only we had thought to record those sessions.

The Gairbraid story would be incomplete without special mention of Ken McLachlan, who has devoted much of his life to the working-class cause. He is owed an important debt of gratitude for so readily coming to Gairbraid's aid when, at crucial moments, the community needed him. Thanks too, to Harry Liddell and Davey Brown for their encouragement and willingness to speak at Gairbraid's public meetings. Important also was the assistance received from Jim Maclean and Peter Robson who were forever prepared to rush to Gairbraid whenever their services were required.

Raeburn Mackie and Alan Brown of BBC Television earned the gratitude of the people of Gairbraid, as much by the way they conducted themselves in the area as by their sympathetic portrayal of the area in their 'Current Account' film. Much of the success of the later campaign may be traced to that television programme. The residents were deeply shocked at the news of Raeburn Mackie's tragic death in a car accident: they felt that they had lost a friend.

Community action intervention in Gairbraid was financed by outside sources. Although those responsible have not always agreed with my point of view, I very much appreciate their generous support. I am also extremely grateful to Professor Martin and members of his staff, Department of Social Administration and Social Work, University of Glasgow, for kindly providing office space and use of facilities. In particular, I wish to thank the secretaries who so willingly helped produce many of Gairbraid's leaflets. I am also extremely grateful to Bob Holman for reading the draft manuscript and for encouraging publication.

I am immeasureably indebted to my wife Sue for so patiently bearing with my long absences, for her encouragement and interest, and for her willingness to undertake the proof reading and correcting my spelling and grammar. The family of a community worker is not to be envied and I thank Lucy, Selina and Scott for so readily accepting it all.

I would also like to express my appreciation of Alice Brown and May Ling Wee who typed various versions of the script. A great many other people who I have been unable to acknowledge contributed either to the Gairbraid campaign or to the preparation of the book. To them and to all the committee's well-wishers I am sincerely grateful. Although I have drawn on the insights of many, needless to say, I alone bear responsibility for the opinions, conclusions and mistakes expressed here.

Finally, I end this preface by pointing out that Glasgow's Housing Management Department is located at Clive House and is referred to as such in the text. For non-Scottish readers I must also explain that 'house' has been used interchangeably with 'flat' throughout the book. Thus, although most, if not all, the Gairbraid residents moved to what the English would call flats, they without exception refer to their new homes as houses. Also, the entrance to tenements in Scotland is called a 'close' which, as defined by the Oxford dictionary, is an 'entry from street to court at back'. 'Wean', meaning 'wee ane', little one, is a child. Hopefully, all other words used in the book will be comprehensible south of the Scottish border.

S.J.

Chapter 1

HOUSING: SHORTAGE, DEMAND AND BUREAUCRACY

Ever since the development and growth of our large cities during the
Industrial Revolution, Britain has been in the throes of a national
housing crisis. The worst of the squalor and degradation which so
marked urban life in the past has now been mostly removed by widespread slum clearance and house building programmes - 'to have
provided over three million new houses since the war, and demolished
¾ million slums (involving the rehousing of over two million people)
since 1955, is no mean achievement'. (1) Yet, the housing problem
remains, in Lord Goodman's words, (2) 'a hideous sore on modern
society'. Every city in the country has its areas of poor and
unsatisfactory housing and for many, the problem seems almost intractable. Cullingworth, for instance, cannot see Scotland's
housing problem (3) 'being solved this century'. The national
housing need is, as Frank Allaun writes, (4) 'colossal' - one and
a half million homes unfit for human habitation and a further four
and a half million dwellings which either lack one or more of the
basic amenities or are in need of serious structural repair. At
an average of three per house, Allaun estimates that eighteen
million people in Britain live under such conditions.

Clearly, large numbers of the British working class are still
inadequately housed and this is likely to continue for several more
generations unless there are drastic and unforeseen changes in
government policies and priorities. Quite simply, not enough is
spent on housing. 'Of the £1,000 million that successive govern-
ments have put into the British Aircraft Corporation to finance
Concorde', Michael Barratt Brown observes, (5) 'we could have
built 250,000 houses, or a thousand comprehensive schools or several
hundred hospitals, and that was only the cost of development and not
of manufacture of this white elephant'. However, more money for
massive clearance and improvement schemes, unless linked to meaningful local participation, is only a partial solution to the housing
problem. In a vicious circle, shortage together with pressure of
demand breeds bureaucracy. Housing departments everywhere must
somehow cope with a seemingly endless queue of applicants and for
each family who, with justice, seeks priority there will be another
whose rehousing claims are even more urgent. There is no simple
solution to the housing crisis.

Slum clearance signifies progress but is more than a logistical problem of bricks and mortar, of politics, finance and statistics. Demolition and rehousing is also synonymous with the uprooting of communities, with the destruction of the social fabric of working class life and with bureaucratic insensitivity. It is a machinery that once in motion may have little regard for individual needs or preferences, kinship, age, employment, schools, transport, recreation and the like. Shelter (6) investigated slum clearance in Liverpool, Leeds, Salford, Newcastle, Nottingham, Birmingham, Sheffield, Glasgow and London, and in none was the process found to be satisfactory. Indeed, the housing problem in any one of our cities tells essentially the same story of crisis. This book is about rehousing from a Glasgow clearance area. Glasgow has a reputation, on most criteria well founded, of having the worst social problems of any city in Britain. However, Glasgow's problems, although sometimes more extreme, are basically no different from those of anywhere else. In housing, Glasgow reflects the national ills.

GLASGOW IN THE NINETEENTH CENTURY

Despite a massive post-war house clearance and building programme, Glasgow still has an acute housing problem and tenement-type dwellings still predominate in the inner city. By 1851, John Butt notes, (7) 'Glasgow's municipal authorities had already recognised the existence of a housing problem... and dangerous slum property was already being demolished.' The impression to be gained in the 1970s is that Glasgow has since been doing nothing else but demolish and despite periodic claims that the solution to the housing problem is in sight - the latest forecast being 1981 (8) - poor, insanitary, inadequate and overcrowded housing still remains a major feature of the Glasgow scene.

The growth and development of Glasgow as a great seaport and trading centre, like Bristol and Liverpool, began with its involvement in the Slave Trade. 'Not until the Act of Union of 1707 was Scotland allowed to participate in colonial trade. That permission put Glasgow on the map'. (9) Its growth in the eighteenth and nineteenth centuries was phenomenal: the city's population rose from 30,000 in 1770 to 359,000 in 1851 and 1,088,000 in 1931. (10) 'The elegance of the eighteenth century city of Glasgow', Butt writes, (11) 'was ravished by the industrial revolution.' Between 1931 and 1961, the population of Glasgow remained static and by 1971, dropped below the 900,000 mark.

House building did not remotely keep pace with the massive increase in population, and obviously there were dire social consequences. In 1851, the population density in the city centre varied (12) from 500 to 1,000 persons per acre. Johnston points out that while the Glasgow population rose (13) by 33,031 in the decade 1831-41, the number of houses increased by 3551. Many commentators of the period agree that the misery in Glasgow was unequalled anywhere - even in (14) 'the lowest nooks of St. Giles and Whitechapel, the Liberties of Dublin, the Wynds of Edinburgh'. Lodging houses in Glasgow, accommodating up to twenty people, are described as (15) 'usually so damp, filthy and ruinous, that no one would wish to keep his horse in one of them'.

Hobsbawm feels that during the industrial revolution the (16) 'Scots working class was not merely much poorer than the English, but also, in the vast stony tenements of its towns, filthily and shockingly poor'. Johnston describes housing conditions in Scotland as (17) 'vile, almost beyond belief'. In Glasgow, 100,000 people lived in one-roomed houses, (18) infant mortality was one in every twelve births, 50 per cent of children died under five years of age and the city workman had only an average life of 48 years 8 months. Johnston marks the period between 1866 and 1869 in Scotland (19) as 'terrible years for the working class - the House Proprietors and Factors in Glasgow driving up rents by from 10 to 25 per cent; privies and middens converted into dwelling-houses; 60,000 dwelling houses in Glasgow without water-closet accommodation; one third of the people in single apartments....'

The raising of housing standards in Britain owes as much to economic and health considerations - 'the classless visitation by cholera' (20) - and to fear of social unrest, as it does to purely humanitarian motives. To capitalists of the late nineteenth century the proposition of 'municipal socialism' was to many anathema and the idea of a corporate responsibility for housing was unacceptable, if not still entirely alien, to central and local government thinking. John Butt (21) draws attention to the activities of the City Improvement Trust and the railway companies in Glasgow, who between them had by 1884-5 displaced 30,000 persons, and neither the trust nor the companies had thought it necessary to provide new houses for those displaced - 'the working people were shunted out of slums into the nearest, next-worst property'. Butt tells of the fears expressed: (22) 'if too much help was given to the unskilled labourer, earning 16s to 18s per week in 1901, the mass of untrained labour in the city would increase'. Subsidised housing as a general principle was not on the agenda although there was some support for the idea that (23) 'the Corporation should act as a rescuer and guardian for the feckless, the vicious and the criminal'. In this scheme of things, the bulk of the working class was to be left to the mercies of the private market.

'The appalling prison-cells of the vast sombre tenement blocks which grew up in the raw smokey fog of Glasgow' was where, as Hobsbawm reminds us, (24) 'one out of every five Scotsmen lived in 1914.' Yet in that year, Chapman notes, (25) 'Glasgow Corporation, more active than most municipal authorities, provided accommodation for no more than 1 per cent of its population.' Clearly, private enterprise was neither willing nor able to deal effectively with Glasgow's housing crisis. A significant increase in the supply of houses in the private market was, and remains, an unrealistic solution, for the vast majority of the working class would have been unable to afford the rent. Butt challenges the notion that poor living conditions were caused by the refusal of the working class to pay an economic rent; rather, (26) 'it was that the income level of labourers in a wide range of Glasgow's industries was too low to allow a man to keep his wife and children in decent accommodation'. In spite of severe overcrowding, 11 per cent of Glasgow's houses were unoccupied in 1911.

The appalling living conditions of the nineteenth century have
largely disappeared and the slum dweller of those times would probably find the worst that Glasgow has to offer now highly preferable
to the wynds of his day. However, in the midst of what we choose to
call the 'affluent' society, it is little solace for the family in a
rat-infested room-and-kitchen to know that their grandparents were
even worse off. A wealthy nineteenth-century industrialist would
have been as unlikely then, as his descendent would be now, to consider a Glasgow tenement as proper accommodation for himself. That
a room-and-kitchen was considered by the Victorian elite as adequate
for a working-class family does not mean that it actually was adequate, or that the problem arises now because the middle class no
longer think this. Neither does the problem arise because the
working class themselves have become less inclined to accept grossly
inferior houses as normal places in which to live and bring up their
families. The fact that the worst houses today are preferable to
much that existed before, simply states that progress has been made.
It does not reflect on houses presently unfit nor does it allow for
any measure of complacency. To say that the Calcutta pavement
dweller would be better off in a British slum in no way makes that
slum tolerable; it merely admits that conditions could even be
worse as indeed they are for the country's countless homeless
families.

During the nineteenth century, there were undoubtedly many
individual acts of defiance against living conditions and rent increases but generally, the labour movement in Scotland was said to
have been (27) 'notably feebler and less stable' than in England.
However, by the outbreak of war in 1914 the Clyde was the most
important munitions centre in the country and Clydeside became (28)
'the synonym for revolutionary agitation'. In the community, particularly in those areas near the shipyards, an attempt by the
Factors to increase rents, from 11 to 23 per cent, (29) was
fiercely resisted by the women, supported by their men who threatened industrial action. Committees in each tenement affected were
organized with two women from each close: (30) 'meetings were held
in the streets and in the back courts, bells were rung, drums were
beaten, and trumpets were blown, all to draw the women out.'
Gallacher describes the 1915 Glasgow Rent Strike as (31) 'such as
had never been seen before or since' and gives an account of its
victorious climax when a mass of people invaded the city centre to
protest outside the Sheriff Court. This action caused Lloyd George
to intervene, forcing the Government to control rent in the private
housing market.

Community work became fashionable in Britain in the 1960s and
professional community workers sometimes assume that working-class
militancy outside the industrial sphere dates only from that period.
This neglects a long and rich history of community struggles in
Britain of which the working-class communities in the west of
Scotland were often in the vanguard. The 1915 Rent Strike and
those that followed on the Clyde are probably still without
parallel in British working-class history. Glasgow has a heritage
of poor housing; it also has a heritage of community militancy,
neither of which have completely disappeared. The former, however,
is now very much more in evidence than the latter; the memory of
the 1915 Rent Strike has all but faded from the streets of Glasgow.

GLASGOW TODAY

No one can arrive in Glasgow without in some way being aware of the
city's housing problem. There are derelict houses almost everywhere in the inner city, both north and south of the Clyde. When
Edward Heath visited Glasgow, he was (32) 'shocked' at what he saw
and as a result five out of the £8 million allocated to initiate
an environmental improvement scheme was provided from central
government sources. 'The Times', though, estimate that 'nearer
£200 million is needed ... to make the whole of Glasgow a really
fair city in which to live.'
    Corinna Adam writes that Glasgow (33) 'is said to have the worst
housing in Europe - with a bow in the direction of Naples, it is
hard to disagree.' 'Areas of Need in Glasgow' (34), a report produced by the city's Planning Department, illustrates the extent of
the multi-deprivation existing there. When compared with three
Scottish and five English cities, Glasgow is shown to have the
highest population dependency ratio; the poorest housing; is, on
most counts, the least healthy place in which to live; has, next to
Liverpool, the highest proportion of working class in its population (which may or may not be a disability); and, on the June 1971
figures, was second only to Dundee in its rate of unemployment.
In 1970, it was officially estimated (35) that 75,000 houses in
Glasgow failed to meet the 'tolerable standard' as defined in the
Housing (Scotland) Act 1969. Using different criteria, Cullingworth
and Watson found that (36) only 56 per cent of the city's houses
are without serious defect. The remaining 44 per cent, roughly
138,000 houses, either lacked a bath (2 per cent), had one or more
serious defect (30 per cent), or lacked an inside toilet for the
exclusive use of the occupants (12 per cent). Clearly, there are a
substantial number of houses in Glasgow which even if above the not
very demanding 'tolerable standard' must, nevertheless, be peri-
lously near to it. Whatever estimate is accepted, and even 75,000
equals almost a quarter of Glasgow's housing stock, the city faces
an enormous problem.
    The 1972 housing waiting list (37) in Glasgow totalled 53,565,
an increase since 1971 of 4,284 families. During 1972, Glasgow
Corporation was able to allocate 12,111 houses of which 47 per cent
were let to list applicants. Glasgow's Housing Management Department is clearly under considerable pressure, the gravity of which
is perhaps best illustrated in the figures for homeless families
registered in the city. In 1972, 15,863 families on the waiting
list were classified as homeless, an increase since 1971 of 4,032.
On its 1972 performance, if Glasgow had attempted to do nothing
else during that year but house the homeless, after all the accommodation available within the city had been allocated, there
would still have been 3,754 families left without a home. As it
was, only 3,451 of the homeless were rehoused during 1972.
    Traditionally, rents in Scotland have been lower than in England,
and so too have been wages and living standards. Also traditionally, poor living conditions have been blamed on the relatively low
level of rent paid for accommodation. Pearl Jephcott, for example,
calls for (38) 'a more realistic' attitude towards rent so that the
increase may provide for the facilities lacking in Glasgow's high-

rise flats. Rent increases, however, cause hardship for those most
in need without necessarily benefiting council tenants. A glance
at Glasgow's housing budgets show that far more is spent on servic-
ing interest on previous loans than is actually used for house
building and maintenance. Referring to the 1970 figures for
Glasgow, Hart (39) points out that of the roughly £30 million housing revenue account, almost two-thirds went to repay interest on
outstanding loan debt and more was in fact collected in rents (£13
million) than was spent on housing (£11 million). Clearly, an
increase in council house rents is not a panacea to cure Glasgow's
housing ills but rather a revised system of housing finance is
needed which will build houses and not mainly subsidize the building societies and money-lenders.

Glasgow's present housing needs must be contrasted with the
tremendous efforts made by the city, particularly since the war, to
provide decent accommodation for its population. Pearl Jephcott
writes that (40) 'the city's current plan for redevelopment is
claimed to be the largest urban renewal scheme in Europe'. Between
1945 and 1972, Glasgow has issued (41) almost 55,000 orders for
closing or demolition of houses, a process accelerated in the five
years 1968-72 when over 31,000 such orders were issued. Since the
war, well over 100,000 municipal houses have been completed in the
city. Clearly, in the last quarter of a century, the face of
Glasgow has been substantially altered. For example, where people
in the Gorbals (42) used to live at a density of 450 to the acre,
the old tenements have now almost completely disappeared. The
rebuilding of Glasgow has in many ways been a remarkable achievement.

Detracting from the enormous strides made in the public housing
sector is the failure of central and local government to consider
the social implications of housing policy. 'They make a wilderness
and call it comprehensive development'. (43) The results are sadly
and unmistakeably attested to in the grey, soulless uniformity of
countless housing estates, spread throughout the country, which if
they have not already become so, promise to be the slums of the
future. Housing is more than planning and providing for purely
physical needs. Undoubtedly, local authorities faced severe problems after the last war and can thus be partially excused for
embarking upon their massive house building schemes with little or
no regard for the social implications of what was involved. In
reviewing the mistakes of the past, ignorance is often pleaded of
the consequences which were likely to accrue from the neglect of
social factors in housing policy. However, many private house
developments of the period can be indicated where the mistakes made
in the public sector were avoided: these were planted with trees
and provided with open space, schools, shopping centres and recreational facilities, all absent from so many areas of working
class housing. Easterhouse, in Glasgow, with a population in the
1970s of over 55,000, provides an example of the deprivation
existing in a working-class estate which resulted from official
neglect rather than ignorance. The first house was opened by
Clement Attlee in 1956 and fourteen years later, Graham Noble was
able to write: (44) 'even now, the small area around the house
opened by Attlee remains one of the few properly landscaped parts

of the estate.' In 1970, in Easterhouse, there were
no public toilets, no public washhouse, no banks, no cinema,
no theatre, no public dance hall, no government offices, no
internal transport system, no community centre, no cafes or
restaurants and no shopping centre. In the area with the
population of a major town there is one pub....It is necessary to travel nearly four miles to Parkhead to claim sickness
or unemployment benefit and in the opposite direction north
into Springburn to claim supplementary benefit - both return
journeys ... taking up to two hours.

Although many of the amenities listed have since been provided in
Easterhouse, it was not before a whole generation there had grown
to adulthood. Indeed, even now, in spite of all the accumulated
evidence, social factors still tend to be ignored and newly built
housing estates are often without the amenities that are regarded
as essential in middle-class suburbia. The difference between
private and public housing seems to be the difference between
making decisions and having decisions made for one, between wielding power and being powerless.

It is still widely held, even by council tenants themselves,
that private is better than public housing. All too often local
authority homes are allocated as a matter of privilege rather than
as of right. The dominant consensus, continually reinforced by the
mass media, is that the council tenant owes everything to the
subsidy of the owner-occupier. Housing policy is influenced as much
by ideology as it is by moral, social and financial considerations.
Dennis suggests that working-class estates, built on the periphery
of our cities, were once thought preferable to high-density central
development as the latter were (45) 'too favourable to revolutionary
activity' and he goes on to add, 'town planning was at one time,
but is no longer, conceived of as "the third alternative" to the
old order or to Bolshevism'.

Some observers of the Glasgow scene, among them Mansley, (46)
the city's former Director of Planning, suggest that because houses
on some estates have become difficult to let, the demand for
Corporation houses is 'rapidly diminishing'. Such opinions, however, confuse housing need with rising expectations in terms of
both the quality and situation of local authority housing. It is,
as Hindess notes, (47) 'no longer the case that all public housing
estates are considered as desirable and normal places to live,
even by those who can afford nothing else.' Indeed, Mansley
writing of Drumchapel as a district (48) 'typifying the city's
peripheral post-war areas' notes that the area is 'grossly short'
of both educational and open space. These estates in large
measure lack most of the institutions which the inner city has and
which help distinguish a community from a mere collection of
houses. The reluctance of anyone to move to an outlying estate
cannot be taken as an indication that their present housing needs
are not urgent. Neither is it merely a matter of distant estates
with no facilities; in the inner city too, some areas are considered
'better', and are often demonstratively so, than are others.
Glasgow has its fair share of unwanted housing estates which,
rightly or wrongly, are considered tougher and less respectable,
less desirable places in which to live, than are others.

The houses, difficult to let in Glasgow, are either of inferior quality, are situated in an environment considered undesirable or else, if physically in good condition, are located anything up to seven miles from the city centre. Despite what the pundits claim, there is a severe housing shortage in Glasgow. From the figures available, it is difficult to imagine a different conclusion being drawn. Statistics alone, however, do an injustice to the real complexity of the housing problem in Glasgow for not only is there a shortage and an enormous demand for housing, the demand is essentially for decent houses in decent areas. It is no longer enough to merely count the number of houses available and equate these with the number of people in need of rehousing and thereby, predict the solution of the problem. It is also necessary to equate peoples' priorities with the houses made available. The Corporation's failure, or perhaps inability, to do so, is as much the crux of Glasgow's housing problem as is the shortage of houses.

REHOUSING THROUGH COMMUNITY ACTION

From the shipyards on the upper Clyde in 1971 the call for 'the right to work' reverberated around the country. Adapting the UCS slogan to their own situation, residents in the tenements of Gairbraid, Maryhill, in the north-west of Glasgow, demanded 'the right to a decent house'. Gairbraid did not fire the national imagination or make an impact beyond Glasgow. It did not even particularly interest local trade unionists and the Gairbraid campaign is hardly comparable to that of UCS, but for all that, the principles involved are none the less fundamental. The people of Gairbraid wanted a decent house for themselves but from this basic demand, inevitably other, more general issues were evoked: the right of people to participate in the decisions made about their own futures; freedom of choice; consultation; rights of appeal; access to and the accountability of authority; the role of the councillor; and local government democracy.
    Consisting of two blocks of tenement property, housing over a thousand people, Gairbraid was a small, densely packed working-class community of the kind ordinarily to be found throughout Glasgow. The events that occurred in Gairbraid describe community action in a housing clearance area. It is the story of a community under stress and recounts, from the local perspective, all that happened during the rehousing process. The history of Gairbraid details the intervention in a working-class area of outside community workers and tells of the emergence of a local leadership and the growth of their organization. It is about a people's belief in their own worth and ability, their insistence on their democratic rights and their long struggle against Glasgow Corporation which, in their own eyes at least, they ultimately won. UCS was about the right to work, community action in clearance areas is about the right of working-class families to live and bring up their children in surroundings of their choosing.
    Every city or area is obviously different from any other and many of the details of the events in Gairbraid are as unique to it as are the people who lived there, but such local differences are

essentially marginal to the basic common problems inherent in the
rehousing process that occurs everywhere.   Even though Scotland has
a different legal system to that of England and Wales, the consensus
of evidence available gives little reason to choose between being
rehoused in Granby, Islington, Notting Hill, St Ann's or Moss Side
rather than in Leith, Gorbals or Gairbraid.   The rehousing process
in Gairbraid was even remarkably like that, described by Gans, (49)
of a clearance area in Boston, Massachusetts in the 1950s.

Chapter 2

FROM YOUTH WORK TO COMMUNITY ACTION

Gairbraid is situated just off the Maryhill Road, one of Glasgow's main artery routes, which stretches from near the city centre to the north-west boundary. At the Maryhill Road and Gairbraid Avenue intersection there is a traffic island with a subterranean 'gents' toilet where old men and 'winos' hang about. At one corner is the old Maryhill Burgh Hall, remembered as a 'great social centre' but long since converted into a police station. Opposite is the public library and the local Labour Party rooms which were used by the Gairbraid committee's pre-school playgroup. There are shops and four pubs close together in the vicinity. Along Maryhill Road, towards the city, is the enclosing wall of the former Maryhill barracks, now the Wyndford housing estate with its tower blocks looming large. Almost opposite the main entrance stands the Maryhill Trade Union Centre where the Gairbraid committee held most of its public meetings. In 1970 the tenements, built above the shops which line Maryhill Road, seemed infected with decay. Gairbraid was by no means the worst area in the neighbourhood. Nearby, Rolland Street, Arden Street, Vernon Street, Oran Street and many more, were half-empty and derelict long before Gairbraid was even designated a clearance area.

Few Gairbraid tenants wished to be rehoused in the surrounding inter-war council estates. North of Gairbraid is Maryhill Cross, the heart of the old village before it was absorbed by Glasgow in 1891, and beyond is a glimpse of the new Maryhill as tenements give way to modern Corporation flats. There is Maryhill 'B' and at the edge of the green belt the Acre Road Scheme. For many the Gairbraid campaign was about the right to be rehoused in these new estates.

YOUTH WORK

The project, sponsored by an independent foundation and employing two full-time fieldworkers, started in September 1970. The first months were spent 'getting to know' Maryhill. Although first-hand knowledge of an area is important, there is perhaps a tendency to over-emphasize a project's initial period when too much time is spent 'going native' and too little in clarifying and discussing objectives. The impression gained of Maryhill after months of walking its streets were similar to those first formed, and not surprisingly, for, bar local details, one inner-city area is very much like another and their working-class populations suffer from the same deprivations: low incomes; unemployment; lack of job opportunities; inferior education and early school leaving; poor housing; inadequate amenities; few recreational facilities; in short, the whole host of closely related factors which are associated with multi-deprivation. As Coates and Silburn point out, (1) the causes of poverty do not lie in the districts themselves.

The intervention in Maryhill began as a youth work project but changing to include the adult population, finally evolved as community action in a housing clearance area. It was assumed that the problems facing the young were essentially similar to those faced by the rest of the community. To focus singularly on youth while ignoring more obvious and basic defects is to control rather than to attack the existing inequalities of our society. Saul Alinsky perceives the intrinsic weakness of the traditional youth work approach when he writes: (2)

> You don't, you dare not, come to a people who are unemployed, who don't know where the next meal is coming from, whose children and themselves are in the gutter of despair - and offer them not food, not jobs, not security, but supervised recreation, handicraft classes and character building! Yet that is what is done! Instead of guaranteeing the right to work for a little bread and butter we come to them with handouts of bats and balls!

Youth work in Maryhill would have meant encountering an adolescent from a large family, living in an overcrowded room-and-kitchen with grossly inadequate facilities, whose parents were unemployed, who had left school at the first opportunity and had little prospect for the future, who, in other words, suffered from all the disadvantages of the underprivileged poor, of whom, when he appeared to be a potential delinquent, the question would be asked, 'how can the youth services cater for him?'

All too often, the obvious is neglected in search of a formula which will provide outsiders with an insight into a local community and, in the process, the working-class nature of the population is overlooked. The talk is of 'delinquency', 'the poor', 'problem families', with the prefix 'working-class' usually omitted, not merely as a form of shorthand but because of an absence of a class analysis in the philosophy informing professional youth, social and community workers. The ideology of professional fieldworkers will reflect what - individual maladjustment or the social, economic, and political structures of society - is held responsible for the problems of the working class. Where political motives are denied or, as is most often the case, simply never mentioned, it is usually safe to assume that the underlying philosophy is one which places the onus of poverty on the individual rather than on society. Apathy and alienation are hallmarks of working-class communities in the old inner zones of our cities, but is apathy a cause or a symptom? The answer will obviously colour the perception held of the working class, in terms of both their capabilities and their needs, which in turn will determine the objectives attempted in the field.

If the working class is seen as too apathetic to participate effectively in the democratic process, then, in Mary Morse's words, the need is for (3) 'many more detached workers to offer friendship and help'. The Wincroft Youth Project in Manchester, with perhaps unusual candour, chose not to present their sample of adolescent boys with (4) 'the political choices that they might have to make to change their environment' but instead aimed to achieve 'more effective relationships at the personal level'. On the other hand, if apathy is seen as a reasonable reaction to a society which excludes the working class from decision-making, then the need is not to help those who cannot cope to adjust to that society but, to increase the power of the powerless. Marris and Rein, in their review of the American poverty programmes, report that (5) 'apathy was not as crucial' as was thought. They quote Sargent Shriver: 'the experts said the poor are apathetic, inarticulate, incapable of formulating demands, assisting and diagnosing their own needs. They were wrong. The poor are only waiting for the opportunity to be heard on a subject only they understand.' The view taken in Gairbraid was that the working class suffer from poor housing and schooling, dead-end jobs and unemployment, are apathetic and alienated because they are given no effective choice in a society that is designed to create inequality.

COMMUNITY ACTION

Sociology has, as Worsley points out, (6) been dominated by arguments between proponents of conflict and consensus models of society. Conflict theorists hold that (7) 'conflict is endemic in society because of deep-rooted differences of interest among the various groups and because of the unequal distribution of resources'. On the other hand, the consensus view lays stress on (8) 'the reciprocity which characterizes the relationships between one part of society and another'. In neither theory nor practice is there total disagreement between the two standpoints. In the humdrum of day-to-day involvement in community organizing, the difference between consensus and conflict is often blurred. Both approaches may even share a common rhetoric - 'participation', 'consultation', 'self-help', 'local needs' and 'local leadership'. Nevertheless, in spite of considerable overlap, the difference between them is essentially irreconcilable. Both sides are equally scathing of each other. SNAP, who adopted a consensus model for their work in Liverpool, suggest that to (9) 'depend entirely on local action seemed romantic'. Their report goes on to portray conflict as unrealistic: (10) 'radical social activists eventually demand a quite unacceptable redistribution of resources and power' and even as dysfunctional: 'inasmuch as this type of game polarises issues, it can have the cumulative effect of inhibiting action.' Alinsky, who developed the theory and practice of conflict as a strategy in community organizing, firmly rejects notions of consensus: (11) 'to attempt to operate on a good-will rather than on a power basis would be to attempt something that the world has not yet experienced.' In these terms consensus is viewed as the process whereby professional community workers attempt

to negotiate with professional council officials and councillors
over the heads of the working-class community, at whose expense
only, is agreement possible.

The approach adopted in Gairbraid, although not uncritical of
his theory, perhaps owes more to Alinsky than to any other and
decidedly was little influenced by the consensus model. The
tactics used, however, did not simply arise out of a preconceived
ideology which favoured conflict and thereby rejected consensus but
were determined by the community in response to events in Gairbraid.
According to the demands of particular issues, strategies of conflict and consensus were interchangeably used. Nevertheless,
conflict was seen to be inherent in the Gairbraid situation,
accurately reflecting Coates and Silburn's observation that (12)
'while progress through co-operation is always pleasant to contem-
plate, there are all too many situations where progress is
manifestly only likely to be achieved through conflict'.

Bryant notes that the (13) 'acceptance of conflict as a purposive
organizing and tactical force' distinguishes community action from
other forms of community work. This is not to say that community
action relies exclusively on conflict but rather, as Holman
observes, employs (14) 'a whole range of tactics and strategies'.
He lists the characteristics of community action as: 'location in
deprived neighbourhoods, control by members (rather than an
external agency), operation outside of traditional structures and
the objective of extending the power of the poor.' The Gulbenkian
Foundation, in their study of community work, follow the definition
offered by Bryant: (15)

> Community action may denote a particular approach to organizing
> local groups and welfare publics; an approach in which the
> political impotence or powerlessness of these groups is defined
> as a central problem and strategies are employed which seek to
> mobilize them for the representation and promotion of their
> collective interests.

Community action theory insists that local working-class communities
must define and solve their own problems, control decision-making
and provide the leadership and spokesmen for the organizations
which emerge. Community action is the means through which working-
class groups gain the knowledge, skill and confidence to protect
their own interests. These are cardinal principles against which
all community action must be assessed. Before beginning work in
Gairbraid, it was agreed that the precise nature of the intervention
in the area would be determined by locally expressed needs and not
by the attitudes and values of the professional workers. Arriving
in an area, uninvited and unannounced, with no concrete programme
on offer, the most immediate difficulty is to explain the project's
intentions. The obvious temptation is to avoid the abstract and
to attempt to impose a preconceived scheme onto the community.
When outsiders decide, Alinsky (16) calls it 'a monumental testa-
ment to lack of faith in the ability and intelligence of the
masses of people to think their way through to the successful
solution of their problems'. Indeed, it is sheer arrogance to
assume that local problems can best be decided upon and solved by
outsiders: it also implies the belief that working-class people
either do not know or cannot articulate what is wrong in their own
situation.

The community worker brings to an area all his attitudes, prejudices and preconceived notions and it is as well for him to be fully
aware of these if he is to be at all sensitive to local demands.
For the community worker to assume 'neutrality' or 'academic object-
ivity' is to deny reality. If he holds such views of himself he is
either dishonest or devoid of self-insight and has no business being
in the community in the first place. While he may believe that no
particular value, motivation, ideology or ambition brought him into
the area, the local people will more sensibly think otherwise. It
will mean that after he has listened to all that local people have
to say - and what they say will be determined largely by how he is
perceived - he will inevitably set about establishing his preconceived scheme. If the outsider is seen as neither genuinely
interested nor partisan, if he does not identify with the community's sorrows and joys, with their pleasures, hardships and
anxieties, he will be regarded with suspicion and quite rightly
will be rejected. As one local leader of a Glasgow tenants'
association asks of community workers: (17)

> Were they genuinely concerned about the community or were they
> trying to establish some degree of authority in the community
> so that their concept of how things should be done, what
> changes should be made, might be the prevailing one as dis-
> tinct from how the community themselves felt about it?

Canvassing local opinion is all very well but it is meaningless if
it only allows for agreement to decisions already made, or if it
merely seeks confirmation of the plans that outsiders have for the
area. Town planners, architects, housing department officials,
youth and social workers, and, let it be said, community workers,
are often guilty of presenting communities with a fait accompli
where the only effective choice offered is acquiscence. Whatever
the claims made for this type of exercise, in any meaningful sense
of the concept, it does not constitute participation.

This is not to say that in every circumstance the community
worker must adhere to anything that the community proposes. For
example, it is conceivable that a racialist Powellite demand could
be made by a local group which conflicts with the organizer's own
personal values. Here, the criterion for deciding whether or not
to support a local initiative is that community action should not
be used as a vehicle by one under-privileged group against another
and clearly, every effort should be made to oppose any bigoted or
discriminatory campaign. This one proviso aside, the decisions
in the community must absolutely be made by the people themselves
no matter what the outsider's attitudes and feelings toward these
are, he must wholeheartedly support them.

It is neither desirable nor possible for the community worker to
remain detached or indifferent to the problems of the area and his
role is not simply to discover 'local needs', as if they were to be
found under a stone, and then, in computer-like fashion, to propose
a programme that will provide a solution. Identifying local needs
is in fact not a simple matter, for anything larger than a single-
person community is bound to be heterogeneous and will contain
within it a complexity of different interests, attitudes, needs and
priorities. Furthermore, as Alinsky points out: (18) 'one of the
great problems in the beginning of an organization is, often, that
the people do not know what they want.' This does not contradict

what was stated before about people knowing what is wrong in their
situation but voicing grievances is a different matter from being
both willing and able to isolate a problem and its causes, deciding
upon a solution and then acting accordingly. Dennis, in his
Sunderland study, asked people if they expected to do anything
about stopping their homes being demolished: (19)

> while many informants expressed strong attachment to their
> homes and unequivocal opposition to demolition, often in
> vivid and forceful language, these questions were almost
> without exception met with something amounting to incom-
> prehension. The impression frequently left was that it
> would be as meaningful to talk about doing something to
> prevent the ebb and flow of the tides.

Alinsky realizes that (20) 'if people feel they don't have the
power to change a bad situation, then they do not think about it'.
It is an obvious lesson in survival, and history is littered with
examples of people in the most hellish conditions, in slave ships
and concentration camps, for no matter how intolerable a situation,
if it cannot be changed, the next best thing is to learn how to
accommodate and live with it. What the wider society calls apathy
is in fact the result of years of resignation and should not be
taken to mean acceptance. The organizer's function is to rekindle
the sparks of revolt which exist in all groups, even amongst the
most impoverished and exploited.

In Bryant's view, (21) 'community action merely makes explicit
the tensions and inequalities which may exist in various situations.' These, it needs to be stressed, are not simply latent,
people are painfully aware of their predicament but it is for the
organiser to channel a pot-pourri of grievances into effective
action by presenting the possibility of success. To draw again on
Alinsky: (22) 'it is when people have a genuine opportunity to act
and to change conditions that they begin to think their problems
through.' The task of identifying 'local needs' is therefore to
present the 'genuine opportunity'.

The aim in Gairbraid was to establish the conditions and situations whereby a local organization, under local leadership, could
emerge. It is pointless to identify local needs if the attempt
at solution is to be controlled by outsiders. For as Alinsky pro-
claims: (23) 'the building of a People's Organization can be done
only by the people themselves. The only way that people can express
themselves is through their leaders.' This truism seems self
evident but as Alinsky goes on to remind us: (24) 'most attempts
at community organization have foundered on the rock of native
leadership.'

Bryant clearly distinguishes between the roles and functions of
the indigenous leadership and those of the outside professional:
(25)

> The local leader is essentially a spokesman, advocate and
> publicist. He represents a community organization to external
> institutions and provides a reference point for the communica-
> tion of local views and grievances. On the other hand the
> professional change agent is a resource person and consultant,
> who provides services and information which would not normally
> be available or accessible to local groups.

Theory rightly allows for little overlap between the roles performed by the local leader and the 'resource person'; however, in
practice the distinction is often delicate and it could be dysfunctional to insist upon a too rigid role demarcation. There
are instances when the outsider needs to assume some kind of
leadership position in the community. Any difference between
practice and theory arises because the community is not set on
demonstrating some esoteric point about leadership. Local people
do not give up of their energies and free time to prove that they
are capable of leadership, their purpose is to win their struggle,
usually on issues that have immediate and profound effect on the
quality of their lives. In such circumstances, the community
wishes to utilize all the resources available to it and when required, the professional worker cannot withhold skills and
expertise on the grounds that this would contravene some purist
notion held about local leadership. Nevertheless, this should not
be made an excuse for perpetuating outside domination. Power
struggles or conflict about control need never arise when the
outsider momentarily assumes a position of prominence, for it is
precisely then that local people should be left in no doubt whatsoever that it is merely both an exceptional and temporary expedient.
That the organization is under local leadership no matter what,
must be fully explicit at all times and should be inherent in all
relationships and situations involving the community. Once this
principle is firmly established only then is it really possible
for the local leaders to flexibly make use of outside expertise
to the best advantage without fear that local control is under
threat.

The question of local leadership basically boils down to common
sense and probably would not even arise if the outside help was
being offered to a middle - rather than to a working-class community. It all revolves around: who controls the organization and
its resources; who decides policy; who are the spokesmen; and
whether the organization represents the views and interest of the
community it purports to serve? If the outsider is in control, if
he alone decides policy, if he represents no one but himself or
at best a small clique, then, whether or not it is called a
'people's organization' and no matter how many committees are convened, the exercise will not constitute participation and invariably local people will be entrusted only with the menial and
back-breaking tasks.

The insistance on local leadership is not merely a dogma to be
achieved no matter what. Rather, it rests on the belief that the
interests and well-being of a community can best be served by the
people themselves. It is not based on a romantic concept of
democracy, it simply recognizes that those personally involved,
who have something to gain or lose, are in the best position to
make the decisions about themselves. People have to do things
for themselves if they are to stand any chance of winning and the
power to win which the working class possesses is in the power of
numbers, depending on their ability and will to represent their
numerical strength in organization. It is in the interests of
the community and not because of some abstract theory that
organization should be under local leadership. The strongest

argument against outside control is that it is not in the people's
interests and that it is less effective than local leadership.
As Bryant observes: (26) 'When outsiders assume leadership roles,
on a permanent basis, they invariably undermine the credibility of
community groups.'
   It goes without saying that the needs of the community can be
better understood, and that the two-way democratic process of
representation is best achieved, when the leaders are elected from
amongst the people themselves. When outsiders assume this role for
themselves they tend to engender suspicion and mistrust. However,
it is in presenting the community to the external world that
professional workers most often feel it necessary to act as spokesmen, usually with detrimental consequences as it severely exposes
the local group to attack. For even where the outside activist
is not in a position of leadership, those in authority will endeavour to present him in that role. This is, partly, because the
power structure, whether Conservative or Labour, often finds it
difficult to relate to the working class on a basis of equal
negotiation, or to accept that people, whom they have customarily
stereotyped as apathetic and feckless slum dwellers, are capable
of independent action. Perhaps more importantly, it is done
because it suits their purpose: the outsider provides a convenient
scapegoat. It is a tactic which, by blaming 'outside troublemakers'
for the community's ills attempts to shift the argument away from
the pertinent local issues. By focusing attention on the outsider
while refusing recognition to the legitimate leaders, the intention
is to undermine the confidence of, possibly inexperienced, local
spokesmen. Further, one of the oldest political tricks in the
book is to split the opposition and the authorities will invariably
attempt to do so by imputing ulterior motives and divided loyalties
to the outsider. The authorities will also attempt to present the
organization to its potential allies as one that is controlled by
outside interests and which is not a genuine local movement. For
example, trade unions, would, quite rightly, be reluctant to offer
support to a group if it was not locally controlled.
   Whenever there is conflict, the charge that the outsider is in
control is always bound to be made: the activist must be in a
position to refute such allegations or else the local group becomes extremely vulnerable. Even if community workers do not
always appreciate that their control severely exposes the local
organization, those in authority are seldom under this misconception and will invariably seek to exploit the situation to their
fullest advantage. The need for local leadership is not merely an
article of faith, nor is it merely the means whereby local people
are encouraged to realise their potential, it is a necessity if the
organization is to deal successfully with the power structure.

RESEARCH

The project was initially conceived within an action-research framework which basically required the fieldworkers simultaneously to
wear research and activist hats. As Marris and Rein report, the
community action programmes in the USA found that (27) 'it was

impossible to be inventive, flexible and expedient on the one hand
and at the same time do careful, scientific, controlled research
on the other'. In Gairbraid, the research-action dilemma was resolved by focusing on the process of action itself. This meant
that the fieldworkers kept a daily diary of events which recorded,
documented, analysed and evaluated the project as it moved through
its various stages. Essentially quantitative material was sacri-
ficed for the impressionistic. An orthodox research programme to
satisfy the scientific purist was neither feasible nor even
desirable. Gans calls for social experiments which alter conditions
and then see how people react rather than empirical research which
he suggests, does not adequately investigate the (28) 'culture of
the poor'. Although impressions were continuously gained during
the fieldwork and most of Gairbraid's public meetings were tape-
recorded, personal interviews were only conducted after the action
part of the project had been completed. Although it is possible
to argue that long-term views are as valid as those obtained in
the heat of the moment, much valuable information was obviously
lost. The systematic attempt to interview the local leaders was
postponed until the end because to have done otherwise would
have been to place an intolerable demand on the time of both the
local people and the fieldworkers.

Several social surveys were conducted in Gairbraid by the local
organization, under its own auspices and for its own purposes.
The results, although fragmentary, are used in the assessment of
the project. More thorough fact-gathering exercises were dis-
allowed; no matter how interesting data may be, the testing of
hypotheses must relate to the immediate needs and interests of the
community. People have a premium on their spare time and much
that can be achieved in the community is limited only by this
factor. It is therefore crucial that the demands of the local
organization take priority over research. Local initiatives tend
to attract academics and others eager to test theories and the
impression sometimes gained in an area is that there are more
outsiders than locals. The presence of too many outsiders, engaged
in a diversity of pursuits, usually has demoralizing effects on the
community. The working class are not guinea pigs and community
action should not be the means by which researchers gain easy access
to them.

The local people involved in community action must be allowed
to express their feelings about it. The local perspective of the
events in Gairbraid was wanted, not only because of the added insight and further dimension that their views would contribute but
also to help offset the tendency of professionals to describe what
ought to have been rather than what actually occurred. This
possible bias was perhaps not wholly avoided as the interviews had
to be conducted by the fieldworkers themselves. Most of the main
personalities who emerged during the Gairbraid campaign were
interviewed: (29) the typed transcripts of these totalled over 600
foolscap pages. Although obviously selected, their views are
given expression throughout.

Any account of the events in Gairbraid will inevitably focus on
the local leadership but, at least as much is owed to the mass of
anonymous residents as it is to the activists. Without the

sustained support and encouragement of the ordinary people of
Gairbraid, the campaign would not have been possible. The elected
leaders were invested with the legitimacy to act on the community's
behalf and hence, mass local support provided the organization with
its source of power. The local leaders who appear frequently in
the pages that follow are: the committee's office bearers; the
chairman, John Moir; the vice-chairman, Jimmy Gallagher; the
secretary, Annie Mallon and, Georgina Atkinson, Davey and Jeannette
Bouse, Ella Donnelly, Isa Hanlon, Adam and Margaret Hobson, Eileen
Kelly, Jackie Moir, John Smith and Hugh and Eileen Thompson.

Chapter 3

REHOUSING AS AN ISSUE

The Maryhill (Gairbraid Avenue) Housing Treatment Area, comprising 399 houses and eight business addresses, was declared in October 1970. When rehousing began in July 1971, only 352 dwellings were occupied, so that, at an estimated three persons per house, the total population of Gairbraid did not then much exceed a thousand. The property consisted of four-storied tenements, sub-divided into twelve, or in a few cases, sixteen dwellings each. There were thus three and sometimes four houses per floor in each tenement. The residents shared lavatories which were situated on the landings between the floors. Now shared lavatories can be a particular misfortune for the childless couple living next-door to a family with a large number of young children. None of the houses had bathrooms and some did not even have hot water. It was a world where men shaved at the kitchen sink looking into hand-mirrors. Gairbraid provided its residents with a minimum of privacy and space. Most of the houses were room-and-kitchens with both rooms containing bed-alcoves, necessary as families of four, five and even six children were not all that uncommon in the area. A few of the houses had two rooms and a kitchen while others were only single-ends. Although tenements of this type are increasingly being replaced by modern Corporation houses, a substantial number of people still live under such conditions and certainly, of Glasgow's working-class adult population, the majority were born and bred in room-and-kitchens if not in single-ends.

The whole treatment area was only two blocks of tenements, each enclosing a large backcourt, entered from the closes, which could be used as a drying green and as play space for children. In Gairbraid, the conditions of the backcourts had deteriorated making such activities hazardous. Ashbin shelters or, more commonly, middens were also situated in the 'backs'. Glasgow's Cleansing Department collects rubbish from these by the archaic method of men carrying baskets into the courts. There, the bins are tipped into the baskets and whether or not the contents actually find their way into them rather than being scattered seems to depend as much on the direction and strength of the prevailing winds as it does on accuracy of aim. As a result, backcourts are often littered with rubbish for which, invariably, the local residents

are blamed. When Hugh and Eileen Thompson moved into Gairbraid in
1967 conditions were still reasonable, 'you could hang a washing
out the back which was a thing you couldn't do latterly'. In both
backcourts there could be found pools of stagnate slime, sometimes
fed by burst drains. The dividing walls had crumbled and loose
bricks and stones lay littered on the ground. The close entrances
were painted with gang slogans. Tiny children turned out immacu-
lately would return minutes later, having played in the backs,
covered in dirt. The alternative was to allow them to play in the
streets. Yet there were still patches of green in the backcourts,
a reminder of when they had once been fully covered in grass, and
of how they could still have been but for neglect, poor drainage
and current methods of rubbish storage and collection.

The treatment area was built on a slope and the two blocks of
tenements were divided by Balfour Street. The outer boundaries
were formed by parts of Gairbraid Avenue, Guthrie and Burnhouse
Streets. Shops were spread throughout the area, including a
butcher, a fish and chip shop and five dairies selling everything
from milk and fruit to newspapers and cigarettes. None of the
proprietors lived in the area although they did tend to employ
local people. Once the Gairbraid Housing Committee had been formed,
its notices were displayed in the local shops which become focal
points for disseminating and obtaining information. Ella Donnelly,
a committee member and Jessie Moir, the wife of a member, worked
in the Balfour Street dairy and the one in Burnhouse Street
employed another member, Georgina Atkinson.

THE HOUSES

Most of the property in Gairbraid was privately rented although a
sizeable proportion was owner-occupied. Key money was alleged to
be a feature of house letting in Gairbraid. Tenants told of having
to pay a 'backhander', sometimes as high as £50, in order to secure
their tenement home. As Jackie Moir remarks, 'I wouldn't say it
was such a good district that you had to buy your way into it - it
was because houses were scarce that people could be exploited by
having to pay key money.' The normal procedure of house buying
for the Glasgow working class is deposit down and the balance
plus interest paid off in monthly instalments. In this way, until
the full price is paid the purchaser incurs all the obligations
but few of the advantages of being a house owner. In clause after
clause, the would-be owner signs away rights and takes on respon-
sibilities for any expenses that may arise. For instance, an
agreement signed by a Gairbraid resident stated: 'You will furnish
me with a Pass Book in which there shall be entered the amount of
the purchase price and all rates, taxes, Insurance premiums, Feu-
duty, Ground Annual and other disbursements made by the Seller on
my behalf.' In this agreement, seven days after being one monthly
instalment in arrears, the factor was entitled to begin eviction
proceedings. The 'Sunday Mail' (1) featured the activities of one
company which owns 600 properties in Glasgow yet, in 1973, took
out 375 eviction orders. Failure to comply with the conditions
of 'rental purchase', the 'Sunday Mail' points out, means that the

occupants 'can be thrown out: without compensation, without rights to the property, without return of the deposit or the money already paid'. Furthermore, if the property is acquired by the local authority for demolition before the purchase price is fully paid, the company rather than the occupants receive the compensation due. The situation in Glasgow does not seem totally dissimilar to the dispossession rackets current in Chicago in the early 1900s, so vividly described by Upton Sinclair (2) in his novel, 'The Jungle'.

The area was in a varying state of repair: some houses seemed structurally perfect while others suffered from dry rot and rising damp requiring, at the least, annual wallpapering. However, most of the houses in Gairbraid appeared to have only minor defects, if any at all. The condition of Jimmy and Betty Gallagher's house was probably the worst in the area. It was a single-storey dwelling sandwiched between two tenements in Burnhouse Street. Over a period of time, with the help of a local councillor and the Health Department, they were 'constantly fighting the factor to do repairs - we got to the position where the room was falling in with dry rot'. In addition to making the floor completely unsafe, the spreading dry rot ruined their furniture. They were forced to evacuate the room and live only in the kitchen, about half of which was taken up by a bed. The Gallaghers were typical of Gairbraid residents: in spite of almost impossible conditions, they main- tained their morale and their one room, full as it was with furniture, was always neat and tidy. Indeed, in house after house, with a minimum of space and a total lack of facilities, people brightly decorated and furnished, making the best of what they had. Often the houses were improved, if not entirely maintained by the tenants themselves rather than by the factors. Many closes and stairs, notwithstanding the slogans sprayed on the walls and the constant mud puddles in the backcourts were, somehow, always spotlessly clean. Despite the stereotype that labels all tenement property as slums, the unkept house in Gairbraid was very much the exception.

In Glasgow, whether or not a particular individual lives in a council house or a tenement is very often merely the result of an arbitrary official decision to redevelop one area rather than another: it is simply a matter of chance. In Gairbraid, there were people who had been on the waiting list for thirty or even forty years without ever being given the opportunity of a Corporation house. Joining the waiting list in Glasgow - over 50,000 in 1972 - is not exactly the most expedient means of obtaining a new house and buying their way into the suburbs is, for most working-class families, highly improbable. For the newly wed, a home of their own usually means, where it can still be obtained, a room-and- kitchen in an inner-city tenement. Yet, the myth still widely persists that people live in tenements through some fault of their own. To classify all or even most people who live in tenements as problem families, is grossly to distort reality. If this were true, it would account for at least a quarter if not a third of Glasgow's working-class population, which suggestion is preposterous. Certainly, for the vast majority in Gairbraid it was patently un- true: the residents there differed from those on a 'typical' housing estate probably only in the quality of the accommodation

they occupied and there is no reason to believe that Gairbraid
significantly differed from any other tenement area in the city.

THE PEOPLE

Whenever a house became vacant in Gairbraid, it was usual for
existing tenants to appeal to the factor, for possession of the
house, on behalf of a relative or friend. It is an informal system
of acquiring tenancy similar to the (3) 'custom of speaking for
relatives' described by Young and Wilmott, in the East End of
London. Thus, many people moved into an already established social
network. Among the committee members, John Moir was well known
among the residents, having once been the local 'insurance man'.
His sister lived across the landing from him and their cousins,
Jackie and Jessie Moir, across the road in Balfour Street. Ella
Donnelly lived opposite her daughter, Eileen Kelly. Davey Bouse
was born in Maryhill and his mother lived in neighbouring Oran
Street. Betty Gallagher's mother lived in the nearby Wyndford
estate. Although the Hobsons had only lived in the area for two
years, Margaret was born in Gairbraid. On the other hand, Hugh
and Eileen Thompson came from the south side and knew relatively
few people in Maryhill. Thus, among residents of Gairbraid,
commitment to the area varied from almost total attachment by those
who were born and bred there, to others who were newcomers and
therefore relatively indifferent to remaining in the neighbourhood.
    Before Gairbraid was declared a housing treatment area, the
consensus of opinion was that conditions were at least reasonably
tolerable and although the basic amenities were mostly lacking,
there were definite compensations for living there. It was convenient, the town was readily accessible and there were plenty of
shops along the Maryhill Road. Gairbraid was a close, compact
area, teeming with life. For many there were friends and relatives
nearby, and neighbours were generally interested in one another.
As Annie Mallon expressed it, 'there was a homely good crowd of
people who stayed - good tenants.' However, it would be mistaken
to think of Gairbraid, on the village model, as a completely
integrated community. Life, as could be expected, revolved around
many different things for different people and rather than a
community, Gairbraid could more accurately be described as consist-
ing of various, not necessarily connected, sub-groups. People were
mostly able to recognize each other at least by sight but by no
means was everyone in the area known to everyone else. Living there
did not instil a special Gairbraid identity in the residents and
there was no particular reason why a strong localized identification
should have developed. After all, Gairbraid was simply two blocks
of tenements and until the authorities grouped them together in the
treatment area, all that they had in common and different from
other tenements, was their close proximity. Community, in any real
sense of the word, encompassing a majority of residents, only arose
after the Gairbraid committee had been formed and, as far as may be
gathered, there was no previous history of organization in the area.
    Whatever else it was, Gairbraid was not a homogeneous community.
There were different interest groups in the area: tenants and owner-

occupiers, those who were born and bred there and those who wanted
to leave. There were old age pensioners living alone and families
with young children. In fact, the possible permutations of interests that existed in Gairbraid were almost infinite. Although
the people in Gairbraid, above all else, were working-class,
represented in the area were all shades of status groups, from
'ultra-respectables' to 'roughs'. Most people though, seemed to
fall in between these two extremes. In employment, the range was
from the relatively well paid and highly skilled through the
ordinary labourer and the recently redundant to the chronically
unemployed.

Gairbraid was a religiously mixed area: there were Protestants
and Catholics and those who were only nominally attached to either.
A conventional wisdom held of Glasgow is that it is seething with
undertones of religious conflict. Religion, however, was never a
factor in Gairbraid and status, the dichotomy between 'roughs' and
'respectables', was potentially much more disruptive. This is not
to say that there are not distinctive Protestant and Catholic
communities in Glasgow. These clearly exist but their importance
should not be exaggerated nor be allowed to mask the essentially
over-riding class nature of the population. In Scotland, it is
an accepted fact of life that Protestant and Catholic children are
educated separately in religiously segregated schools. Besides
education, the other great religious divide in Glasgow is football.
Celtic football club fly the Irish tricolour at their stadium and
Rangers are said never to have fielded a Catholic player. In their
support for these clubs, Catholics for Celtic and Protestants for
Rangers, Glaswegians are sometimes quite fanatical. For example,
Rangers supporters on the rampage in Barcelona were reported to
have shouted at the Spanish police not, as may have been imagined,
'fascist' but, 'fenian bastards'. While this does reflect a degree
of religious bigotry and a dismal political consciousness, it
represents just one aspect of the massive complexity that is the
Glasgow working class. In Glasgow, football rivalry notwithstanding, religion is ordinarily relatively unimportant. Indeed, there
seems to be a minimum of religious friction between the two
communities with a great deal of social mix in evidence. Moreover,
in Maryhill, both Celtic and Rangers supporters are united in at
least a sentimental attachment to the local team, Partick Thistle.

In Gairbraid, where the population seemed to be about equally
divided between Catholics and Protestants, religion never assumed
any importance and it played no part in the Gairbraid campaign.
When asked whether or not religion was ever a factor in their
struggle, the committee members, without exception, strongly
denied it and were even offended that the possibility implied in
the question could have been conceived. The committee was in
fact about equally representative of both groups.

CONTROL OF OCCUPATION

People expected that at some time or another redevelopment would
reach Gairbraid, but few in the area could have imagined that it
was to be so soon. Jackie Moir, for instance, thought that it

would be about ten years before the area was touched. Gairbraid
seemed in far better condition than other property in the vicinity.
There were, for example, the tenements opposite the police station
in Gairbraid Avenue, where Paul and Eileen Kelly had previously
lived but had been forced to leave because they were over-run with
rats, and yet those buildings were not included in the treatment
area. It was thus reasonable to predict, in view of conditions
elsewhere, that Gairbraid would not be a priority for demolition.
Moreover, as a considerable amount of clearance was then already
underway in Maryhill it was rational to expect that these would
first be completed before new areas were started.

When word came from the Corporation, reactions were mostly
ambivalent. People welcomed the prospect, particularly after many
years of waiting, of decent accommodation with a modern kitchen, a
bathroom, an internal WC and space, and yet many felt reluctant to
move away from the neighbourhood. Some of the old people, simply
wanting to be left in peace, refused to acknowledge that anything
at all was about to change in the area. In general though, there
was an air of excitement and expectation in the area, tempered by
apprehension about the future. Whatever the individual reaction,
all seemed taken by surprise.

Whether or not it is correct to regard Gairbraid as an integrated community, many of the people living there felt it to be so
and its passing was deeply regretted. John Moir, describing the
area says:

'We were very happy there and people couldn't believe that
they were taking the place apart. It's a funny thing; you
have got to go into the place to get the atmosphere of it.
To me it was like a wee village and everybody knew what was
happening to people and everybody was interested in each
other. It was like a death sentence that kind of thing
coming to us.'

In December 1970, every resident in Gairbraid received control of
occupation orders. These were headed 'The Housing (Scotland) Act
1969', sub-titled 'The Maryhill (Gairbraid Avenue) Housing Treatment
Area Control of Occupation Order 1970'. The document informed the
residents that:

Whereas the Corporation of Glasgow, the local authority
under the Housing (Scotland) Act 1969, (hereafter referred
to respectively as 'the local authority' and 'the Act'), have
of this date passed a resolution declaring an area in their
district to be a housing treatment area, which area is known
as the Maryhill (Gairbraid Avenue) Housing Treatment Area.

Now therefore the local authority in exercise of the powers
conferred on them by section 16 (1) of the said Act, but subject to section 16 (3) of that Act, hereby prohibit the occupation of the houses in the said area except with their consent.

Other than provide a list of the addresses affected, no other information was provided and the control of occupation order quoted
above remained the only attempt made by the authorities to commu-
nicate with the residents. It caused total bewilderment in the
community. Isa Hanlon for one, 'hadn't a clue' what it was all
about and simply 'threw the paper in the drawer'.

By prohibiting people from moving into areas that have been earmarked for clearance, the local authority aims to curtail 'queue jumping' on to the house waiting list and is thus able to 'freeze' the numbers whom it has a responsibility to rehouse. Had control of occupation been thought unnecessary, it seems reasonable to conjecture that the residents would have received no information at all until it was time for them to be moved. As it was, the authorities never provided an explanation of what 'housing treatment' meant nor of what was intended in Gairbraid. The residents were not told how they were to be affected nor when events were likely to begin and further enquiries were not invited. Quite clearly, Glasgow Corporation viewed the control of occupation order solely as a means of protecting their own interests and they did not even manage that properly as they sent out the wrong document. (4) Further, it was sent out almost three months after the treatment area resolution was passed, instead of within the statutory 28 days. Certainly, it was not regarded as an opportunity to inform, consult or in any way involve people in decision-making about their own futures. An accompanying explanatory leaflet would have avoided much confusion. Instead, the people of Gairbraid were kept totally in the dark and no one knew what was going to happen, let alone how or when.

Under the 1969 Act, houses may be dealt with either by demolition, improvement or by a combination of both. Gairbraid had been designated a housing treatment area for total demolition. The people living there, however, were not informed of this fact and left to their own devices they, naturally enough, interpreted 'housing treatment' to mean improvement. Where demolition is intended 'housing treatment' is a singularly unfortunate choice of phrase: in Gairbraid it caused nothing but confusion. As rehabilitation was an innovatory aspect of the 1969 legislation, the mass media tended to concentrate upon it and house conversion is what tended to remain in peoples' minds. The press and television, though, cannot be blamed for the local authority's failure to inform. The assumption universally held in Gairbraid was that three houses were to be knocked into two so as to provide bathrooms. One of the Maryhill councillors who was then a member of the Corporation's housing committee - the body responsible for the decision to treat Gairbraid - when asked, incredibly reaffirmed the locally held misconception that the area was to be improved. Eileen Thompson, who was one of those who made the enquiry, believes that the councillor 'honestly did not know'. Although someone in authority must have known that the intention all along was to demolish Gairbraid, this was not communicated to the people living there nor, it seems, to the local councillors. As Georgina Atkinson expresses it, 'we were just left sitting there, nobody knew what they were doing, we didn't know if the buildings were getting done up, coming down or what would happen.'

Although the belief that the area was to be improved was firmly held, the possession of this 'knowledge' did not decrease the uncertainty felt but, rather, contributed to it. Jackie Moir, for instance, thought that 'they were going to improve the houses but I had no idea it would mean moving.' Improvement in fact poses innumerable possibilities and these were variously speculated upon in Gairbraid. Converting three houses into two requires a decrease in

population density and, therefore, some residents at least could
not be given the option of a house in the new Gairbraid. Indeed,
would people be given any say at all about whether they stayed or
moved? Could people continue to live in the property while work
was in progress or would they need to be temporarily rehoused and
if so, for how long was that likely to be? These and similar
questions were anxiously the subject of many heated arguments. As
the decision to demolish had long been taken, the whole debate was,
of course, totally irrelevant. Nevertheless, the lack of explanation was so complete that it is still widely believed by former
Gairbraid tenants that 'housing treatment' means 'improvement' and
it is thought that what happened in Gairbraid was that at some
point the authorities changed their minds and decided, instead of
treating the area, to 'condemn' it and, therefore, the property
was demolished.

Where house moving is likely to be a once and for all affair,
as it is for so many Corporation tenants, then the process needs
to be handled with a maximum of sensitivity. Rehousing in Gairbraid
was commonly perceived in terms of 'wanting to better myself'. As
John Moir describes his experience:

'Honestly, you have got to be in the position just sitting
there and not knowing what is happening. It's a great important
thing when you change your house. You only do it a couple of
times in life, especially us working-class folk. We don't
often move much and to know you're moving, it might be for good.
So then suddenly you get a letter saying you're moving. That's
all you hear. You don't know when, or what's happening and
suddenly you notice that your place is not getting repaired.
But you're still paying away rents. Then a burst pipe remains
burst. To me the worst thing is the lack of information.
They don't tell you anything.'

The official silence in Gairbraid was absolute, no word at all
followed the control of occupation order and no clarification was
ever attempted. The mood in the area of excitement, anticipation,
preparation, or trepidation that was caused by the initial communication, when nothing else was heard, soon gave way to the gloom
of anti-climax. The change was in the sudden stagnation of a
community. People continued their daily business as before but in
an atmosphere of total uncertainty. Then and throughout the entire
rehousing process in Gairbraid, the authority's failure to inform
the residents of what was happening had the effect of alternately
raising and lowering expectations, damaging morale and making the
area susceptible to rumour and hearsay.

The immediate result of being kept ignorant of the future is that
long-term planning, surely a necessary pre-condition of ordinary,
stable life, becomes increasingly hazardous. Questions such as
whether or not to cancel the summer holiday; the advisability of
redecorating or improving the house; buying new furniture; the
children's schooling, and so forth, all become clouded in uncertainty. A precise date was not required, merely an approximation
of when rehousing was likely but this the authorities steadfastly
refused to provide. For instance, if only a matter of months then
obviously redecorating would not be worthwhile but if a longer
period was involved, then life could be made more bearable if

damp-prone walls were repapered. While such matters may be relatively inconsequential amongst high income groups, to the average
working-class family, not to mention the old age pensioner, they
are of immense importance. Jackie and Jessie Moir, for instance,
missed the opportunity of a house while away on holiday, while
others who decided to cancel their holidays against such an event-
uality did not receive any offers during that period. One 72-year-
old woman packed her things months in advance of being rehoused.
People who decided not to incur any additional expenses on their
homes found that they were not rehoused for at least a year. In
this way, the Corporation bears responsibility for the early onset
of the blight in Gairbraid.

The control of occupation order with its complicated legalese,
confusion and non-information, exemplifies the Corporation's
attitude to the local community throughout the entire rehousing
process and provides the background to Gairbraid's decision to
form its own organization.

Chapter 4

FORMING THE GAIRBRAID HOUSING COMMITTEE

Gairbraid was selected as the area in which to work on essentially arbitrary criteria and almost any other working class district in Maryhill or, for that matter, Glasgow, could equally have been chosen. Nothing especially propelled the project to Gairbraid, other than that it had to be located somewhere and the area seemed as suitable as any other. Being relatively isolated, Gairbraid constituted a geographical entity if not an actual community. The area is bounded on four sides by physical barriers which give it a sense of enclosure; on the one side there is the wall of the Wyndford estate and on the others the River Kelvin, the Forth and Clyde Canal and the busy Maryhill Road. The Gairbraid area contains examples of the most prominant types of working-class housing in Glasgow - inter-war council, a modern multi-storey block of flats and privately owned tenements. This diversity attracted the project to Gairbraid as, at that stage, rehousing had not yet emerged as an issue.

The project, in attempting to acquire premises in the area, thought of a disused shop but were informed by Glasgow's Planning Department that all the possible shops in the district were located within what had recently been declared a housing treatment area for demolition. In this way, the project first became acquainted with the fact that demolition was intended in a part of Gairbraid, but the implications of this were not then appreciated or even considered beyond the limitations it placed on the search for premises. Eventually, a top-floor room-and-kitchen in tenement property was bought, situated at 36 Burnhouse Street. Opposite is the Gairbraid primary school and just up Burnhouse Street, at the corner of Gairbraid Avenue, was the treatment area. The flat was initially occupied by one of the fieldworkers so as to provide a base for the project rather than as a resource for the community. Later, when made vacant, the flat became the Gairbraid committee rooms and it, plus its telephone, proved indispensible during the Gairbraid campaign.

On first entering the Gairbraid area early in 1971, the community workers attempted to seek introductions to people living there who were thought likely to be interested in the project. It was a difficult task, perhaps the most difficult of the entire programme.

Having agreed that the nature of the work should be locally decided, the project had nothing concrete to offer and the obvious
question, 'What is it about?' was not easily answered. In practice
it meant knocking on a stranger's door, somehow attempting to make
it all sound credible and not like a visitation from the Archangel
himself, ready to solve everyone's problems at the drop of a hat.
One early response from a Gairbraid resident was, 'Is this something
to do with the Communist Party?' A difficulty is that people who
are approached in general terms are bound to respond with generalizations. The initial problem was not to discover someone who could
articulate a formula to cure Maryhill's ills but rather, simply to
make contact in the area so as to demonstrate the project's serious
intentions. Only when people gain confidence in the outsider are
they likely to voice their genuine grievances.
    The first positive lead towards making contact in Gairbraid was
provided by Ken McLachlan, an activist of long standing, who was
chairman of the Maryhill Ward Committee and of the Wyndford Tenants'
Association. In the months ahead, he was to provide invaluable
assistance to Gairbraid. On that occasion, he suggested that a
trade union colleague of his, Sean Mallon, might be interested in
the project. It just happened that the Mallons lived in that part
of Guthrie Street that had been included in the treatment area.
The stage was set for a housing campaign.

SEAN AND ANNIE MALLON

The Mallons were visited and the warmth of their welcome, in the
traditional Glasgow working-class manner, showed all nervousness
and prior rehearsing on how best to introduce the project to have
been unnecessary. Very soon the lack of facilities in Maryhill was
being discussed in the cosy comfort of their home and later this
discussion continued in a nearby pub where a great deal of Guinness
- 'the national beverage' - was consumed. Sean Mallon, who has
spent most of his adult life in Scotland, is Irish born. It is a
sobering thought that had the community worker been a teetotaller,
the course of the project might have been very different; it
certainly would not have been as enjoyable. Sean and Annie Mallon
had lived in Guthrie Street for seventeen years and both were very
active in the local Catholic church. They were well known in the
area and both had interest in and extensive knowledge of the
community. The project was indeed extremely fortunate in making
early contact with them.
    After several visits when the problems of Maryhill were dis-
cussed with the Mallons and some of their neighbours, Sean produced
the Gairbraid control of occupation order which everyone in the
area had already received and which no one understood. While not
being able to enlighten them about its meaning, the community
worker was able to inform them that according to the Planning
Department the area had been earmarked for demolition. The Mallons'
reaction was of such disbelief that the Planning Department had to
be recontacted and the information confirmed.

THE PETITION TO THE HOUSING
MANAGER

A member of Glasgow University's staff, knowledgeable in housing
procedure, was brought to the Mallons' home so that Gairbraid's
possible future could be discussed. A further meeting was arranged,
in the Maryhill Trade Union Centre, so that more of Mrs Mallon's
neighbours could be invited. Thirteen Gairbraid women attended and
although all had at least some idea, either through their own experience or from that of relatives and friends, of what to expect
during rehousing, none had a complete picture of the entire process.
The meeting agreed that there was an urgent need for precise information on what was going to happen in Gairbraid. On the suggestion
previously made by Sean Mallon, the group decided to send a petition
to the Housing Manager requesting information and a public meeting
with an official of the Housing Department.
    Once the contents of the petition had been agreed, it was decided
that the community worker should draw up the final version, to be
vetted by the Mallons, and that he should provide the duplicated
forms. Thus, from the beginning, the community worker assumed the
role of 'local scribe' which continued throughout. The signatures
for the petition were collected by the younger of the women present
in door-to-door canvassing of the area. Among those who participated was Georgina Atkinson who later became the GHC's treasurer.
    The forms, containing 144 signatures, were handed in to Mrs
Mallon: through misunderstanding some were lost. Many people later
complained about not being given an opportunity to sign and very
few actual refusals were registered. The petition was hurriedly
and unsystematically gathered and under these circumstances, 144
was considered a respectable total.
    The petition read: 'We, the undersigned residents whose houses
are to be demolished, request an official of the Housing Department
to address a public meeting and answer residents' questions about
rehousing.' The covering letter was couched in especially polite
terms so as not to inadvertently cause offence. The tone of the
letter was designed to imply that the lack of information supplied
had been an oversight.
    The petition was sent off on 1st April 1971. The authorities,
when confronted with the lack of local participation during the
rehousing process, invariably protest that while full participation
is desirable and indeed a policy objective, it cannot be foisted
upon an apathetic community which is unorganized and, by implication, perhaps even incapable of organization. Where a consensus of
opinion is unrepresented, the argument continues, there is no
identifiable group to whom officials may address their pleas for
participation. The Gairbraid petitioners presented the authorities
with the opportunity to put into practice their often stated
rhetoric, for here was a group of residents, in tenement property,
who were interested and keen to participate in decision-making about
their own futures. The reply from the Housing Department was thus
eagerly awaited in Gairbraid.
    Writing in his 1971 Annual Report, Glasgow's Housing Manager,
claims that: (1) 'The Department has become involved with Tenants'
Associations ... to an extent hitherto unknown .... It is essential
to maintain liaison even in the most difficult or sometimes hostile

circumstance.' In the 1972 Report, he again writes: (2) 'The
"in" words are "communication" and "participation", and members
of my staff readily apply themselves to meeting the demands of
Tenants' Associations and Community Groups....' As applied in
Gairbraid, there was no correspondence between official rhetoric
and practice: the Housing Department's response to the Gairbraid
petition was simply to ignore it.

There was a precedent in the area for official non-reaction:
some time previously, a petition to have a bus re-routed was
ignored. The bus used Gairbraid as a means of turning around and
the residents complained when it knocked down a child in the area.
They, however, did not receive a reply to their petition and the
bus continued thereafter to endanger the lives of the children
playing in the streets. Gairbraid was determined that a similar
fate would not befall their housing petition.

After waiting over three weeks for a reply, a complaint was made
to a Maryhill councillor. Further, a delegation of Gairbraid women,
led by Annie Mallon, attended an election forum which presented the
local candidates in the 1971 municipal elections. The Gairbraid
people, none of whom had previous experience in public speaking,
very vocally drew attention to their grievances, particularly to
the Housing Department's failure to respond to their petition.
The councillors acted promptly and it must remain a matter of
speculation whether or not a reply would ever have been received
had it not been for their intervention.

In early May, a letter arrived from the Housing Department.
After acknowledging receipt of the petition, it stated:

The question of procedure in Housing Treatment Areas scheduled
for demolition has been referred to the Town Clerk for clarification of legal implications of the Housing (Scotland) Act
1969.

As soon as a ruling has been received, I will notify you and
your request for an official of this Department to address a
public meeting will receive consideration.

The oblique reference to 'treatment areas scheduled for demolition'
was the first official communication received that informed residents that the area had not been earmarked for improvement.
Gairbraid was never able to ascertain what aspects of procedure
required legal clarification, nor was notification of the ruling
ever received.

Although there were very real grounds for complaint, the spirit
of the petition sent to the Housing Manager was simply a request
for information: it attempted neither to question nor challenge
official policy. The reply finally received made no attempt to
remedy the abysmal level of information provided and clearly, the
authorities did not wish to avail themselves of the opportunity to
involve local residents, in any way, in the rehousing process.
The authority's failure to provide the most basic information in
Gairbraid, even when politely petitioned to do so, contributed
greatly to the early growth of the local organization: people felt
angry at being ignored.

FORMING THE COMMITTEE

The petition had been hastily gathered on the assumption that rehousing might begin at any moment and under these circumstances,
it was felt that obtaining information about the authority's intentions should be the major priority in the area. With little time
to organize, it was thought that the proposed public meeting could
function, in addition to eliciting information, as a forum to elect
a local representative committee. While the initial reaction to
the reply received from the Housing Manager was acute disappointment
at the apparent official attitude of non-cooperation, on second
thoughts, it was realized that the community had been allowed a much
needed breathing-space in which to organize. As a ruling about
procedure was required from the Town Clerk, rehousing was not as
imminent as had been previously feared and thus, a local committee
could be elected before the process was started.
     During the period, from when the treatment area was declared in
October 1970 to when Gairbraid decided to form a committee, fully
seven months elapsed and the only official communications received
by the residents were a virtually indecipherable control of occupation order and a curt letter from the Housing Manager in response
to a petition. There was every indication to suggest that simply
appealing to the Corporation for fair treatment was insufficient
and that, in itself, such a tactic was extremely unlikely to
produce positive results. If local interests were to be protected,
it was essential that Gairbraid should be able to bargain from a
position of organized strength. The difficulties encountered when
the petition was collected, by a relatively small number of people
living in only one part of the area, clearly demonstrated the need
for a solidly based committee, representative of the whole community. Local spokesmen were required who could both unite the
community and represent their various interests. There had been
obvious disadvantages in sending the petition to the Housing
Manager before a power base had been established in the community.
However, the experience gained in the process convinced those who
had been involved of the necessity for local organization and thus,
when the Gairbraid committee was formed, it was not imposed from
outside, rather, it was demanded by the people themselves.
     It was decided to call a meeting, open to all the residents of
Gairbraid, for the purpose of electing a committee to represent the
area during the rehousing process. A newsletter was distributed
throughout Gairbraid which gave a summary of the events which had
occurred so far - the facts without embellishment were sufficient.
The newsletter was compiled by the community worker, helped by the
Mallons, and he provided the paper, typing and duplicating facilities - resources not readily available in Gairbraid.
     It was decided that Annie Mallon would open the meeting by pro-
posing that a committee be formed. It was to be suggested that the
four streets which comprised the treatment area should be represented, if possible, by at least three members each. The meeting
was deliberately left unstructured so that its form could be
determined by those present. A room was booked at the Trade Union
Centre, Maryhill Road, and subsequently most of Gairbraid's public
meetings were held there. A crowd of about 30-40 was anticipated

and rather than have the demoralizing effect of a half empty hall,
a relatively small room was booked.

At the Trade Union Centre, on the appointed night, the community
worker's first reaction was that he had arrived at the wrong meeting. Twenty minutes before the advertised starting time, the room
was already full. Barely had arrangements been made to move upstairs to a larger hall than this too was seen to be inadequate and
a second move was necessary. At least 100 people were present; one
estimate was as high as 150. With only 399 houses in the whole
area, not all of which were occupied, a third and probably more of
the families in Gairbraid were represented at the meeting. In fact,
there seemed to be considerably more people at the Gairbraid meeting than had been at the election forum with all of Maryhill for its
constituency. The high turn-out was symptomatic of the degree of
anxiety felt in Gairbraid about rehousing. However, it must not be
imagined that a notice in a corner-shop announcing a meeting is all
that is required to achieve support - three months' work preceded
the formation of the Gairbraid committee.

The atmosphere at the meeting, in a crowded, smoke-filled hall
was noisy, friendly and good-humoured. An informal chat with
relatively few people had been planned and no preparations had been
made for the large turn-out. It was thus inevitable that chaos
should ensue and indeed, chaos tended to the tenor of the meeting
throughout. The lack of formality and direction had its advantages
as it was obvious that people were not there simply to endorse the
candidature of an already established clique - clearly, no such
group existed. Everyone who wanted it was allowed the opportunity
to participate and no-one dominated the proceedings.

After some delay, Annie Mallon, protesting that she could not
get up in front of so many people, opened the meeting. In the
months to come, Annie Mallon was to speak on many such public
occasions. She stood, not much more than five foot tall, engulfed
in the body of the audience, and spontaneously delivered a stirring
speech, calling on the people to organize. Contributions were then
called from the floor and after each, the meeting lapsed into a
buzz of private conversations as the points raised were considered.
There was no doubt that the unanimous and loudly enthusiastic
opinion was that a committee should be formed with representatives
from each of the four streets. Eventually, volunteers were called
for, though some like Jimmy Gallagher were nominated. In all,
twenty people came forward. Votes were not actually cast because
it was felt that since not all the candidates were personally known
by everyone present, an election was pointless. Furthermore, twenty
was considered a good number and accordingly, all twenty candidates
were popularly acclaimed to be members of the Gairbraid Housing
Committee - the GHC.

Once the hall had emptied, the committee gathered around a table
to elect office bearers and to arrange their next meeting. The
election which took place seemed quite random, as may have been
expected from a group of people coming together for the first time.
For instance, Annie Mallon, who had to leave early, was not chosen
simply because she was not present. The community worker was
offered the chairmanship which he declined on the grounds that the
committee, if it were to achieve success, required to be under local

leadership. This explanation was immediately accepted without
dissent: leadership is seldom forced upon an outsider as is sometimes claimed. As Jimmy Gallagher saw the purpose of the meeting,
'it was to get the people to form their own committee because only
they were able to express what kind of conditions they lived in.'
    The committee started with £1 in the kitty, donated by an
official of the Maryhill Trade Union Centre. It was a gesture of
solidarity much appreciated by the committee's members. At all
subsequent public meetings held there Gairbraid was usually charged
only a nominal fee for use of the premises.

THE COMMITTEE MEMBERS

It had been anticipated that, when the euphoria of the previous
night had given way to the cold reality of the morning after, some
of the people who joined would begin to have second thoughts about
their continued membership of the committee. The first casualty
was the secretary who resigned two days after being appointed on
the grounds that membership was incompatible with her employment
by Glasgow Corporation. She was replaced as secretary by Annie
Mallon. Three others never attended meetings at all, one of whom,
because of ill-health, felt unable to climb the three flights of
stairs to the committee rooms. A further seven of those recruited
attended no more than two meetings each before dropping out for
reasons such as being placed on night shift or simply lacking
interest. Thus eleven, or more than half the original number of
recruits, ceased almost immediately to function as committee
members. From the very beginning, the group was reduced to nine
active members and of these, only five were to become leaders in
the community. Throughout their campaign, the GHC was geared to
recruit additional members and residents continually joined to
reinforce the existing core of activists.
    The reasons given by the main activists for joining the committee
were negative past experiences with the Housing Department together
with the belief that their aspirations could only be realised
through organization. As Hugh Thompson expressed it: 'I had heard
so many stories about Glasgow Corporation browbeating people, I
thought a wee bit of united action was for our own benefit.'
Eileen Thompson's sister had had a 'rough time' being rehoused -
'she just would not get off their backs, she was up there practi-
cally every day until she got what she considered a decent offer'.
Betty Gallagher's mother, in spite of forty-three years tenancy,
needed eight offers, all 'worse than the house she was leaving',
before she was successfully rehoused. She was told that 'she'd
have to get out, they were threatening her and she was seventy-odd'.
The experience taught Betty Gallagher that 'you held out for what
you wanted and didn't give into them'. In their own dealings with
the Housing Department, the Gallaghers were told that if they refused an offer they would have to find their own accommodation.
They saw old age pensioners going away in tears with the treatment
they were getting from the clerks. The Gallaghers asked to move to
Maryhill 'B', then being built, and were told that they 'hadn't a
chance'. (3) Jimmy Gallagher joined the committee feeling that

'they wouldn't be able to treat the mass of people the way they
treat a monority'. In addition, he felt that the committee's
purpose was 'to make sure that the councillors were doing something for the people as they were nominated by the people'.

Two close relatives of John Moir's, his aunt and grandmother,
had separately had wretched experiences during rehousing. His
aunt advised him to form a local organization in Gairbraid:

'That aunt of mine, she was in the same predicament years ago.
She said: "you better get to grips - get the people together."
They had done this years ago further down Maryhill. It came
out of the blue for them and then they were left hanging.
They plucked one or two from here and there and the place
collapsed round about them. This went on for two or three
years. The place was condemned but they were in the building
for say three years at the very least without any repairs
being done, water cut off. There was a do-it-yourself sort
of thing, tradesmen who lived in the street repaired all the
pipes themselves. Eventually, they got together and formed
a committee and badgered away and eventually they got success.
So she had said, "you would be better to try and form some
committee", and then, this letter came through the door saying
there was a meeting, this was ideal for me.'

Recalling his grandmother's difficulties with Glasgow Corporation,
John Moir remembers:

'Unfortunately, I had been in the army at the time and she was
in the house with my sister. The same thing happened again:
they plucked two or three out and left. They came and more or
less threatened her. She took the first offer. Never even saw
the house. Didn't even know where it was or nothing. She
never went out when she moved up there. She was a very active
woman and she never went out. That was her stranded in that
house. I'll always remember that, she never left the house,
very, very seldom because there was a tremendous hill. She
didn't want the place but the chap came showing her the empty
houses getting boarded up - "it's a very quiet place and you'll
be left here" and mice flying all over the place and all the
rest of it. "It must get worse and there are only four or five
of you left and the chances are you will be the only one left."
He said to her the other four had accepted but probably they
didn't, he probably had not seen the other four. He had said
that to the lot of them. It was up a tremendously big hill, so
the old people she was friendly with couldn't come and see her
and vice versa, she couldn't go see them. I feel this was only
one instance, there must be thousands of cases like that. I
feel that a younger person could have taken that house on the
hill quite easily, it was a three apartment, and my gran could
have been rehoused on the main road and she would have been okay.
But she actually broke her heart in that house. She just went
right down the hill altogether, just lost interest in everything. Well, these things you do remember, I could see this
happening again - the idea of the committee seemed to me
fantastic. I feel, through these two experiences, with that
aunt but more so my gran, I wanted to join the committee.'

The large number of people annually dealt with by Clive House is

often used by them to justify criticism, arguing that under the
circumstances, the occasional complaint is only to be expected.
However, no amount of official denials can hide the testimony of
vast numbers of working-class Glaswegians who over many years have
suffered during their rehousing. Most people in Gairbraid knew
of past experiences almost identical to their own. In the treatment it received, Gairbraid was not exceptional, either before or
since, in the long history of Glasgow's Housing Department. The
residents showed great tenacity in opposing official policy but
even in this, as illustrated by John Moir's aunt, Gairbraid was
by no means the first to resist. Organized opposition against the
Corporation is not necessarily dependent on outside community
action support. While the fieldworkers provided the spark for
organization in Gairbraid, the potential already existed and no
outside force was required to create discontent.

ORGANIZING TO CONSOLIDATE

On 20 May 1971, two days after it was formed, the GHC held its
first committee meeting. Thirteen of the twenty elected members
turned up to begin the sober business of organizing in the community. The period from then until the beginning of rehousing about
eight weeks later, although unspectacular, was a vital phase of the
compaign in which the foundations of the local organization were
built. In the lull before the storm, the committee's survival hung
in the balance as people reconsidered their commitment and weighed
the odds of success, deciding whether or not the effort required
would be worthwhile. During those first few months it was not at
all certain that organization would be sustained in Gairbraid.
The issue was in fact decided by only a handful of residents who
undertook the preparatory work and carried the committee through
its formative period. By the time rehousing started, they had
formed a cohesive group, ready to lead the community in its
struggles. The GHC needed to establish its credibility as a viable
organization in relation to both the Corporation and its own
community. The committee had to gain recognition from a local
authority which was unwilling to concede even the slightest legitimacy or status to the group. At the same time, the committee
had also to win and sustain the support of the majority of Gairbraid
residents who were clearly sceptical about the chances of success.
It was an initial vicious circle: the authorities would ignore the
committee unless forced to do otherwise by the power of the local
protest which, however, was likely to be muted until the committee
had proved itself and demonstrated its ability to achieve positive
results. Thus, the committee, if it were to survive, had to
operate on two levels - externally in dealing with the power structure and internally within the community.
    Gairbraid faced a powerful machine, insensitive to local needs
and unused to having its decisions questioned. As far as it was
concerned, at that stage, the area's future had already been sealed.
It is, therefore, not surprising that many in the community, including some of the committee members, felt that any attempt to oppose
the Corporation would prove to be a pointless exercise. The

committee had firmly to establish in the community a two-way democratic process between the leadership and the ordinary resident.
Close links between the committee and its constituency were
especially vital in Gairbraid: being a clearance area, rehousing
was bound to continually weaken the local organization by removing
activists from the scene and thus, if- the GHC was to conduct a
sustained campaign, replacements from the community would be constantly required. The danger was that the members would be rehoused
before the committee had created a life of its own independent of
individuals. The GHC needed quickly to gain an initial success to
raise committee morale and to reinforce local support. The early
strategies devised all aimed to consolidate the committee's position
as a group representative of the community which would be able to
intervene on their behalf when the expected crisis arose at the
start of the rehousing process. However, before it could appear to
be a viable force to others, the GHC had to become one. The first
priority was thus organizing within the committee itself.

During the early days, there was the danger that the committee
members would come to represent no one but themselves. Very
patently the area was not organized and the GHC was not so much a
group as a mere collection of individuals who had joined together
out of differing motives and expectations with none too clear an
idea of how best to achieve success. The excitement of the public
meeting notwithstanding, the birth of the GHC heralded no immediate
changes in the community and the committee had to make its presence
felt quickly if it were not simply to be forgotten. With the
exception of one active trade unionist, Jimmy Gallagher, the pooled
organizational experience of the members was slight. In the beginning the unity that the GHC represented as a group and as the
collective expression of local aspirations seemed extremely fragile.

Before it could even begin to formulate policy, the GHC had to
consider such details as how often and on which night it should
meet. After some trial and error, Mondays were found to be the day
fewest people worked over-time. Weekly sessions were decided upon
and for the next sixteen months, Monday in Gairbraid became committee night. The meetings were held in the flat in Burnhouse Street,
and the premises, together with its telephone, proved indispensible. The first committee meeting was conducted in an informal,
friendly atmosphere where the members discussed their own and the
community's problems. This set the tone of all subsequent meetings and although there were periodic pressures from a few of the
committee members to have the discussion directed through the
chair, with minutes being taken and read, such moves were always
resisted by the majority. The decision to maintain informality
had important and positive repercussions, as it allowed a feeling
of group identity to develop, new recruits were able to be easily
integrated, and large numbers of non-members were able to attend
and contribute freely without being made to feel outsiders or
inhibited by unnecessary ritual. The regular attenders came to
enjoy the opportunity to chat and discuss the weekly events and
the meetings themselves acquired a positive social value. Whenever possible the meetings were ended before closing time -
10.00 p.m. in Scotland - to enable the men to rush off to the pub
while the women remained to chat. The committee could not to a

certain extent avoid becoming an in-group; however, it is a tribute
to the good sense of John Moir and Jimmy Gallagher, the main office
bearers, that this tendency was minimized and the committee was
never allowed to sever its links with the rest of the community.
Unstructured meetings, although often an irritant, resulting in
repetition and wasted time, seemed best suited to Gairbraid's purposes: whether or not a similar procedure is adopted elsewhere
would seem to depend on the issues and personalities involved.

There, of course, could be no guarantee of success, but if there
was to be any chance of it the members had to have confidence in
their own ability and to transmit to the community their belief in
ultimate victory. The working-class population of Gairbraid were
used to official neglect, they had never been consulted about anything and were only ever remembered by anyone in authority at
election time when candidates vied for their votes. A reluctance
to demand participation was not so much a matter of apathy as a
realistic assessment of the existing balance of power. Jackie Moir
says, 'this stems from away back, people believed that you would
never get anywhere fighting the Corporation.' On paper, the odds
were stacked against Gairbraid, but this was reckoning without the
depth of feeling that existed among the people, their sense of
justice, their grit and determination to see the campaign through.
Gairbraid also had the advantage of being among the first to mount
a co-ordinated challenge to the Corporation, who, when faced with
the unfamiliar, simply did not know what to do. Gairbraid's
strategy throughout was to present the authorities with a choice
where it would be easier for them to rehouse the community quickly
than to resist local demands.

There were some in the community, particularly among the elderly
who felt that to become active on the committee was to risk victim-
ization by the Corporation. The logic of the situation, however,
suggested that activists were more likely to be rehoused quickly
so as to deprive the community of its leadership. The GHC confronted a prevalent feeling of powerlessness. Widespread in the
area too, was an attitude of cynicism: 'once rehousing started,
solidarity would disintegrate as people clamour to obtain the best
houses for themselves.' Eileen Thompson remembers one woman
saying: 'they must be communists, nobody does nothing for nothing
in Maryhill.' The system is hardly designed to create feelings of
fellowship; basically, the whole apparatus is geared towards dishing
out houses to an endless queue in a situation of acute scarcity
where every man must be for himself. John Moir perceives it as a
competitive world where altruism and the best intentions are necessarily made suspect:

'When you are dealing with houses, you are dealing with people's
feelings. It's not as if you have plenty of money and can take
a bad house and say, well I've made a bloomer, I'm off. People
moving houses, working-class people, they know its more or less
for a life time. You very seldom move again. I would say the
biggest majority of people, when they move, that's it and they
know that. So you're dealing with a very tricky situation.
It's hard to convince people that you think of them as well as
yourself.'

The committee had thus at all times to act with the utmost care and

responsibility, never to jeopardize anyone's chance of a house: its
task was to build up trust and a store of goodwill in the community.
      On the one hand, residents felt that 'the committee has been
elected, let them get on with it'. On the other, members felt that
many residents 'couldn't be bothered, they just sit back while we
do all the work for them'. In a situation where unity was impera-
tive, such attitudes, had they remained prevalent, would have
created an inseparable gulf between the committee and the rest of
the community. All sections had to realize that the community itself, in co-ordinated action, was the area's only available source
of power sufficient to influence the rehousing process. It is
difficult to ascertain accurately the role played by the non-
active residents during the initial stages but there is no doubt
that the committee stimulated interest and discussion in the area.
Often people could be seen, at street corners and in the local
shops, gathered to assess the committee's prospects. There was
continual feedback to the committee members, from their friends and
immediate neighbours as well as from relative strangers asking them
about the latest activities. The reports back to the committee
varied from strong encouragement, to pessimism that the whole
enterprise was doomed to inevitable failure. It was clear that
the committee had not only to act on the community's behalf but
also had quickly to be seen to be doing so.
      The community were kept informed through newsletters which
appeared almost monthly during the committee's active life. Soon
after the committee was formed, all the names and addresses of the
members were listed in a newsletter. The residents were invited
to contact members to pass on information, ideas, suggestions,
problems or whatever, and this invitation was repeated in all the
newsletters. Without exception, the committee members regarded
the newsletters as a vital element of their campaign. Eileen
Thompson, for instance, believes that the newletters were 'most
important because people felt a part of it - people were always
kept up to date, they knew exactly what was going on.'
      Many in Gairbraid had definite ideas of what the committee should
be. One of the first problems which arose was that two of the
twenty who volunteered to join the committee were considered, because of low status, unsuitable for membership. There was some
pressure from both within and without the committee to have them
excluded. Potentially, a classical 'roughs versus respectables'
clash was in the offing and at that early stage the committee could
ill afford any disruption. Whether or not it would have developed
beyond mild ostracism was never determined as the matter was resolved when the two women, after attending the first two meetings,
allowed their membership to lapse. One moved away from the area
soon after and the other had serious personal difficulties and it
is doubtful whether she could have remained active even if encouraged to do so. Many of the members were unaware of these events
but, nevertheless, the committee faced a potential crisis which,
had it arisen, might have posed a serious dilemma: the two women
represented a section of the community, albeit a minority, and thus
had a legitimate claim to membership. Later, the committee did
accept new recruits from all sections of the community as full
members which suggests that the roughts-respectables dichotomy,

although important, was perhaps no more than a latent force in the area. It is too simplistic to label this lack of solidarity as 'false consciousness'. Particularly in tenement property, where even one un-cooperative family can cause a whole stair to deteriorate rapidly and make life generally miserable for all the other inhabitants, antipathy towards such individuals is not unreasonable. However, as with all prejudices, generalizations are made and a whole section or sub-class in the community becomes tainted because of the anti-social behaviour of a few. Some degree of conflict between 'roughs' and 'respectables' is bound to occur in all communities. The working class is not homogeneous and it is as well for community activists to realize this from the outset.

From its inception until the start of rehousing, the GHC held seven committee meetings and each was attended on average by almost seven members. During this period the active membership was reduced to nine of whom the most prominent were: John Moir and Hugh Thompson in Balfour Street, Annie Mallon and Georgina Atkinson in Guthrie Street and Jimmy Gallagher in Burnhouse Street. Of those who had dropped out, David Bouse was to rejoin and play a crucial role during the later stages of the campaign. He left because 'there were plenty of people on the committee'. Although numbers were never consciously restricted, the active membership never exceeded twelve, which probably reflects the maximum who could perform useful functions at a given moment. A larger membership would have eased the problem of door-to-door visits in the area, and well attended meetings helped maintain the morale of the members, but essentially people were reluctant to fill either menial or passive roles. This is particularly true of working-class populations where people have to work over-time to earn a living wage.

Chapter 5

ORGANIZING BEFORE THE CRISIS

At the first committee meeting, three main topics occupied the members: the need to obtain information; the role of the councillors; and the factors' responsibility to maintain the property. These were to remain the dominant issues until overtaken by events when rehousing started.

THE LACK OF INFORMATION

When questioned about the reasons behind their timing, the authorities simply insisted that under the Housing (Scotland) Act 1969 they were under a statutory obligation to demolish in Gairbraid. However, Glasgow cannot simultaneously treat all the houses under its jurisdiction which fail to meet the tolerable standard. The GHC was never able to ascertain the reasons behind their area, by no means the worst in Glasgow, being among the first to be singled out for demolition under the 1969 Act.

The right to know what is going to happen to you, when it is likely to happen and the provision of a reasonable choice of alternatives, so readily taken for granted in a middle-class milieu, are in working-class areas like Gairbraid issues for struggle. Although not always articulated in this way, the demand, at this basic level, for human rights, is what the Gairbraid campaign was all about. It was certainly the point at which the campaign was initiated. Without consultation, a community is seriously disadvantaged: Gairbraid was forced to operate within a severely curtailed range of possibilities. In that the people were presented with a fait accompli, they were not given the option of being rehoused in the new estate that was to be built in Gairbraid. It was also too late for them to demand that they be rehoused together elsewhere so that the community could be maintained. By the time they became aware of what was happening, the basic decisions about their future had long been made. The die had already been cast and it was then no longer possible that the community would be even partially maintained. 'Rehousing the community en bloc', although later demanded by the GHC, was never more than a slogan and none of the committee members ever had any real expectation that it could be achieved. The authorities, by withholding information until the last moment, effectively eliminated communal rehousing as an option open to Gairbraid. Under the circumstances, the best that the GHC could hope to achieve was that the residents would be decently rehoused in the shortest possible time and, in the alternative accommodation offered them, that they would receive a maximum of choice.

In conditions of constant rehousing, an individual, whether or not he believes it desirable that the community should be maintained, dare not refuse a decent house when it is offered him. Thus, the fact that the residents accepted dispersal is not evidence that Gairbraid lacked a sense of community, it simply indicates that the people were given no other option. Random rehousing over a lengthy period of time were the terms dictated by Glasgow Corporation. It was imposed on the community. It certainly was not chosen by them. The GHC was thus forced to operate within an already defined situation and could aim only to ameliorate the worst effects of official policy. The committee's strategies were developed largely in the context of, and in response to, Glasgow's rehousing policy and practice. Of the options open to the GHC, the obvious activity was to increase pressure on the Housing Department to ensure that the public meeting, first proposed in the petition, took place as quickly as possible. However, by then, the meeting had become a means rather than an end in itself. It was quite apparent that as a source of accurate information, very little could be expected from the meeting as the Housing Manager appeared unwilling to co-operate. Rather, the GHC, by bringing a Housing Department official into the area when it was clear that he would not come on his own accord, hoped to gain credit and thereby establish some credibility for itself in the community. The meeting was also viewed as a means of giving notice to the authorities of the community's strength and determination to oppose official policy. Finally, it was to be a rallying point for the community to enable the committee to gather local support.

Two months after the petition had been sent and a month after the reply had been received, Gairbraid still awaited an official clarification of their position. Accordingly, the GHC again requested that a public meeting be held in Gairbraid. The letter was sent to the Town Clerk's Office to be passed on to the appropriate Corporation departments and committees so that councillors in addition to officials would be involved. The letter also raised questions about the content and timing of the intended treatment programme and pointed out that complicated issues concerning both tenants and owner-occupiers urgently required attention. Finally, a copy of the Corporation's resolution declaring the treatment area was requested but this was never received. Failing satisfaction, the authorities were advised that an approach to the Secretary of State for Scotland would be contemplated. An acknowledgement was promptly received and then nothing else was ever heard of the letter. It seemed that the Corporation had adopted a policy of ignoring Gairbraid, possibly in the hope that the GHC would fail to pursue the matter. Quite obviously, the GHC could not simply sit back until such time as the Housing Manager agreed

to hold the proposed meeting. Without constant pressure it was
extremely doubtful if the meeting would ever take place and moreover, building the local organization was essential in the time
allowed before rehousing started.

THE COUNCILLORS

At the committee's inception, Maryhill was represented by two Labour
and one Scottish Nationalist councillors, but almost immediately,
at the 1971 municipal election, the Labour Party won control of all
three seats. That election saw the return of a Labour Party
majority in Glasgow. Although the initial decision to declare
Gairbraid a housing treatment area was made under a Conservative
administration, actual rehousing was started and completed while
the Labour Party held an absolute majority in the city. It may
be argued that Labour inherited a mess in Gairbraid and, therefore,
responsibility must lie with the previous Tory administration.
However, even given the totally incompetent and insensitive way in
which Gairbraid was initially handled, the damage already done was
by no means irretrievable by the time Labour took office. Few, if
any, even among staunch Labour Party supporters in the area, could
detect the slightest departure in rehousing policy from previous
practice after the Labour victory in the city. Gairbraid, in fact,
did not witness any visible difference between the policies of the
two main political parties.
     The councillor is very often in the difficult position of having
to represent diverse and sometimes conflicting interests. In
Maryhill, for instance, the early rehousing of a Gairbraid resident
might have meant delay for a family in a similar predicament else-
were in the ward. The councillors had also to balance party
loyalty with local interests. The Maryhill councillors faced
criticisms of rehousing policy for which their own Labour Party
was responsible. The councillors thus contended with various
irreconcilable interest groups, each demanding loyalty in a
situation where neutrality was likely to earn scorn from all sides.
     Where the functions of local organizations and councillors
overlap both tend to compete for the same constituents and, therefore, a certain amount of conflict between them is only to be
expected. Gairbraid's concern with housing was clearly within the
councillor's domain and thus the GHC's very existence could have
been interpreted as a reflection both of the councillors' inability
to cope, and of the failure of the democratic processes of local
government itself. Indeed, were the councillors able to represent
adequately all the people living in the ward, an almost impossible
task when these number tens of thousands, there would be little
reason in the first place to form local action groups.
     Many people in Gairbraid felt that had the councillors been
really interested in the welfare of the community they would, on
their own initiative, have visited the area. In the nine months
available, from the moment the treatment resolution was passed
until rehousing started, there was sufficient time for the three
Maryhill councillors between them to cope with the 399 Gairbraid
households. It was thought that the councillors should have

visited or even leafleted each of the families in the area, to
provide information and explanations of procedure and to note
and follow-up grievances and special cases. Such action would
have made the GHC appear superfluous, however, and even if willing,
it is debateable whether this is the proper function of a councillor. If it is not, there is no real contradiction between the
roles of councillors and action groups and the best solution would
seem to be for both to work in conjunction with each other. Be
this as it may, the Maryhill councillors did not deem it necessary
to intervene in the rehousing process unless individually requested
to do so. On the assumption that the official machinery would
operate fairly and satisfactorily for the bulk of the population,
the councillors' attitude to rehousing seemed to be that, provided
they were first approached, their services were available to the
few who might not manage on their own. However, even disregarding
the fact that those most in need are usually those least likely to
seek assistance, there is nothing in Glasgow's past to suggest that
rehousing may be undertaken in anything other than an extremely
insensitive and bureaucratic manner. The councillors thus failed
to respond to the local crisis.

In Gairbraid, attitudes towards the councillors tended to be
ambiguous. On the one hand, there was a deference for their
status and an appreciation of their power to help individuals
through their access to officialdom. On the other hand, political
cynicism was widespread and many thought that with rare exceptions
councillors do nothing for the people. The tone of the relationship between the GHC and the councillors was set by the latters'
initial inactivity. Although mutual feelings sometimes lapsed
into a state of semi-hostility, contact with them was always
maintained. Throughout the Gairbraid campaign, the Maryhill
councillors were sent copies of all GHC correspondence: they were
not to be allowed to claim ignorance for failure to act on the
community's behalf.

At the first committee meeting it was decided that the GHC's
role was to bring the councillors to Gairbraid. One of its
functions was defined as maintaining and extending the channels of
communication between the community and their political representatives. It was agreed that the councillors could perform an
important intermediary role between the community and the power
structure and thus every effort was to be made not to antagonize
them unnecessarily. The committee felt that the councillors were
elected by the people to represent their interests and since
Gairbraid was a community under stress it was reasonable to expect
every co-operation from them. The committee sought to inculcate
into the community the belief that people had a real democratic
right to demand and receive attention from their elected representatives, and that assistance obtained was definitely not to be
regarded as favours bestowed. It was one of the GHC's early
achievements that deference for the councillors quickly passed
and they were no longer regarded as a privileged elite but rather
as persons elected to serve the interests of their constituents.
Time spent with the ordinary citizen in Gairbraid was seen to be
as much part of their job as was devising grand schemes for the
city.

Although many in Gairbraid had at various times been in contact with individual councillors, most of the people would have been hard pressed to recognize or even name their representatives. The mere presence of a councillor in the area was still unusual enough for the committee to gain credit for having invited them and as such, bringing the councillors to Gairbraid was an early means of establishing credibility. However, an invitation to the councillors to attend a committee meeting was postponed to give the members time to gain sufficient experience and confidence to enable them to maintain control of the proceedings. This was simply a precautionary measure to ensure that the councillors did not assume a position of leadership in the community although the danger was probably minimal as none of them had shown any readiness to identify with either the local people or their problems. The committee felt strongly that, in Gairbraid's interests, the community should provide its own leadership. If progress was to be achieved at all, Gairbraid had to define its own priorities and this excluded councillors, community workers and all other outsiders, from decision-making.

HOUSE REPAIRS

Once an area is earmarked for demolition, almost overnight repairs are no longer undertaken as, quite understandably, owners are reluctant to incur additional expenses on property which only has a limited life. This, however, does not take account of the fact that tenants are forced to live under ever-deteriorating conditions. The Corporation refused to disclose how long the buildings were likely to remain in use and, therefore, it was difficult for tenants to convince the house factors that even temporary repairs were worthwhile. Many of the factors refused to do any repairs although the tenants were still required to pay rent. In this situation the only satisfactory solution was for the Corporation to take immediate responsibility for the upkeep of the area. However, compulsory purchase orders were only issued after Gairbraid had been completely cleared. Thus, throughout the period when the treatment area was occupied, responsibility for the maintenance of the property remained with the factors.

Repairs were thus an issue which immediately confronted the GHC. Forcing the factors to do repairs was, again, a means of establishing credibility in the community, particularly where these had not been done for some time. Another advantage was that it provided the members with a set task while the reply was pending from the Housing Department. Until the crisis broke with the onset of rehousing it was essential that the committee did not disintegrate through inactivity although, of course, tasks could not be artificially created. Complaints about repairs were collected by the members in a door-to-door canvass which was a way of re-affirming the GHC's presence in the area, giving them the opportunity to become known in the community.

While the problem of repairs could not be ignored, the possibility of over-involvement needed to be avoided. After all, the main quarrel was with the Corporation and not with the factors.

Legitimately, rents could have been withheld until repairs were satisfactorily completed but this might have resulted in threats of eviction and lengthy court appearances. The committee thus decided to avoid, if at all possible, a confrontation with the factors. The strategy adopted was that those factors who had failed to undertake repairs would be threatened with legal action in the hope that this in itself would be sufficient to induce them to do at least some remedial work on the property. At that stage, the committee had no intention of instituting legal proceedings in case this deflected energies away from the rehousing process. It was decided that only in the event of rehousing being delayed would the committee become fully committed to the problem of repairs. It was an unsatisfactory even if necessary compromise for some of the factors had clearly neglected their duties. However, once warning letters had been sent, if there had been a delay in rehousing, action against the factors could have then started immediately - a skirmish with them might have proved a useful preliminary issue around which to unite the tenants for the major campaign ahead.

Owner-occupiers in Gairbraid were naturally enough less keen on an enthusiastic pursuance of a repairs campaign than were tenants. While the factors may have neglected to undertake common repairs so too had some of the owner-occupiers and they would not have thanked the GHC for involving them in additional expense just prior to their rehousing. Therefore, a taboo was placed on common repairs such as roofs, stairs, drains and so forth, for which factors and owner-occupiers shared responsibility. Above all else, the committee wished to avoid splitting the community so that it came to represent the tenants as opposed to the owner-occupiers in the area. For the same reason at that stage no attempt was made to put pressure on the Corporation to maintain the area. If successful, such action, almost certainly, would have resulted in expenses being claimed from the owner-occupiers. As it was, Hugh and Eileen Thompson, who owned their house, had already received notice from the Corporation demanding that they remedy a choked drain. A letter sent in response, under the auspices of the GHC, requesting full details of the Health Department's extensive examination of the drainage system, was never acknowledged but it did silence any further claims that the Thompsons might be responsible for the upkeep of the drains. As most tenements in Glasgow contain both tenants and owners whose interests do not always coincide, if the latter are not to be alienated any campaign to have the property properly maintained must proceed with the utmost caution.

The GHC were advised by two lawyers although neither were practising at the time. They helped compose the letters, in legal language, sent to the factors. They also advised on other legal matters such as bogus repair bills. The lawyers offered to place their services at the committee's disposal so that a legal advice centre could be started in the area. Although both of them attended several sessions, there was never enough interest in the area to maintain the service. However, the advice given by them to the committee proved invaluable, as did the occasions when they rushed to the area to deal with individual legal problems. Although

mostly unnecessary, as the law played little part in Gairbraid,
legal expertise was not readily available in the community and
the backing of the lawyers, particularly their assurances about
aspects of the law which were in doubt, helped the committee
members gain confidence during the initial months of the campaign.

Only six of the committee members were involved in the door-to-
door collection of complaints, and at that most of the work was
done by three of the members between them. Thus, the list of
repairs collected was by no means complete. Of the four streets
in the area, only Balfour and Burnhouse Streets were systematically
visited. Guthrie Street was only partially covered and Gairbraid
Avenue not at all. This reflected the unequal distribution of
committee members in the area: Gairbraid Avenue had then only
one representative.

The complaints collected varied from relatively minor defects
such as cracked or broken windows to more serious grievances like
dry rot, dampness or 'no fireplace in the bedroom - just a hole
through which the rain comes in.' Many of the tenants were
satisfied with their factors and by no means all complained about
outstanding repairs. Frequently, tenants had done the work themselves - 'I had to put in my own window cords after numerous
requests to the factor.' Of those who did have outstanding complaints, all had previously drawn their factor's attention to them
without ever receiving any satisfaction. The GHC notified four
factors of outstanding repairs that required immediate attention,
failing which legal proceedings would be instituted against them.
Only one of these replied saying that they 'resented the threatening tone' but nevertheless instructed their tradesmen to begin
work on the required repairs. Nothing further was heard from the
other factors though soon afterwards activity was observed in the
area as some long-neglected defects in the property were attended
to. Georgina Atkinson, for example, reported that dampness in her
house, about which she had complained for about three years, was
then finally remedied. The committee had thus gained some, even
if limited, success in their attempt to have the property maintained. Some of the required work was never completed as factors
never got beyond sending tradesmen to inspect the defects. The
matter, however, was not pursued because soon thereafter the
rehousing process began.

THE ARRIVAL OF THE HOUSING
VISITORS

In late June, the committee had to take cognizance of the approaching summer holidays. During the Glasgow Fair fortnight much of
the city closes down and it was anticipated that many of the residents would either be away on holiday or else would be entertaining
friends and relatives at home. It was thus desirable to avoid any
major activity during this time. It was decided to withhold
pressure on the Housing Department until the end of the summer when
a renewed campaign would be started to ensure that the promised
public meeting took place as quickly as possible. To maintain local
interest over the holiday period of inactivity, the committee

proposed that, instead of again inviting the officials, a public
meeting be organized with only the Maryhill councillors present.
It was to be held in early July before the holiday break and it
was viewed as a useful preliminary exercise in which the members
could gain experience for the later, more important, meeting with
the Housing Department. It was to be an opportunity to seek a
commitment publicly from the councillors to work in the community's
interest. All three of the Maryhill councillors were invited but
only one accepted as the other two had already made plans for the
summer. No sooner had arrangements been finalized than word began
to filter through from the community that some residents had received warning from the Housing Department that the Housing
Visitors were about to descend on the area. The whole equation
had suddenly been changed: the arrival of the visitors meaning
that rehousing would soon follow.

Strategy had been based on the mistaken assumption that rehousing would not begin before the autumn, which would have allowed
for a comparatively leisurely build up of organizational strength.
The arrival of the housing visitors created a mild panic in the
committee as alternative plans were hurriedly made: an invitation
was rushed off to the Housing Department for an official to attend
the already arranged meeting with the councillors. Against
expectations, two days before the meeting was due to be held,
confirmation was received that an official would be present. It
meant that the GHC had to rethink its strategy for the meeting.
Nevertheless, the members were elated for, at long last, things
were beginning to happen in the area: after all, bringing an
official to Gairbraid had been one of the committee's major
objectives. The Corporation's timing, however, was extraordinary.
A petition, a reminder letter and finally a third invitation was
necessary before the Housing Manager agreed to allow one of his
officials to address the Gairbraid residents. Although fully
three months elapsed between the initial request and the actual
meeting, the committee was given only two days' notice in which
to prepare for it.

The petition had requested that the meeting be held before the
housing visitors were sent to the area so that the official could
provide the residents with information before the rehousing
process began. To hold it afterwards seemed senseless and illogi-
cal, that is, unless the Corporation preferred that the residents
should enter the rehousing process in a state of ignorance. The
treatment area had been subject to legal difficulties and the GHC
had been promised notification once these had been clarified.
This had in the first place been given as the reason for postponing
the proposed meeting - the Housing Manager had raised no other
objections to it. This promise created a false sense of security
in the community as it was reasonable to expect that the GHC would
receive a communication from the Housing Department dealing with
both the legal question and the proposed meeting before rehousing
was begun. Both the outstanding invitations to send an official
to the area and the promise to inform the residents were ignored.
Had the GHC not acted quickly and again invited the official, there
can be no doubt that the meeting would never have been held. The
lesson learnt was that very little could be expected from the

authorities and that rights, to be obtained, would have to be
demanded. The committee was also disappointed in the local
councillors: either they knew of the impending arrival of the
housing visitors and did not disclose this information or else,
they were kept equally as ignorant as the community, in which
case they were almost as powerless as the GHC.

Notice of the housing visitors' arrival was not simultaneously
sent to all the residents. Where GHC members were among those
notified and others on the same stair were not, some accused the
committee of organizing things so that they would be rehoused
first. These allegations were easily disproved as some members,
including the chairman, were among those initially left out.
Soon thereafter the matter was resolved when notices were sent to
the remainder. The incident was most certainly innocent, probably
caused by nothing more than a postal delay, yet the reaction to
it illustrates the high level of anxiety, mistrust and disunity
still existing in Gairbraid. Rumour also had it, untrue as it
turned out, that one of the new housing schemes then being built
in Maryhill was reserved for Gairbraid. Reactions were not
completely positive as some expressed the view that not everyone
in the area deserved a new house. Clearly, some people wanted
to get away from their neighbours. Just prior to the meeting
with the housing officials, Gairbraid hardly presented a solid
front. In the short time available to it, about seven weeks,
the GHC could not have been expected to unite the community and
certainly, had not managed to do so.

THE PUBLIC MEETING WITH THE
HOUSING OFFICIALS

Although the committee had continually striven towards bringing the
housing official to the area, when suddenly faced with organizing
the event, a common strategy had still to be worked out. The
meeting was ostensibly aimed at obtaining information. While most
of the committee members were sceptical and believed that the
Housing Department would not divulge anything useful, this view
was not on the whole shared by the community who tended to regard
the occasion as an opportunity to plead their own individual cases.
It is only natural that people should be eager to press for houses
for themselves. However, it was highly improbable that the
officials would be able, even if willing, to deal meaningfully
with individual problems. These, if allowed to completely dominate,
would have simply elicited platitudes and the meeting would have
become a public relations exercise for the Housing Department.
The discussion needed to be steered towards points of policy
affecting the whole community and although unlikely to find ready
acceptance, the committee had to use the opportunity to impress
upon the authorities a demand for genuine local participation in
decision-making. While the committee did attempt to ensure that
important points were raised, neither then nor at any subsequent
public meeting, was it thought possible or even desirable for them
to predetermine and control the questions raised from the floor.

The committee, meeting two days before the official was due to

speak in the area, discussed their strategy. It was agreed that
John Moir, who was then vice-chairman, should open the proceedings
with a prepared speech. The official was to be asked four main
questions:

1 When would rehousing begin and how long was the process
   likely to last?
2 Would residents who wished to be rehoused together in the
   new Maryhill estates be allowed to do so?
3 In order to avoid the worst effects of the blight and
   vandalism, would people be moved tenement by tenement
   instead of the normal practice of issuing offers randomly
   throughout the area?
4 How long will it take before house owners receive compensation and tenants well maintained payments? (Under the
   Housing (Scotland) Act 1969, Section 11, either the owner
   or the tenant, whoever maintains and repairs the property,
   is entitled to such payments.)

The committee intended that the opening speech, by demanding
definite statements about policy rather than about individual
grievances, would set the tone for the meeting. The event was
planned as a show of force, aimed at demonstrating the local re-
solve to challenge the Corporation's authority to exclude Gairbraid
from all decision-making. The strategy was to focus on the housing
officials without being critical of the councillor, to give him
the opportunity to side with the community, and not with the
Housing Department. Many of the notices advertising the meeting
were distributed before it was known that the official would be
present. Nevertheless, the councillor was considered to be a
sufficient draw and a large turn-out was confidently expected.
On the night of the meeting, however, there were far fewer people
present than anticipated, about eighty in all, of whom a large
proportion were elderly. It did not augur well for the outcome
of the meeting and indeed, almost everything that possibly could
went wrong for the GHC. The fault was a combination of inexper-
ience, poor organization and pure bad luck.

As the advertised starting time ticked by, the chairman, the
only person briefed for the job, had not yet appeared. After
anxious delay, it became apparent that the meeting would have to
start without him. None of the members had ever organized a
meeting before let alone been called upon to take the chair.
Without being in any way prepared, at a moment's notice, Hugh
Thompson had the chairmanship thrust upon him. Unusually for
Glasgow, it was swelteringly hot and stuffy. Many of the people
were dressed in their formal best as working-class respectability
and tradition seems to demand on such occasions. Cigarette smoke
filled the room as people impatiently waited for the meeting to
begin - it was started in a hushed silence. The audience strained
to hear above the drone of the traffic below in Maryhill Road, as
John Moir began his speech - it was his first-ever public address.
Everyone seemed receptive, there was no coughing or shuffling as
they listened. The first of the committee's demands was read out:
'When was the Corporation going to start and when were they likely
to finish in Gairbraid?' Whispered approval could be heard in the
audience. The official, obviously flustered, apologised for not

anticipating the type of meeting it would be. He provided no information but rather described the difficulties of his job and how the Housing Department was blamed for everything and then he called on the councillor to give his views. The chairman allowed the councillor to speak and at that point the committee lost control. John Moir was never able to finish his address. To the committee's surprise and chagrin, the councillor proceeded to deal with every point that John Moir had intended to raise. It later emerged that one of the members had naively told the councillor of the committee's prepared statement. He dealt with each point in turn, at great length, lightheartedly disposing of them. The gist of his argument was that the demands being made on the Housing Department were unreasonable, that everyone was doing their best for the community and in the end, with patience, all would be satisfied.

By the time the councillor sat down, amidst applause, the official had regained his confidence. Without committing himself to anything definite and without providing any information, and by way of numerous anecdotes about his childhood, the official assured the people of the Housing Department's good intentions. Most of the questions raised were either dismissed out of hand or completely evaded. He told the gathering that the housing visitors would have completed their work within a week, that rehousing would begin soon thereafter and that the process was likely to continue for at least two years. He complained that too many people had listed Maryhill as the only area in which they wished to be re-housed. For those who had not yet been seen by the housing visitors, he strongly recommended that, in order to increase their chances of an early move, they should give as wide a choice of preferred areas as was possible. As it turned out, where a wide range of areas was listed, residents were invariably offered houses in the least desirable of them. Often residents expressed a wish to be rehoused in a particular area for which they easily qualified, but said that if none were available there, at a last resort, they would agree to move elsewhere. These people seldom found that they were offered a house in the area of their first choice, irrespective of the accommodation available there. The committee asked the official, in view of his assurances, for an undertaking to address another meeting in the area after rehousing started. This he refused to do, claiming that it was unnecessary. Many of the audience drifted away before the end. It was a disappointing night, as a means of obtaining information or as a show of force, the meeting was a failure.

The inevitable post-mortem continued for days. Hugh Thompson blamed himself for not wielding greater control but this was unfair; being inexperienced and unprepared, all agreed that, under the circumstances, he did remarkably well. For the future it was realized that a strong and experienced chairman was absolutely vital. There was some bitterness that the chairman had not turned up - he had to work over-time. He was asked to remain on the committee but he soon fell away and was rehoused fairly quickly afterwards. John Moir feels: 'He was so embarrassed at not turning up. I still think he would have been okay. He is quite a nice fella, to this day, I don't know what happened.' John Moir was

elected as the committee's new chairman, with the vice-chairmanship
going to Jimmy Gallagher. The committee had reached a hiatus, and
the real struggle was about to begin with rehousing. It was
apparent that greater efforts at organization were required in the
community. A difficulty was that the committee members, through
their dealings with the authorities, had gained a wider perspective
of the problem than had the ordinary resident and thus, in a sense,
the community lagged behind the leadership. To a greater degree
than before, the committee had to involve everyone in its activities. Perhaps the GHC, after being in operation for less than two
months, had been over ambitious in its expectations. Certainly,
in retrospect, the public meeting was not an unmitigated disaster.
Important organizational lessons were learnt and the mistakes made
then were never repeated again. For instance, at future meetings
the committee members were dispersed in the audience rather than
being seated on the platform where they were unable to contribute
to the discussion. The meeting was in fact no more than a temporary
set-back from which some advantage could even be gained. Contrary
to what the official promised, the committee had warned that the
offers of accommodation would tend to be of poor quality. On the
one hand, if the official version of satisfaction for the bulk of
residents was substantiated, all would be well but on the other
hand, if the committee's predictions proved accurate, its standing
and credibility in the community would increase while the Housing
Department's would fall. Everything in fact depended on the
quality and speed of the offers received. There was not much for
the committee to do but issue a newsletter giving details of the
meeting, and then to adjourn for the summer break.

In the newsletter, the committee pointed out that while the
official had called for patience he had suggested that rehousing
might take as long as two years, and the GHC's demands had been
dismissed as unfair. The gist of the argument was reproduced and
the community asked to judge for themselves. Clearly, the
community, but neither the official nor the councillor, lived in
room-and-kitchens and it was for them to decide. Finally, the GHC
re-stated its policy: residents who received satisfactory offers
of alternative accommodation were urged to accept but equally
those who were unhappy with their offers were urged to refuse and
were promised full committee support in their actions. Decisions
on whether or not to refuse an offer had obviously to be left to
the individual concerned and it was a matter of principle if not
common-sense that the committee never attempted to influence
individual decisions. As the moment would soon approach when
activists would be rehoused, the GHC's immediate priority on
reassembling was the recruitment of new members - with the resignation of the chairman, these numbered only eight. In the meantime
it was simply a matter of wait and see. In the final analysis, the
committee would be judged, not on a particular event like the
public meeting, but on its ability to influence the rehousing
process, then about to begin.

Chapter 6

THE START OF REHOUSING

The Victorians, even in their tenements, built to last. Under the
1969 Housing Act with its provisions for improvement, Gairbraid
appeared a likely candidate for rehabilitation, for, outwardly
at least, the stone looked extremely solid. This, however, could
not have impressed the experts as they opted for demolition. In
the struggle of age, and physical wear and tear against paint,
wall-paper and patchwork repairs, Gairbraid had slowly and
undeniably been deteriorating for years. Some thought that this
pace of decline, if left to itself, could have continued for a
decade or more before the balance was irretrievably tipped and
conditions became intolerable. The issue was finally decided by
the standstill suddenly created by the control of occupation
order: repairs increasingly came to be neglected and houses
vacated in the normal course of events remained empty unless taken
over by squatters. By the time rehousing started in Gairbraid,
47 or roughly 12 per cent of the 399 houses were unoccupied.
The fact that so many were empty made little impression on the
area; it had occurred gradually and was hardly noticeable. The
streets seemed always full of people and there was nothing particular about the place to suggest that the community was about to
collapse. The summer holidays were in full swing when the rehousing process began. The equilibrium which had for so long been
maintained was forever shattered. Almost immediately, as the
first offers of alternative accommodation were received, people
began to move out. Removal vans, loaded to over-flowing, became
a permanent feature in Gairbraid. They left behind empty houses
and a trail of destruction as the blight took hold and the vandals
moved in.
    The GHC, when it re-convened at the end of July, faced a crisis
situation. The bulk of the offers received were even worse than
had been anticipated. Gairbraid buzzed with reports of gloom, of
people being offered grossly inferior houses, either in a state of
total disrepair and/or situated in unasked-for and undesirable
areas. There was an acute awareness among the people that, over
time, conditions in Gairbraid could only worsen and therefore to
many it seemed sensible to accept any offer which appeared at all
reasonable, and to move out as soon as possible. Those who refused

offers faced abuse and threats of eviction from the counter staff
at Clive House. There was thus considerable pressure on people
to comply by accepting the accommodation offered them, no matter
how imperfect nor how profoundly these houses disappointed their
aspirations. The GHC, on the side-lines, seemed marginal and
unable to influence the course of events. All the GHC's efforts,
until then, had clearly failed to make an impression on the
authorities. The offers received were no different from what they
would have been had there been no local organization in the area;
they certainly could not have been any worse. The committee,
facing its first test, was very much on the defensive in the knowledge that failure then to exert an influence over the rehousing
process would have certainly meant its demise. Overwhelmingly the
community felt its lack of power. It was for the committee to
provide a sense of solidarity and the support necessary for people
to feel sufficiently confident to refuse unsatisfactory offers.
The committee had to neutralize the external pressures placed on
people, by ensuring that the area was properly maintained and that
the minor officials, the ordinary residents' sole contact with
authority, behaved correctly when dealing with members of the
public.

OFFERS OF ALTERNATIVE
ACCOMMODATION

Under section 1(2) of the Housing (Scotland) Act 1969, where houses
fail to meet the tolerable standard the Corporation is instructed
to have regard to the 'alternative housing accommodation likely to
be available for any person who may be displaced from houses as a
result of any action proposed by the local authority'. While
obviously designed to protect the interests of those dispossessed,
such clauses, if they are not to remain entirely ineffectual, must
spell out in detail the precise obligations of the local authority.
In Gairbraid, judging by the quality of offers initially received,
the suitability of the alternative housing accommodation was left
to the discretion of Glasgow Corporation only at the expense of
the local people. Other than force as many people as possible to
accept unwanted houses in undesirable areas, Clive House transpa-
rently had no plan for Gairbraid. The authorities did not have
regard for individual preferences or needs but rather simply
endeavoured to fill empty council houses, no matter with whom.
    The main complaint in Gairbraid was that insufficient account
had been taken of the availability of alternative accommodation.
Very few questioned the need to demolish. Professional expertise
was hardly necessary for people to know that the property was
inadequate and that sooner or later something would have to be
done about it. What they were angry about was that they felt that
they were being rehoused before the Corporation was properly able
to do so. While by no means perfect, most houses in Gairbraid were
capable of withstanding several more years of use until such time
as adequate accommodation was available. They argued that since
rehousing was already in progress in various parts of Maryhill
these ought to have been completed before a start was made in

Gairbraid. A case in point was the area around Oran Street, a
short walk away from Gairbraid, where the property was infested
with rats and had long been in a state of extreme decay due to
rehousing started years before. For humanitarian if for no other
reasons, these clearances should have been completed before others
were started. Generally, people tend to opt for rehousing in or
close to their own areas. Gairbraid and Oran Street residents
were both after the same houses but this situation of a large
number of people wanting houses in a vicinity where few were
available was precisely what the local authority's action in
Gairbraid precipitated. Dennis describes a similar situation in
Duke Street, Sunderland, (1)

> An expanded and accelerated programme would mean even less
> choice and/or an even longer wait under clearance-area
> conditions of vandalism, theft and arson .... The existing
> staff of the local authority was unable to cope with the
> current programme. They could not cope with an even larger
> programme, except at the expense of the families affected
> by it.

Although largely of their own making, Glasgow Corporation was able
to use the existing scarcity of houses in Maryhill to explain and
justify delays in the rate of rehousing. A standard expedient used
in Clive House was to reject requests for particular houses on the
grounds that they were to be allocated to people in other areas who
had priority over Gairbraid. Gairbraid residents were frequently
told that they could not have houses in Maryhill because they were
reserved for Oran Street people, who, in turn, were told that the
same houses were for Gairbraid.

No records were kept of the numbers rehoused from the treatment
area during the first wave of offers, but at a rough guess somewhere between thirty and fifty families moved out then. (2) It
is also not known how many offers were made at that time, the
proportion of refusals, or how many of those who accepted were
satisfied with the houses they received. There is evidence to
suggest that a considerable number accepted houses they did not
want. One instance which particularly upset the committee members
was the case of an old man of about eighty. Hugh Thompson
remembers:

> 'That old man wanted to stay in Maryhill. He was actually
> threatened, if he didn't take this house, he would get no
> other house. Now to an old man like that, he took the house
> in panic. You see the old man, he's very old now, wandering
> up to the corner, where the toilet and the three pubs are
> and he's standing there nattering to his old friends. He's
> going up there every day. That's the old man's life.
> Gairbraid Avenue, that's his world, where the people of his
> world lived. I think he was actually born in Balfour Street.'

It was clear that the old, the timid and the weak were particularly
vulnerable. The committee were under no illusion about what to
expect from Clive House and were determined to ensure that no other
people were forced to accept accommodation against their will.

Many in Gairbraid refused offers, among them Eileen Kelly who
describes the condition of the house offered to her:

> 'The meter had been pulled out, a bedroom was full of ashes,

cans and bottles. It was about three feet deep in rubbish.
In the kitchen, the sinks were broken. The taps had been
taken off. There was no wiring in the house, it had all
been ripped out. It was just an absolute mess.'
John Smith, in similar vein, describes his first offer:
    'The smell of the house, as soon as we went in, would have
    killed you. The ashes and paper, the stink of the house
    would have made you sick. When we looked in the three
    rooms there wasn't a bit of (wall) paper together. The
    bathroom was black. The windows were all smashed. I was
    sick and I went and handed the keys back. The house was
    full of rats, you could smell them. The women in the
    stair told us that there had been about twelve rats taken
    down by the rat catcher.'
The house in poor condition was typical of the offers first received
in Gairbraid and even where the property was in good order, there
were other complaints, like the family with five small children who
were offered accommodation on the twenty-ninth floor.

THE COMMITTEE ON THE DEFENSIVE

A committee member was among those first rehoused from the area but
his early move was expected as he had set out to obtain a re-let
rather than a new house. Together with another irregular attender
finally dropping out, his departure reduced the active membership
of the GHC to only six. During this period, the committee's
energies were mostly inner-directed, aiming to bolster morale within
the community. In an attempt to influence the rehousing process,
the refusal of unsatisfactory offers was then about the only option
available to the residents. If a disproportionately large number
of refusals were registered for Gairbraid as compared to other parts
of the city, then Clive House would have to take note. The degree
to which people would be resolved to 'sit it out' until they
received suitable offers depended to a large extent on the committee's ability to ensure that conditions were not allowed to
deteriorate too rapidly. There was a danger of defeat, not by the
authorities but by vandalism. One family after viewing a house
decided to reject it only to return to Gairbraid to find that in
the meantime the water pipes in the empty flat above had been
stolen, causing their home to be completely flooded. As a result,
they immediately accepted the offer they had previously rejected.
The authorities neglected Gairbraid, doing, virtually nothing to
stem the decay of the property. The GHC had to ensure that a
reasonable standard of life was maintained for the residents.
    The area was falling apart, literally day by day. Several of
the committee members stood in the middle of Balfour Street on a
cold, wet autumn evening, silently witnessing the destruction of
their homes. The actual advance of the decay was almost percepti-
ble. On either side, water gushed down the stairs and into the
street from two separate closes. The authorities had been informed and so had the councillors but no one had come. The group
was joined by others who reported more floodings elsewhere in the
area. The feeling of powerlessness was complete. Conditions had

already become impossible although rehousing had barely started
and there was still the winter to come. The residents, however,
did not give up and somehow they managed to cope. The committee
members collected complaints, telephoned the councillors and the
Corporation's emergency services and more often than not mended
burst water pipes themselves. Floods could be dealt with by
turning off the supply at source which deprived everyone in the
building of water and sometimes it took weeks before they were
re-connected. (3) Jimmy Gallagher produced his own wood and nails
and boarded up empty houses for his neighbours which the authorities had neglected. Hugh Thompson and John Moir on one occasion
worked knee-deep in water, and as a result of being thoroughly
soaked John Moir was off work ill. It reached a point where some
people, rather than deal with an emergency themselves, would call
on a committee member. None of the committee members were either
plumbers, electricians or joiners and while they did not mind
helping old people or others who could not manage on their own,
they did resent being dragged out of bed in the middle of the
night by people as capable as themselves of dealing with the problem. Night after night, the committee members could be seen
working in the area and among these, Hugh Thompson was particularly
active. With fantastic energy and enthusiasm he dealt with problem
after problem. To the amusement of bystanders, he was once seen to
drag a councillor up Balfour Street by the sleeve, pointing to the
decay and yelling 'we elected you, do something'. The committee
stood up to the blight and slowed it down. The authorities were
forced to take note and reluctantly they made some attempt to
maintain the area.

On the question of having empty houses secured, the Corporation's
method of boarding up with corrugated iron was ineffective as it
was easily ripped off. Moreover, if attended to at all, empty
houses were invariably sealed only long after they had been vandalized and all the pipes stolen. The committee suggested that doors
and windows should be bricked up and one of the Maryhill councillors agreed to put this proposal to the appropriate authorities.
After months of being 'under consideration' the councillor finally
announced that the suggestion had been rejected as impractical and
too expensive. Over a year later, a team of workmen suddenly
appeared in the area and proceeded to brick up the by then almost
deserted and totally ruined property. In one instance, the cement
had hardly dried before a demolition squad arrived to pull down
the newly sealed building. Had empty houses been bricked up from
the very beginning much suffering could have been avoided, averting
not only floods but danger from gas leaks and fires which plagued
the inhabitants until the very end.

Gradually, the committee's campaign began to have effect. All
complaints about poor quality offers and official neglect in the
area were passed on to the councillors who were constantly
pestered with a bombardment of individual complaints. A newsletter
was issued in which people were urged to refuse unsuitable offers.
Residents were advised to take witnesses with them whenever they
went to Clive House and to report any clerks guilty of misconduct.
Gradually, the quality of the offers seemed to improve although it
is not known whether this was due to the committee's efforts. Clive

House seemed to have a policy of trying to get rid of their worst
houses first and thus, over time, some people were bound to receive decent offers. More and more people began to turn to the
committee for support and the rate of refusals increased. The
members grew in self-confidence as their efforts began to produce
positive results.

Although some residents accepted houses which they might have
refused had local support been forthcoming, the community survived
the initial onslaught. Having managed to catch its breath, the
GHC decided to assume the offensive. As a first step, a public
meeting, to be attended by the local councillors, was arranged.
It was to provide a forum for reinforcing local solidarity, a
platform for recruiting new committee members and finally, it was
to be a means of placing pressure on the councillors and thus,
indirectly, on the housing authorities. It was held on the
25 August, seven weeks after the previous public meeting and during
this time, the members had gained enormously in experience and
tactical sense.

THE AUGUST PUBLIC MEETING

Since their first attempt, the GHC came to appreciate that a great
deal more was involved in organizing a public meeting than simply
booking a hall and inviting speakers. In preparing for their next
meeting, the GHC decided to invite Ken McLachlan to take the chair.
As chairman of the Maryhill Ward Committee, Ken McLachlan could
legitimately perform this function for Gairbraid without being
accused by the councillors of meddling in matters that did not
concern him. The GHC thus obtained the services of a highly experienced and skilled chairman, completely sympathetic to the
local cause. Moreover, Ken McLachlan's presence freed the committee's own chairman, John Moir, from platform duties, enabling him
to contribute and fully participate from the floor. Two of the
three councillors agreed to attend the public meeting which was
announced to the community in a newsletter, followed by a reminder
notice distributed throughout the area. These spelt out the
committee's tactics:

It is vital that as many people as possible turn up. The
committee is your committee. Support it and we can all
get the houses we want. If we create enough fuss, publicity and organize well, we can succeed. The Corporation
does not want publicity and will try to avoid it .... It
is essential that people who have already refused offers
come and state their grievances. The time to speak out
is now.

The committee members encouraged those in the community who received particularly bad offers to attend the meeting. Annie
Mallon, Hugh Thompson and John Moir were extremely active in the
community during this period.

Up until the beginning of rehousing the committee had considered
that prematurely involving the mass media would serve only to
unnecessarily antagonize the authorities. The quality of the
offers received removed all such inhibitions. The committee felt

that they had built up a good case, they had tried all the conventional means of achieving redress for their grievances, from
petitions to pleading and had in return been ignored by the
authorities. Clive House could hardly complain that they had not
been given sufficient opportunity to act. A reporter said to be
sympathetic to the working class was contacted but his response
was 'so you have a housing problem, all of Glasgow has a housing
problem'. All of the city's daily and Sunday newspapers were
informed about the public meeting but none of them covered the
event. A just case was clearly not enough; if Gairbraid was to
achieve publicity, the community would have to create its own news.

The GHC, at its normal weekly session just prior to the public
meeting, heard reports from the members of a community, angry and
determined and a well supported gathering was confidently expected.
The members worked hard, and small details were remembered, such
as providing a jug of water and glasses for the speakers. Although
perhaps basically insignificant, such touches give an impression
of organizational competence. A leaflet was prepared for distribution at the meeting which, referring to the offers received,
stated:

> Would officials in the Housing Department accept these
> houses for themselves? Why then do they expect us to
> accept them? These houses are an insult. We deserve
> better and we will get better. We, the committee, affirm
> the right to a decent house for everyone.

The hand-out went on to call for new committee members and suggested
the establishment of a 'close representative' system, whereby one
person was responsible to the committee for all the people on his
stair. It was an attempt to involve more people in the GHC and
to facilitate communication between the community and their leaders.
Close representatives were not expected to attend the weekly
committee meetings and thus it gave those unable to fully participate the opportunity to become involved.

The hall filled slowly. Unlike the previous occasion where
the committee members aimlessly milled about, each had a role to
perform. There were tables to be manned, for recruiting new
members, and close representatives, for listing repairs and one of
the lawyers was present to provide legal advice. Above all,
committee members mixed with the crowd, discussing problems,
explaining and urging people to voice their grievances. When John
Moir began his opening address, there was standing room only at
the back. The estimated audience size was between 100 and 120
people, indicating a high degree of support, as by then there could
not have been many more than 300 families left in the treatment
area. John Moir gave a brief history of the GHC's activities and
a summary of the community's grievances. His words struck a
common cord; people mumbled about the offers they had received.
Clive House, by sending out poor offers and by their treatment of
people generally, had proved to be the GHC's best organizer. The
authorities had given the people no alternative: they had either
to accept Clive House's terms or to turn to the committee for
support. Being present, the councillors rather than the housing
officials bore the full brunt of the people's anger.

After John Moir's opening address, the meeting was immediately opened to questions and comments from the floor. Ken McLachlan ensured that the councillors' replies were kept brief and to the point. One after another the residents, in vivid detail, described the defects of the houses they had been offered - 'I wouldn't put a pig in it.' The mood throughout, although calm, was angry and aggressive. The tendency was to deride, sometimes strongly, the attempted explanations, advice and justifications offered by the councillors. Amidst loud applause one resident ended his contribution by advising all to stay put until they had received decent houses in Maryhill. In all this, Ken McLachlan as chairman maintaining tight control throughout, contributed positively to the proceedings whenever possible.

The committee members, dispersed through the body of the hall, were prepared to intervene but this proved unnecessary as all the important issues were spontaneously raised. While skilled chairmanship and careful organization are crucial, success in the last instance depends on the willing and intelligent support given by the community. The people of Gairbraid, after what they had been through, did not need words put in their mouths. The GHC provided the right conditions, the community seized their opportunity.

Even in finding the meeting disagreeable, the councillors could not but be impressed by the community's show of force and it was hoped that this message would be passed on to the housing authorities. Ken McLachlan extracted a promise from the councillors to attend a follow-up public meeting to be held within the next month or two. A constant worry in the community was the threat of eviction and the councillors confirmed the GHC's contention that the Corporation did not have this power - as the compulsory purchase orders had not yet been issued, they could not evict from property they did not own. The councillors further assured the community that statements by housing officials which suggested that evictions were imminent, that only one offer would be made per household, that no new houses would be available for Gairbraid residents and so forth, were all completely untrue. Lastly, the councillors advised people to refuse houses which were in poor condition. The councillors were placed in the position where they had no alternative but to endorse the committee's advice to the community.

THE AFTERMATH OF THE MEETING

The public meeting in itself did not produce any houses for the community. Although nothing tangible was immediately achieved, the event was a symbolic turning point in the area's fortunes. The GHC, having for the first time proved its organizational ability, emerged with strengthened morale and confidence. The people had demonstrated a degree of unity and determination to question authority. The councillors had been forced to listen and had promised to act on the community's behalf. No longer isolated, everyone had the assurance of being in the same boat as everyone else. The meeting had as a collective demanded decent houses for the community and had dispelled the previous feeling of total powerlessness. The people had endorsed the committee's programme and this expression of support had made ultimate success seem a reasonable expectation, quite within the organization's capabilities. As a show of force, the meeting achieved its aims. However, it had failed to achieve any press publicity. Thereafter, the GHC concentrated on seeking press coverage as a means of pressurizing the housing authorities, while, internally, it turned towards strengthening its own organization and consolidating local support. The major struggles were obviously still to come.

Before tactics and the week's events were discussed, it became usual for the GHC to devote the first part of its meetings to dealing with individual problems. Members often presented the committee with long lists of complaints which they had gathered the previous week. Residents attended meetings to explain their grievances although some came simply out of curiosity to see for themselves what progress was being made. The issues brought to the committee's attention covered the whole range of housing problems, the most common being either dissatisfaction with offers received or requests for rehousing in particular areas. People approached the committee with requests for houses which they knew to be empty, usually situated near to where a relative lived. While some had already received several offers, others had received none at all and for this, they demanded an explanation. A large number of people objected to the behaviour of the clerks at Clive House while others, already rehoused, complained that the authorities had not carried out promised repairs to their new homes. Information about special cases, of a member of the family being medically unfit or of an old person living alone, were reported. With offers being randomly distributed throughout the area, some closes emptied sooner than others and very early on there were appeals for urgent rehousing from families left stranded in virtually desolate property, often without the essential services. Owner-occupiers inquired about compensation, about which they had been given no information at all. Indeed, there was not a single aspect of the rehousing process about which a large number of residents did not have cause for serious complaint.

The committee passed all the requests and complaints it received to the councillors in addition to also encouraging people to see and telephone the councillors themselves. In extreme cases, the councillors were urged to visit people in their homes to see for themselves the conditions under which they were forced to live. In all instances, the committee followed up complaints until each had been satisfactorily settled. At almost every committee meeting, the councillors were telephoned and details of new complaints dictated to them. The councillors objected to being telephoned, sometimes several times during the day and night. However, the committee considered that this inconvenience to them was little when compared with what the people in Gairbraid suffered. The calls continued unabated. Indeed, the councillors' home telephone numbers were printed on the newsletters to encourage more people in the area to contact them. As the number of individual complaints accumulated, the councillors were frequently invited to attend committee meetings where these were discussed and their willingness to do so was appreciated. However, the councillors were sometimes reluctant to accept the committee's invitations and on these occasions it was apparent that more than pure dedication brought them to Gairbraid. The feeling among the members was that the GHC's organizational power had at least something to do with the degree of co-operation achieved with the Maryhill councillors. (4)

There is no doubt that due to the GHC, the councillors were more active in Gairbraid than they would have been had there been no local organization in the area. Certainly, more of their energies were given to Gairbraid than elsewhere in the ward. This prompted the councillors to protest that the GHC selfishly de-flected attention away from other areas where problems were equally if not more pressing. This argument is based on the improbable assumption that, left to themselves, the councillors would have transferred the time spent in Gairbraid to other areas. It is far more likely that had the GHC never existed, all the clearance areas in Maryhill including Gairbraid would simply have been equally neglected. The councillors had after all not shown much interest in the treatment area before the committee was formed. It was thought that the councillors too readily accepted the decisions made by the officials. Thus, where an individual's qualification conformed with those deemed necessary by the authorities, the councillors were generally able to hurry the process along. However, where an individual did not qualify or where their grievance was not acknowledged by Clive House, the councillors usually seemed eager to drop the case, apparently unwilling to challenge official decisions.

The GHC thus operated as a kind of 'middle-man' between the community on the one hand and the councillors and the Corporation on the other. The frequent presence of councillors at the commit-tee meetings must have created an added incentive for non-members to attend. The fact that people increasingly turned to the GHC for help reflected both the worsening crisis and the organization's growing reputation. In addition to attending the GHC meetings, the councillors held regular surgeries where they were available to be seen by their constituents. These, however, are quite in-adequate to cope with crisis situations in clearance areas. If residents in such areas are to be properly represented, throughout the period of the clearance programme, special meeting places need to be arranged to give residents easy and frequent access to their councillors.

THE COMMITTEE'S PLEDGE

In spite of considerable effort, only two new committee members, Isa Hanlon and John Smith, were recruited at the public meeting. Several close representatives joined and of these Eileen Kelly was soon to become a full committee member. The close represen-tative system was never to function perfectly and by no means all the closes in the area were represented. In some instances, no sooner did someone volunteer to represent a close than they were rehoused. In a situation of constant flux it was almost impossible to ensure that every close in the area was represented and the system functioned better in some parts of Gairbraid than it did in others. For instance, Jimmy Gallagher organized representatives in all the closes for which he was responsible in the top end of

Burnhouse Street. In constant contact with his close representatives, Jimmy created an extremely efficient system of communication which contrasted with other parts of the treatment area, where there were few or no representatives at all. The system was designed to provide a communications network in the area. It was also hoped that in the event of a large number of key activists being suddenly rehoused, close representatives would provide ready replacements. Although an acute emergency of this nature never arose, the system was thus viewed as a second line of defence. To have functioned more adequately, however, close representatives would have needed to be organised before rehousing commenced.

Soon after the public meeting, both John Moir and Jimmy Gallagher received offers of alternative accommodation from the Housing Department. Thus at one moment, the committee stood to lose both its chairman and vice-chairman who were its main spokesmen and by then already seasoned campaigners. Although not situated in Maryhill, in both instances the houses were only about a year old and were among the first reasonable offers to be received in Gairbraid. On the grounds of being unsuitably situated, neither the Moirs nor the Gallaghers accepted. The long expected threat constantly hanging over the committee of having its key members rehoused had been temporarily averted. The members attempted to protect the committee by pledging themselves to remain active in the event of their being rehoused. The pledge provided only a partial solution because once rehoused a member is not only deprived of daily contact with the community, his circumstances change and he becomes an outsider who no longer personally stands to gain or lose from the committee's activities. Furthermore, where rehousing is at a far distance from the old community, travelling to and from meetings places an enormous strain on the committee member who must at the same time adjust to his new environment. However, the pledge did allay fears in the community that the members were only after houses for themselves. It also helped committee morale, enabling long-term planning to go ahead without the threat that any moment the whole organization would collapse. The pledge was indeed an article of faith. It was put to the test in early September when Hugh Thompson accepted an offer and became the first key committee member to be rehoused.

The Thompsons moved north of Maryhill to Milton and given an indifferent bus service, the journey back to Gairbraid from there is both tiring and time-consuming. The couple have a lot of commitments: they have five young children; Eileen Thompson was soon active as a founder member of the Milton Tenants' Association; and Hugh has little spare time, being a long-distance lorry driver. All these were ample reason to withdraw and few in the community would have blamed them if they had quietly allowed their committee membership to lapse. However, in spite of all, the Thompsons somehow managed to honour their promise and remain active in the GHC. For over six months after they were rehoused first Hugh and then Eileen regularly attended the weekly committee meetings and even afterwards they could always be relied upon to help whenever needed. Their action confounded the cynics who prophesied that the committee would collapse as soon as members were rehoused. The Thompsons set a high standard of integrity which tremendously raised the

committee's esteem in the community. Unlike the situation later,
it was especially crucial that the first to move should not
immediately abandon the committee. The GHC owes a great deal to
the solidarity of Hugh and Eileen Thompson.

Hugh Thompson had been extremely active in Gairbraid and his
departure from the area was a blow to the committee. It had
always been dreaded that as a matter of deliberate policy, the
authorities would try to rehouse activists as quickly as possible.
Although it is only possible to speculate, many in Gairbraid
strongly suspected that this was indeed Clive House's intention.
Hugh Thompson at the time of his rehousing was with John Moir and
Jimmy Gallagher one of the most active members of the committee.
The fact that all three received relatively good offers early on
might or might not have been pure coincidence. Hugh Thompson had,
through his boundless energy, become the 'eyes and ears' of the
community and was a veritable thorn in the flesh of councillors
and officials alike. With his departure this role, fortunately
for the GHC, was quickly assumed by Isa Hanlon. Strangely perhaps,
within the next few months after she had established herself 'Big
Isa' was the next committee member to be offered a house.

THE DESTRUCTION OF THE MIDDENS

The saga of Gairbraid's middens, or ashbin shelters as they are
officially called, began in early August when the Corporation
decided that many were in a dangerous condition and had them
demolished. No one in the community was consulted or informed
prior to this action being taken, the shelters were one day just
simply knocked down. Whether or not the shelters constituted a
real danger was never demonstrated to the community, although
residents did observe that it took several men, wielding hefty
sledge hammers, almost a whole day to complete the demolition
which suggested that the shelters were hardly likely to collapse
on their own accord. Be this as it may, it is totally beyond
dispute that, by the act of demolishing the middens, the
authorities created distress, difficulties and dangers for the
people in Gairbraid, and at best, one set of dangers were merely
replaced by another. The bins, being unprotected, were kicked
over by children playing in the backcourts with the result that
these became increasingly littered with rubbish. Cleaning the
backs, however, was made impossible as after the demolition, the
resultant rubble was not removed but left lying about in piles.
Little children clambering over these invariably fell and hurt
themselves, and the rubble also provided a readily available
supply of ammunition which encouraged window-breaking. Mothers
feared that sooner or later a child would suffer serious injury.
Furthermore, the mounds of rubble threatened to provide breeding
grounds for rodents.

To people in the community it seemed only logical that empty
houses be boarded up before rather than after they were vandalized, and if to be done at all it was pointless unless done
securely so as to provide a serious obstacle to break-ins. Sheets
of corrugated iron fastened with a few nails presented no problem

to even relatively small children. Few people found such
inefficiencies surprising as on the whole very little was expected
from the authorities. It was more or less accepted as a fact of
life that the Corporation would do little or nothing to maintain
the area; nevertheless, it came as a shock to realize that they
were actually participating in its destruction. The demolition
of the shelters and the subsequent refusal to have the rubble
removed were regarded in the community as acts of official
vandalism designed to make living conditions as difficult as
possible. It was felt to be an attempt to shatter morale and
weaken local resistance. 'By pulling down the middens, leaving
the rubble and empty houses', John Moir said, 'we feel the
Corporation is trying to throw us out quicker.' Probably pure
incompetence was responsible but under the circumstances the
community could hardly be blamed for feeling paranoiac. The GHC
complained to the councillors and were referred, in turn, to the
Health Department, the Office of Public Works, the factors and
again to the Health Department. Inter-departmental contact and
co-operation seemed to be almost nil and the GHC, after considerable effort, was back at square one. While none were willing to
assume responsibility for the rubble, the number of grazed knees,
broken windows and the accumulation of filth in the backcourts
continued to increase.

The matter was again brought to the attention of the councillors
at the public meeting. Soon after, a letter from the Chief
Sanitary Inspector was forwarded to the GHC, in the councillor's
words, 'so that you can see action has been taken'. The authorities, after a site meeting, had agreed to remove the rubble. The
GHC accepted the letter as a statement of intent and the councillors did not bother to verify whether or not action had been
taken. After a fortnight, without a single stone having been removed, the GHC informed the Health Department that unless the
rubble was removed forthwith, a complaint would be made to the
Secretary of State for Scotland. In the meantime, it was threatened, if any child sustained serious injury legal advice would be
sought and the Health Department held responsible. They were also
advised that if satisfaction was not obtained, the residents would
be compelled to remove the rubble themselves. It was left to
their imagination as to how and where the residents would dispose
of it.

The GHC also took the opportunity to complain about the
authority's failure to seal empty houses adequately, offering to
provide the Health Department with information about when houses
were to be vacated so that they could be immediately boarded up.
The Health Department, like the housing officials, factors and
councillors before them, placed most if not all the blame for the
deterioration of the property in Gairbraid on vandalism. Indeed,
this view seems to be a conventional wisdom held by the authorities, the mass media and the public at large. By focusing on
vandalism, it firmly places the onus for the upkeep of the property
on the residents themselves and essentially ignores housing policy
and official neglect which in the first place not only makes
vandalism possible but also positively encourages it. Clearance
areas provide an apprenticeship and training ground in vandalism

for adolescents and younger children who live in and around the
affected area. It is unlikely that a child who over a period of
years has participated in the systematic destruction of derelict
property, stealing and selling lead and other metals, will cease
to engage in vandalism when he is moved to a new council estate.
As Gairbraid deteriorated, the council property adjacent increasingly suffered from vandalism. Teenage gangs tend to congregate
in clearance areas and derelict houses are used for such purposes
as truancy, the consumption of alcohol, drug taking and sexual
promiscuity. Vandalism costs Glasgow £1 million a year. (5) Much
of the worst effects of vandalism could have been avoided in
Gairbraid had the area not been allowed to decline for want of
essential repairs. Other than a few belatedly produced sheets of
corrugated iron, the authorities made no attempt to tackle the
problem. Prolonged rehousing, sometimes over a period of several
years, ensures that the effects of vandalism will be severe.
Although a police station was located only a few hundred yards
from Gairbraid, police surveillance of the area left much to be
desired, being totally inadequate to cope with the problem.
Vandalism seems to be symptomatic of a national ill. The point
here is not to provide a diagnosis but rather to affirm that local
residents are not responsible for combating vandalism.

Chapter 7

A WEEK OF ACTION

September was a busy period in the community. Although not as
quickly and thoroughly as was desired, progress was being made.
The extreme pressures of the previous month seemed to lift.
Through frantic efforts, the GHC had stemmed the rate of decline
in the area and increasingly more people began to receive satisfactory offers. Nevertheless, there was a vague ·feeling of
dissatisfaction; that nothing important was happening, that the
GHC was too dependent on councillors and officials and that it
still too often operated within the narrow confines of the housing
regulations. Alinsky's rule (1) 'keep the pressure on, with
different tactics and actions, and utilize all events of the
period for your purpose' needed to be applied in Gairbraid.

MAINTAINING THE MOMENTUM

As conditions in the backcourts deteriorated, young children were
no longer allowed to play there and thus many remained cooped up
in room-and-kitchens for most of the day. The community workers
suggested that a pre-school playgroup be formed, to which the GHC
readily agreed, feeling that besides providing a much needed
facility, it would also help maintain morale, extending the GHC's
contacts and influence. One of the community workers undertook to
investigate its feasibility, obtain equipment and act as the initial supervisor. Sessions were first held in the GHC's flat in
Burnhouse Street which the playgroup soon outgrew and it moved to
the Labour rooms in Maryhill Road. It was held regularly four
mornings per week and at its height was attended by twenty-four
children, divided into two groups. Although started exclusively
for the residents of the treatment area, as the population there
declined, children from elsewhere in the neighbourhood began attending. Residents who at various times were active in both the GHC
and the playgroup included Jeannette Bouse, Isa Hanlon, Margaret
Hobson, Eileen Kelly and Cathy White. With the help of the Glasgow
Pre-school Playgroup Association the playgroup continued to function
in a local church hall after the treatment area was completely
cleared and thus it survived the GHC. Several jumble sales and

children's parties were also organized in Gairbraid. Annie Mallon
and Georgina Atkinson held a raffle and a weekly bingo session was
started by Isa Hanlon. The bingo was later taken over by Ella
Donnelly and then by Jessie Moir who continued with it almost to
the very end.

The GHC began a door-to-door collection of signatures for a
petition to the Secretary of State for Scotland. It was a threat,
made on several occasions, that the GHC finally felt compelled to
carry out. Another of Alinsky's rules, (2) 'the threat is usually
more terrifying than the thing itself', needs qualifying in that
threats without action quickly lose potency. Assisted by the
committee's legal advisers, three principal grounds for complaint
were formulated: lack of consultation and inadequate information;
unsuitability of the alternative accommodation offered; and accel-
erating deterioration of the area caused by Corporation policy.
In the local opinion the Corporation had misconceived its duties
by failing to exercise the powers given them in the community's
interest. While it was thought unlikely that the complaint would
directly influence housing policy, the GHC believed it would at
least embarrass the Corporation. The petition itself was considered worthwhile because it provided the GHC with a further
opportunity to involve the community. In an incomplete coverage
of the area, 203 residents signed the petition.

Jimmy Gallagher undertook to have a resolution sent to the
City Labour Party through his branch of the National Union of
Vehicle Builders (since amalgamated with the Transport and General
Workers Union). It complained about 'malpractices' in the Housing
Department and listed charges relating to rehousing, the lack of
maintenance and the behaviour of the staff at Clive House. (3)
Many considered that the implications of involving a trade union
were potentially more important than the complaint to the Secretary
of State. The support gained from the Vehicle Builders is at
least symbolic of the labour movement's involvement in community
affairs. It is an area of co-operation that future community
action could with advantage seek to extend.

The councillors had already committed themselves to attend
another public meeting and one was planned for early October.
To avoid a repeat performance of the previous occasion when residents harangued the councillors it was decided also to invite
officials from the Housing and Health Departments.

Throughout September, the committee continued in its attempt to
obtain publicity which provided an element of excitement in what
was otherwise a relatively dull period between meetings. Contact
was made with a 'Daily Record' reporter who attended two committee
meetings and was shown around the area where she took copious
notes. An article seemed certain and in the weeks that followed,
sales of the paper must have greatly increased in the area - until
it became apparent that Gairbraid was not going to be featured.

In addition to seeking publicity, the GHC explored the possibilities of linking up with other groups in similar situations to
their own. It was Gairbraid's misfortune that at the time no other
clearance area in Glasgow was known to be organized. Contact was,
however, made with the people of Newcraighall, a mining village on
the outskirts of Edinburgh, whose houses were threatened with

demolition. Many of the mining families had lived there for generations but Edinburgh Corporation proposed to disperse them in a
large, nearby housing estate, Craigmillar. Local people felt that
their demolition order was being brought forward because of the
large number of empty houses, difficult to let, in Craigmillar.
With the support of the local Miners' Institute and their councillor, Davey Brown, who lived in the area, the residents refused to
accept dispersal, insisting that new houses be built for them
within the village. (4) The GHC invited Councillor Brown to speak
at their October public meeting - to foster solidarity between the
communities and to contrast his strong commitment to the local
struggle with that of the Maryhill representatives.

    The first positive contact made with the mass media was through
a friend of the community worker who knew Raeburn Mackie of BBC
television. He was particularly interested in Glasgow's housing
visitor's report, a copy of which the GHC had fortuitously
obtained. He wished to do a programme dealing with the effective-
ness of the Housing (Scotland) Act 1969 and was already familiar
with the situation in Newcraighall. Gairbraid presented the possibility of doing a joint programme, featuring communities under
stress in both Edinburgh and Glasgow, a process that Raeburn Mackie
was later to describe on 'Current Account' as (5) 'more like the
Highland Clearances of 150 years ago than slum clearance in Scotland
today'. Before committing themselves to a programme, Raeburn Mackie
and his colleague, Alan Brown, visited Gairbraid several times and
both greatly impressed the community by their sincerity, care and
tact. After speaking to many of the local people and attending
one of the GHC's weekly meetings, they finally decided to go ahead
with the film. The committee's role was to interest the BBC in
the area and to outline its main grievances, but once the programme had been agreed, the selection of issues dealt with became
the prerogative of the television team. Left to the GHC the
importance of local organization would have received greater
emphasis. Similarly, in the choice of those interviewed, the GHC
had only an indirect influence in that several non-members, whose
experiences seemed relevant, were asked to attend the committee
meeting at which the television people were present. Of the six
Gairbraid residents who appeared on the programme, only John Moir,
Annie Mallon and Isa Hanlon were committee members. Ella
Donnelly and Eileen Kelly joined soon after and Mrs Jackson, an
old age pensioner, was never involved. Thus, many of the most
active and articulate in the community, including Jimmy Gallagher,
the Thompsons and Georgina Atkinson, were not interviewed.

    Excitement mounted with the appearance of camera crews in the
area. The GHC decided that its various planned activities should
be organized so as to coincide with the television broadcast,
scheduled for Friday 15 October. The public meeting was held over
until the Monday of that week. At this, Jimmy Gallagher was to
announce his trade union's resolution condemning the city's housing
policy and practice. The committee also decided to postpone until
that week its petition to the Secretary of State for Scotland so
that handing it in could be filmed for the programme. For this
purpose, John Moir, Isa Hanlon and Georgina Atkinson, were dele-
gated to make the journey to the Scottish Development Department

in Edinburgh. It was a time of great activity in Gairbraid as
preparations were finalized. In the fourteen-day period between
27 September and 10 October, where two committee meetings would
normally have been held, five were convened. Press releases were
sent to all the local newspapers. The public meeting was widely
advertised in the area and every effort was made to ensure a
large turn-out. The GHC eagerly awaited the public meeting to
begin their week of action.

THE OCTOBER PUBLIC MEETING

'We will not be pushed around', John Moir declared, 'we will not
accept inferior housing in poor areas.' The audience, numbering
well over a hundred, listened attentively to the opening speech.
Ken McLachlan was in the chair and beside him on the platform were
two of the Maryhill councillors, Councillor Brown from Newcraighall
and an official from both the Housing and Health Departments. A
certain amount of pleasure was gained from the fact that the
housing official was the same individual who three months previously at the first public meeting had said he would not return
to Gairbraid. John Moir stressed that the 400 new houses then
being built in Maryhill could easily accommodate the roughly 150
Gairbraid families, about 60 per cent of those left, who wanted
both a new house and to remain in Maryhill. 'We will never leave
here', he proclaimed, 'you can't force us out and we won't leave
until these houses become ours.' The need to reduce population
density as an argument against rehousing communities together
disregards the fact that a degree of dispersal tends to occur
naturally - in Gairbraid between 30 and 40 per cent of the residents either desired a relet or a move away from Maryhill.
     The meeting was disrupted when one of the councillors objected
to her speech being tape recorded. People jeered and shouted
their disapproval and it was with great difficulty that Ken
McLachlan managed to restore order. The residents were obviously
in militant mood and the officials, in their turn, received a
noisy reception. In contrast, Davey Brown was cheered as he
called upon Gairbraid to 'stick together as the only way to win
your campaign'. The official from Clive House informed the meeting
that in the three months since rehousing started, 245 offers had
been made of which eighty-seven were accepted. As almost two out
of every three offers were refused, residents seemed no longer to
be accepting unwanted houses. With eighty-seven already rehoused,
Gairbraid's population had shrunk by approximately 25 per cent,
leaving 265 families still in the area. At a similar rate of rehousing, Gairbraid would be cleared within a further nine months
and although far from ideal, this prospect compared favourably
with the Corporation's past performances. At least Gairbraid
seemed destined to avoid Oran Street's fate of seemingly endless
decay.
     During question time, there were frequent heated exchanges
between the platform and the floor. For instance, it was alleged
that Clive House used length of tenancy to deter people seeking
accommodation in select areas. One woman, claiming that she was

told that she needed thirty years' tenancy to be offered the
Wyndford, asked, 'Why thirty years? My children are young, I
don't want to wait 'till they are grown up. What good is it to
me then? I've lived in Maryhill thirty-four years, I was born
there. I think I am entitled to the Wyndford.' The length of
time taken to complete repairs to relet property was another major
grievance. 'My brother got a house eight weeks ago', a resident
complained, 'his wife had a baby and they thought they'd have
moved in before she had the baby. How long does it take for them
to do repairs?' That, the official replied, was the responsibility
of the Building and not the Housing Department. Similarly,
questions about compensation were referred to the Town Clerk. He
dealt with individual complaints by inviting residents to write for
appointments to see him at Clive House. At this point, supported
by shouts from the floor, John Moir interjected: 'You told us that
at the last meeting, to write in. We wrote in, I don't know how
many people wrote in. We never heard from you, we were told that
you didn't even work there. Did you know that?' The official
responded by claiming that Clive House annually receives about
30,000 letters. John Moir dismissed this argument by saying: 'I've
asked you straight out, if we write in when will we get an answer?
Tell me? You said there were 30,000, what's the use of them
writing if you can't give them an answer?' An old age pensioner
when refusing an offer was told by a clerk at Clive House that 'I
was to take this house or else, if I didn't take the house, I'd
be evicted'. Jimmy Gallagher informed the meeting that the
Corporation being 'responsible for the run-down of the property
were responsible for finding suitable accommodation for the
people'. The reply that the Health Department cannot have workmen
standing by just to nail up empty houses was greeted by a shout
from the body of the hall that 'there are 8,000 joiners unemployed
in the city'.

A disappointing aspect of the meeting was that a few residents
complained that offers received by others should have more
properly been given to themselves. After being rejected for a
particular house on, for example, the grounds of insufficient
tenancy, it is difficult to suppress anger when someone else, who
seemingly is even less eligible, is offered it. A person
struggling to survive in an empty building without any of the
essential services may be excused for objecting when the authorities give priority to another family whose need is less urgent.
In a situation of acute housing shortage where house allocations
are essentially arbitrary, competition and personal resentments
are inevitable by-products of the rehousing process, turning
neighbour against neighbour. There are circumstances where these
are natural and easily understood reactions but whether justified
or not, they are self-defeating and divisive, hindering the growth
of local solidarity. On almost every occasion there was someone
who complained about the unfairness of the system in relation to
themselves when compared to how others had been treated. Although
never expressed by more than a small minority, it was invariably
used by councillors and officials alike to discredit the committee
and was often produced by them to prove that no community solidarity existed in Gairbraid.

The meeting closed with Ken McLachlan calling upon Jimmy Gallagher to read his union's resolution. Although well received, no one else ever put similar resolutions through their trade union branches. An extra bonus to what was regarded as a highly success-ful meeting was that at long last the committee achieved press publicity. A reporter from the 'Scottish Daily Express' had been present and an article under the heading (6) 'Tenants fight threats from City' appeared in the morning paper. Based solely on the press release, 'The Glasgow Herald' also gave mention to Gairbraid. Neither newspaper seemed to regard the public meeting as news-worthy in itself: the 'Express' began its story with an account of the union resolution and 'The Herald' with details of the peti-tion sent to the Secretary of State for Scotland. Clippings from these papers were displayed in the local shops and, if nothing else, provided a morale boost for the residents.

The meeting had served its purpose: from the militancy shown, the committee gained increased confidence in the community's support; as a show of force it had demonstrated to both councillors and officials Gairbraid's determination and ability to continue and, if necessary, intensify the campaign. The committee had proved its competence to organize and perhaps for the first time had really shown that City Hall could be challenged. The Health Department had the rubble removed within days of the meeting. Having stood up to officialdom, people left the meeting eagerly awaiting the highlight of the week's events: the television programme.

CURRENT ACCOUNT

Unprecedented for a Friday evening, the streets in Gairbraid were completely deserted as people waited for the start of the tele-vision programme. 'There wasn't a soul in Gairbraid Avenue', Isa Hanlon recalls, 'from one end to the other.' Very few in the area could have missed seeing it. Gaining coverage in the mass media is one thing, receiving a sympathetic hearing is another and thus people were slightly apprehensive about how the area would be presented. Excitement was intense. The 'Current Account' programme began by asking the question: 'Has Scotland got this whole slum clearance business totally wrong; we bull-doze buildings and call that success but surely to God it's a failure if in the process we smash communities and bureaucrati-cally bulldoze people?' Raeburn Mackie dealt with five areas of complaint: lack of information, the housing visitor's report, offers of poor quality housing, the clerks at Clive House, and the timing of the rehousing programme. On each of these topics, local residents were first interviewed followed by a spokesman for the Corporation, a senior member of Glasgow's Housing Commit-tee. In every instance, he admitted to serious deficiencies in the city's housing policy and practice. On the first, when asked about the control of occupation order - 'Why was this ambiguous legal letter the only communication from the Corporation?' - the councillor replied that he was not aware of the lack of detail being sent. He promised that people will in future be 'made aware

of precisely how they will be affected'. The housing visitor's
report, called by Raeburn Mackie 'an astonishing document' was
the next item dealt with in the programme. The camera zoomed in
for a close up, revealing Glasgow's method of grading tenants.
The system is indefensible and the councillor did not attempt to
seek justification. When asked 'do you think it's right that
somebody should come in and, on the basis of a few minutes' visit,
classify people into a type?', he replied:

> 'I think it's not only wrong, I think it's impossible. I
> don't frankly know what is gained from an endeavour to
> classify people in the way indicated. I will be taking
> that matter up with the Housing Manager in the hope that
> he will be able to provide me with a satisfactory explana-
> tion of this.'

Questioned about offers of alternative accommodation residents
described the poor quality of these. Mrs Jackson, when she found
that she had been offered a place in an old folks' home, 'just
about collapsed in the street'. Ella Donnelly told of her
encounter with the clerks at Clive House:

> 'I went up and I just said to the man I would like to see
> about having a house. He said, "Oh yes, you're in the
> Maryhill treatment area?" I said, "That's right." "You
> haven't had an offer yet?" I said "No." He said, "Oh
> well, the only thing I could offer you at the moment is
> Easterhouse." I said, "I'll take it." He said, "Well,
> ... with your, how long have you been there?" "Twelve
> years." "With your tenancy, you could get something
> better, you could even get Drumchapel." I said, "I'll
> take it." He said, "Well let me think now, what about
> around Stobhill, around about that area, that's even
> better than Drumchapel, I could give you that." I said,
> "I'll take it." "Well, ..." He himmed and hawed for a
> wee while and then said, "Well Mrs Donnelly, as soon as
> I've got something I'll get a card out to you and I'll
> let you know." That's three weeks ago, I've had no card
> yet but I've been offered the whole of Glasgow.'

The councillor was asked 'is there a policy of trying to fill the
really poor houses first, trying to get rid of them somehow?'
'Not an official policy', he replied, 'I shouldn't be surprised
if it was a practice rather than a policy in certain instances.'
In Gairbraid, poor offers were initially received in almost every
'instance'. There is little doubt that Clive House tries to
foist its worst property on families foolish, vulnerable or
desperate enough to accept.

The behaviour of the clerks at Clive House was the fourth issue
dealt with by the film. Isa Hanlon described them as 'really
cheeky' and told of seeing 'an awful lot of old people, not just
from here, from other places as well, going away in tears'.
Eileen Kelly and John Moir were both threatened with eviction.
When Mrs Jackson refused the place in the old folks' home the
clerk threatened her:

> 'I would take that house or he would throw me out in the
> street. I said, "You can't throw me out in the street."
> He said, "We can." I was finished. Now Annie Mallon and

another lady met me in the street and they thought I was
collapsing. In fact they had to go get the doctor for
me.'
'Neither the clerks nor anyone else is authorized to threaten anyone with eviction', said the councillor, and added 'we don't stick
to one offer and there are very many offers in many instances.'
    Finally, Raeburn Mackie posed the question:
    'If the vandalism and the rapid decay have only really
    taken over here since December, if being declared a
    housing treatment area was the kiss of death to the homes
    of this neighbourhood, then why did the Corporation start
    the slum clearance ball rolling if it wasn't ready right
    away to rehouse the people satisfactorily and adequately?'
In reply the councillor could only state that the people would be
'satisfactorily and adequately housed'. The programme on Maryhill
ended with John Moir being asked whether the Corporation was doing
all it could to help: 'They are doing nothing, as far as we are
concerned, absolutely nothing.'

THE AFTERMATH OF THE TELEVISION

People in Gairbraid were thrilled by the programme. 'The Scotsman', in its review, praised 'Current Account' for (8) 'a
worthwhile job ... in exposing what appeared to be considerable
bureaucratic heartlessness and lack of sensitivity.' Continuing,
it considered that 'Raeburn Mackie had collected an impressive
group of tenants ... all articulate, intelligent and genuinely
concerned.' Indeed, the programme had, in its sympathetic treatment of local problems, exceeded even the committee's high
expectations.
    A danger for local groups is that obtaining publicity may
become an end in itself. Very few people are blase about appear-
ing on television and when nothing tangible follows, excitement
may lead to feelings of anti-climax. Publicity should never be
more than a stage in a campaign. In Gairbraid after all, the
objective was not to embarrass the authorities but to obtain
houses for the residents.
    The GHC had greatly increased its status. Strangers approached
residents to find out about the committee, to express sympathy
and support and to tell of their own experiences of rehousing.
Remembering his mother's experience, a taxi-driver, taking Betty
Gallagher home, remarked, 'I'm glad to see somebody at last has
started fighting back'. The strength of the programme was that
it placed the onus of blame on the authorities rather than, as
is more usual in the mass media, portrayed the area as a pathetic,
poverty-stricken slum. Publicity serves to embarrass the power
structure, exposing it to ridicule, forcing it to explain and
justify its behaviour. A community group which demonstrates its
ability to gain access to the mass media obtains a degree of
insurance against arbitrary treatment. For instance, a local
authority will usually think twice about evicting a tenant if such
actions are bound to be observed by the press and television.
    The GHC immediately distributed a newsletter throughout the

community, emphasizing the highlights of the programme. Social
activities were increased in the area. The pre-school playgroup
and bingo sessions were already firmly established, and with the
help of a student on placement, visits to old people were
organized. A hallowe'en party was planned for which cakes were
baked and sweets and toys provided. It was attended by about forty
local children. The GHC accepted an invitation for a 'night out'
at the Miners' Institute in Newcraighall. Organized by Isa Hanlon,
a bus was hired and forty-five Gairbraid people, including eight
old age pensioners who travelled free, made the journey to
Edinburgh. It was a memorable occasion spoken about with pleasure
for a long time after. Without denying the intrinsic value of
these activities, and they were certainly enjoyed by those who
participated, the GHC's prime motivation was to involve as many
residents as possible so as to maintain morale as conditions
deteriorated.

The GHC emerged from its week of action strong and confident.
Of the original membership, Cathy White resigned for domestic
reasons but remained active in the playgroup. Of the old
stalwarts, John Moir, Jimmy Gallagher, Annie Mallon, Georgina
Atkinson and, although rehoused, Hugh and Eileen Thompson still
attended regularly and remained the backbone of the organization.
In addition, new recruits, Isa Hanlon, John Smith and, more
recently, mother and daughter Ella Donnelly and Eileen Kelly, were
active and fully integrated into the committee. Isa Hanlon
was particularly energetic and she assumed Hugh Thompson's former
active role in the community. Ella Donnelly, like Georgina
Atkinson, worked in one of the local shops and was thus ideally
placed to obtain and disseminate information. In an area as
small as Gairbraid with the community beginning to be well
organized, very little could happen without it rapidly becoming
common knowledge. Rehousing had not weakened the committee; on
the contrary, in terms of numbers it was as strong as it had
ever been and in terms of commitment, confidence, experience and
expertise it had grown into a formidable organization. Largely
as a result of the television programme, there was no longer any
difficulty in obtaining press publicity. In the coming months,
five periodicals featured Gairbraid. (9)

The reforms promised during the television programme created
openings for further action. The GHC had temporarily gained the
initiative and needed to keep the issues alive as long as possible so that the promised reforms were not quietly forgotten.
Within a week, the GHC sent transcripts of the programme to the
Housing Manager and to every Glasgow councillor, urging them to
help rectify Gairbraid's 'serious grievances' and to ensure that
'practice did not conflict with policy'. An urgent meeting with
the Corporation's Housing Committee was also requested. Only
one councillor, a Tory replied, asking for further information
relating to specific cases which, clearly, were the responsibility
of the local councillors. To have complied would have been to
raise a hornet's nest of inter-party squabbles: Gairbraid was not
to be used as a political football. As it had been made perfectly
plain that the objective was general reform not individual
remedies, the request was not considered a serious enquiry and was

therefore ignored.

As for Labour, they closed ranks with none prepared to public-
ally disassociate themselves from their party's rehousing policy.
An exception was a Maryhill councillor who, with GHC members
present in the public gallery, raised questions about the housing
visitor's form in the council. He accused the Corporation of (10)
'giving Housing Department officials a great deal of arbitrary
power' and suggested that 'it was quite inappropriate for an
administration representing the working people of the city to have
a system that reinforced class and status distinctions'. In reply,
the spokesman for the Corporation, promised that in future assessments would be made 'on a more reasonable and factual basis'.
Grading tenants, Norman writes, (11) became a political issue in
Glasgow. It certainly was the single most important issue to
emerge from the Gairbraid campaign.

THE HOUSING VISITOR'S REPORT

'Current Account' was the first to expose the visitor's form. It
had never before been opened to public debate or scrutiny.
Although vital to rehousing policy, the grading system had never
been approved by the Housing Committee. It was simply introduced
by officials and the councillors, having had no say in its adoption, hardly even knew of its existence. Being at the heart of
the rehousing process, almost all else which occurs during
clearance flows directly from it. Grading is inimical to free
choice: creating ghettos, it cannot countenance rehousing communities together but produces sporadic offers and is responsible
for prolonged rather than rapid rehousing. Damer and Madigan
stress that (12) 'neither the principle of grading tenants nor
the arbitrary and subjective way in which it is done, is unique
to Glasgow'. The 1969 Cullingworth Report, which is highly
critical of grading, affirms that (13) 'the majority of applicants
are "suitable" for a new house'. The procedures seem so common-
place that they are rarely questioned. Clare Ungerson, (14) for
instance, reproduces Brent's grading system, which is almost identical to Glasgow's, without feeling the necessity to comment on
either the validity of the criteria used or on the ethics of
allocating houses in this manner.

Glasgow's house letting regulations state that (15) 'depart-
mental knowledge concerning the applicant and his family and the
availability of houses will be taken into account in deciding the
type and situation of the house to be offered'. What is meant
but never stated is previous housing record, the counter staff's
impressions and the housing visitor's report. Just prior to
rehousing visitors, aptly described as (16) 'a corps of untrained
middle-aged women' descend on a clearance area. Their function is
to note individual preferences, check rent arrears, length of
tenancy, eligibility for rehousing, income and occupation. Each
household is then graded and this is 'crucial' (17) in determining
the quality of the offer they will receive. The residents in
Gairbraid were graded on a five-point scale from 'very good' to
'poor' on criteria of 'type of people', 'cleanliness' and

'furniture'. The housing visitor specifies the area in which she
thinks an allocation should be made. As Norman observes, (18) 'a
joint policy of grading tenants ... and matching them with a
similarly graded house is institutionalised in the allocations
system'.

Grading in this manner reflects an attitude which has a long
history, being deeply moulded in the 'deserving poor' tradition
of the nineteenth century. Octavia Hill, almost a century ago,
insisted that before letting, (19) 'one must ask for good refer-
ences; the drunkard, the dirty thriftless woman cannot be accepted;
the poor may be received, but not those whose character is
doubtful; the preference is fairly and rightly given to the sober,
industrious and clean'. Nowadays, Cullingworth finds that applicants are graded (20) 'according to an interpretation of their
desert' and that the essential qualifications for eligibility
seemed to be (21) 'moral rectitude, social conformity, clean
living and a "clear" rent book'. The purpose of grading is to
ensure that the best accommodation is allocated to the 'most
deserving' and, by the same yardstick, the 'least deserving' are
either offered the worst houses or even totally excluded from
the public housing sector. The justification is that some tenants,
who as Cullingworth stresses are few in number, (22) 'may not take
care of a new house'. Although such people present an extremely
difficult problem for local authorities and their neighbours
alike, (23) 'it is a far cry from allocating specially selected
houses to unsatisfactory tenants to grading all according to their
"fitness" for particular types of houses'.

A compassionate society, it could be argued, would make life
as easy as possible for those least able to cope rather than
force them to live in the most difficult circumstances - in the
oldest houses, often in a state of disrepair, with a minimum of
modern conveniences, in what are usually 'rough' neighbourhoods
lacking the basic amenities. The rationale may again be traced
to Octavia Hill who, in distinguishing between two types of
tenants, (24) 'the reasonably prosperous artisan' and those 'living on the edge of poverty', believed that for the latter, everything should be made 'strong' and 'simple' - 'I think old houses
far better than the new for training them in'. Such a policy
cannot but result in the creation of ghettos as some estates come
to be used as dumping grounds for problem families, real or
imagined. Woolley claims that every town has its undesirable
council estates where (25) 'only the weakest and more desperate
people are prepared to go' and he suggests that 'local authorities have deliberately let schemes run down and turned them into
problem areas'. In Glasgow, Damer and Madigan write, (26) 'many
of the poorer corporation estates have bcome stigmatised, the
outcome of a self-fulfilling prophecy set in motion by the corporation when it created a special category of low amenity
housing estates for slum clearance before the war'. Houses on
these estates inevitably become difficult to let, and as a consequence such authorities must devise punitive measures to fill their
unwanted property.

Although people in Gairbraid did not know exactly what to expect and were not told that they were being graded, most had a

shrewd idea of what the housing visitors were about. There was
a rumour, untrue in Gairbraid as far as is known, that the housing visitors inspect sheets and bedding, that they poke in
corners and under carpets for hidden dust - Cullingworth (27)
found that some local authorities do in fact inspect bedding.
The pending arrival of the visitors created scenes in Gairbraid
of spring-cleaning, washing, tidying and one family was even
reported to have re-decorated. To be too proud to do so, as
many were, could have meant jeopardizing the chance of a decent
house. Damer and Madigan found that (28) 'the younger, larger
and more "disorganised" households did poorly, especially if
they were demanding of the visitor, rather than grateful and
deferential'. Being graded is to have the privacy of one's
home invaded, of having to submit one's self and family to a
barrack-room-type inspection. Cullingworth feels that (29)
'the system leaves too much scope for personal prejudice and
unconscious bias to be acceptable'. Indeed, the housing
visitors seem to have almost absolute discretionary powers to
decide a family's future.

Strong objections were taken by the GHC to the categories used,
as people felt that they had been treated 'like cattle'. An
example of how ludicrous the whole system may appear is provided
by Eileen Thompson who, having then four young children, prepared
for the housing visitor

'... but she didn't come. So the next day because of the
baby, I had to do a washing. I couldn't put it off in a
room-and-kitchen which meant I had the washing machine out
when she walked in the door and I had five piles of clothes
all across the floor. So either she thought I was hellava
clean or hellava untidy.'

The Thompsons' future could have hinged on whether or not that
particular housing visitor had ever had to cope with young
children in a room-and-kitchen. Jeannette Bouse's complaint was
'how do you classify peoples' furniture, you are not going to
put good furniture in a room-and-kitchen that's soaking with
dampness?' Georgina Atkinson points out that 'there could be folk
who keep their house shining all the time but there can be folk
who just clean their house for that kind of day'. Isa Hanlon
remarks , 'does it mean that the likes of me with six weans, who
hasn't got much, is going to be classified as dirty because I
haven't got big fancy furniture? Do I have to get into debt?'
'Type of people' and 'cleanliness' were regarded as outrageous
and judging 'furniture' was seen to favour those who had bought
by hire purchase. In what was a fairly common experience, the
Atkinsons were graded without having been seen by the visitor.
Annie Mallon let the visitor into a neighbour's house while they
were away at work. Being out, apparently was no serious obstacle
to being graded. The system seemed to operate smoothly whether
or not people were actually seen by the visitor, and indeed, for
all its validity, it probably made little difference either way.
On average, the length of time spent with each resident seemed to
be between two and three minutes. In spite of the casualness of
the visits, the grade received largely determined the type and
situation of the house offered.

An aspect which particularly disturbed the committee was that
the unemployed in the community seemed to be discriminated
against. In the west of Scotland it was a time of extremely high
unemployment, job insecurity, weekly lay-offs and massive redun-
dancies. (30) A number of families whose breadwinner had been
made redundant complained about the poor quality of the offers
they received and this seemed to apply irrespective of the condition of their present homes, length of tenancy or rent record.
Although difficult to prove, these suspicions were regarded as
particularly unfair. It meant that after years of waiting on the
housing list, a man who had worked conscientiously all his life
found that at a stroke he had lost both his job and his opportunity for a decent home.
    During the television programme and again in the council, the
Corporation promised to reform the grading system. The 'Glasgow
News', featuring the visitor's report, gloomily predicted that: (31)

    It is very doubtful if the substance of grading will be
    abolished, even if the form of words is altered, because
    the whole machinery of house allocations depends on it.
    The fact is that a great deal of Corporation housing in
    Glasgow leaves a lot to be desired, and some of it is
    just plain lousy ... no one wants to live in these houses
    but - short of knocking them down - someone has to.

The report was amended and, in a letter to the GHC, the spokesman
for the Corporation stated (32) 'I am glad that our joint wishes
have been met'. However, 'Glasgow News', in inviting its readers
to 'spot the difference', declared 'grading remains'. It went on
to comment that it is 'difficult to avoid the conclusion that
criticisms by elected councillors have been fobbed off with a
piece of not very convincing window dressing'. Basically, all
that had changed was that 'type of people' was excluded and a
space for 'general assessment' added. The Corporation had
certainly not been able to fulfil its promise of reform but the
'revised' report apparently satisfied the Maryhill Councillor for
he did not publicly renew his criticisms of the grading system.
Those interested in meaningul reform had lost their champion.
    The GHC could not continue campaigning around the issue. The
residents had long been graded and the issue was only one of several major grievances. For the people affected, the whole
rehousing process is a series of crisis and injustices one after
another. Life in clearance areas quickly becomes a matter of
sheer survival and thus people cannot ignore immediate threats
in order to concentrate on past issues. In so far as people
were poorly graded, the GHC intended to make the system inoperative but such action could only affect the local area and
not the city as a whole. A general weakness of community action
in small areas is that campaigns around single issues tend,
almost inevitably, to be overtaken by events. In crisis situations, local organizations must respond to changing circumstances.
The GHC had at least succeeded in exposing Glasgow's grading
system and it was left to future local organizations to continue
the struggle. Three years later, the residents of the Oatlands
(33) treatment area held a widely publicized demonstration,
demanding that 'tenants should not be graded and herded from a

slum area to a sprawling housing scheme simply because the Corporation have to fill empty and boarded-up council houses'. The
Residents' Association asked 'why does the Corporation persist
with the grading system and why is housing regarded as a privilege
and not as a right?' Since Gairbraid, Glasgow has faced considerable criticism of its grading system: Shelter's national
report on 'Slum Clearance' (34) reproduces both the old and
revised visitor's report.

A senior member of the Housing Committee justifies grading by
claiming that (35) 'the same types of people naturally draw
together anyway'. In view of the fact that the Labour Group
seemed determined to retain the system intact, other than
continue to complain, there was very little that the GHC could
do. Equally disappointing were the promised changes in the
procedures governing the public's contact with Clive House. After
(36) 'a lengthy report on the Department's counter staff by a
team of senior management officials and councillors' the decision
was taken to replace five clerks with others of 'more mature age'.
Youth in this country has been blamed for many things but never
so unjustly as to bear responsibility for Clive House's bureaucratic administration. The solution to the Department's ills lay,
it seemed, in employing counter staff of age 35 or over, with (37)
'tolerance, imagination and initiative'. Indeed, all this and a
great deal more is needed in a job which essentially attempts to
convince people to accept houses they do not want.

The 'Current Account' programme failed to bring about significant changes in the city's housing policy and practice and no
more could reasonably have been expected. It did achieve a
greater public awareness of what actually does take place and,
for Gairbraid, reinforcing morale and the determination to
succeed, it greatly enhanced the GHC's bargaining power.

Chapter 8

THE THREAT OF MANY GAIRBRAIDS

The television programme over, the GHC resumed its day-to-day
organizing in the community, aware that the campaign needed to
be extended. Gradually the mood moved towards direct action,
but first, attempting to extract all the mileage possible from
the programme, the GHC aimed to achieve a meeting with the
Corporation's Housing Committee.

THE DELEGATION TO THE CITY
CHAMBERS

With the help of the local councillors, a meeting was arranged
with a specially appointed sub-committee to be held at the City
Chambers on the 22 November. Having been in existence for
barely six months, the GHC had, even if begrudgingly, been
granted recognition. From initially ignoring Gairbraid's
petition for information, senior councillors and officials were
now prepared to discuss matters with the GHC. Where appeals for
fair treatment had failed, a sustained campaign to exert pressure,
culminating in the 'Current Account' programme, succeeded. Glasgow
Corporation was forced to take note of Gairbraid.
    Although delighted at having achieved the meeting, the committee
members were keenly aware that Gairbraid was attempting to nego-
taite from a position of weakness. The community could bring no
immediate sanction to bear if its demands were rejected: unlike
a trade union the GHC could not threaten a withdrawal of labour.
All that was open to the committee was to attempt to argue logically and rationally in the knowledge that justice was on its side
which, clearly, was not enough. The GHC anticipated that few if
any concessions would be granted as a direct result of the meeting. The exercise was regarded as merely another stage in the
campaign which, if successful, would demonstrate the community's
determination to persevere until the very end. It was suggested
that the GHC should restrict its demands in the hope that the
Corporation would be more amenable to consider marginal rather
than fundamental change. This strategy was rejected: the GHC
felt morally obliged to place on record the full account of their

opposition to the city's rehousing policy and practice, not only
for Gairbraid but for the mass of Glaswegians without the opportunity to voice their own grievances. To have attempted anything
less would have meant that the GHC ceased to represent the
aspirations of their community. A conciliatory approach had after
all been repeatedly tried without much success. On tactical
grounds, the GHC felt that a demand for fundamental policy changes
would in the long term be more productive as it would pose the
threat of future militant action. Nevertheless, the GHC decided
to avoid creating antagonism. Accordingly, and perhaps mistakenly,
the press was not informed of the meeting at the City Chambers.

A list of the issues which the GHC wished to raise were requested
and these were sent to the sub-committee before the meeting. It
was considered that in each of the demands the people of Gairbraid
had serious grounds for complaint which, by reform, could be
rectified. It was stressed that many of the local difficulties
arose as a direct consequence of the premature start of rehousing
in Gairbraid, that is, before the Corporation had completed
clearances in other nearby treatment areas. The obvious and
ideal solution, it was argued, would have been to provide people
with the option of being rehoused in the new estate planned for
Gairbraid once the old tenements were demolished. As this
solution was no longer feasible Gairbraid's requests were by
necessity only second choices. Seven issues were raised by the
GHC: rehousing communities together; offering new houses before
completion; the housing visitor's report; repairs to relets; the
behaviour of the clerks; the rates increase; and compensation and
well maintained payments.

In its document, the GHC pointed out that the Corporation
itself had attributed the (1) 'stresses and strains' found in
Glasgow's housing estates to the fact that former neighbours were
not rehoused together. The Housing Manager had declared that
the (2) 'serious problems in housing areas ... will only be
solved when communities acquire an identity'. Gairbraid was an
organized, established community. Its people would not have been
dispersed had the Corporation any serious intention of tackling
the many acute problems facing the city. The sub-committee was
reminded of the social and economic consequences of uprooting
communities, and of the family, friendship and emotional ties
that united many Gairbraid people and which bound them to
Maryhill. It was a plea to the Corporation to take its own
rhetoric seriously.

It was predicted, correctly as it turned out, that at least
some Gairbraid people would be offered accommodation in the new
Maryhill estates, and therefore much unnecessary hardship could
be avoided if offers were made in advance rather than at the
last possible moment just before the property was ready for
occupation. Old Corporation houses are offered while in a state
of disrepair, often months before they are habitable, and in the
private market new houses are sometimes sold long before completion, so why not new council houses? Other than create some
administrative difficulties, there does not seem to be any logical
reason why people cannot be given assurances about the area and
type of accommodation that they will be offered before the

rehousing process actually begins. If adopted, such a policy
would alleviate a great deal of suffering because being certain
about the future, people are able more easily to tolerate deteriorating conditions.

The authorities were urged to suspend the housing visitor's
report and immediately inform people of the new criteria adopted.
Gairbraid, it was stated, cannot be expected to accept houses
offered on the basis of an invalid report. On the next point,
it was stressed, that the Corporation's inability to satisfactorily repair relet property within a reasonable length of time
made people reluctant to consider houses which they otherwise would
have gladly accepted. It was suggested that the Housing Department
should provide its prospective tenants with a written statement of
the repairs they were willing to undertake, specifying an approxi-
mate completion date.

The Corporation were made aware of the anomalous situation
existing in Gairbraid where, although conditions had become intolerable and the maintenance of the essential services almost
impossible, residents were expected to pay increased rates.
Furthermore, as rates and rents were paid simultaneously to the
factors, residents were faced with either having to pay both or
neither. Residents could not by-pass the factors and pay rates
directly to the City Assessor. It was suggested that the
Corporation needed to evolve a policy concerning rates in areas
scheduled for demolition.

Those who preferred to purchase another home rather than rent
from the Corporation urgently required payment of the compensation
due to them. The GHC was also concerned that factors, often
contributing nothing to the upkeep of the property, would receive
well maintained payments rather than the tenants who had borne
the expense. It was a situation that would hardly do credit to
a Labour administration. Action was particularly urgent as
assessments would be impossible once the property had been
vandalized. Given the expenses involved in moving, buying new
furniture, replacing fitted carpets and gas cookers with
electric, and the like, all payments due to residents should be
made long in advance. The Corporation, however, did not even
provide residents with information about compensation or well
maintained payments.

It was not expected that the GHC's list of demands would be
well received. The authorities later complained that the document
had been written by an outsider - it had in fact been written by
the community workers in conjunction with the committee members.
As the Corporation, quite rightly, seeks expert advice whenever
necessary, there is no reason why local groups should be denied
the privilege of obtaining any aid available to them. The GHC
had an early disappointment when Jimmy Gallagher was unable to
get time off work and thus had to withdraw from the delegation.
John Moir, Annie Mallon and Isa Hanlon were selected to represent
Gairbraid at the City Chambers. After much discussion, it was
also decided that the community workers should accompany the
delegation, which was probably the worst tactical error committed
throughout the entire campaign. The power hierarchy in the city
was out in full force to meet the Gairbraid delegation. Those

present included the Housing Convenor with two of his senior
councillors, two of the Maryhill councillors, the Housing Manager,
the Chief Sanitary Inspector, the Senior Depute City Architect,
representatives from the City Chamberlain and the Planning Department, plus various others. They were seated in two rows around
the table where there was hardly room to accommodate the Gairbraid
delegation. The authorities had marshalled an impressive gallery
of dignitaries which both bewildered and amused the Gairbraid
contingent. It seemed as if a representative from every
Corporation department even remotely connected with housing had
been squeezed into the room. It was a sure sign that the GHC
were being taken seriously.

The meeting was chaired by the Housing Convenor who, referring
to the presence of the community workers, immediately seized the
opportunity to blame 'outside trouble-makers' for Gairbraid's
problems. A scapegoat was thus provided which allowed the
authorities to avoid discussion of the real issues. From the
start it was obvious that Gairbraid would not receive a fair
hearing, nor was any serious consideration going to be given to
their demands. Rehousing the community en bloc and the request
for early offers were dismissed out of hand. Gairbraid, as
expected, was accused of seeking preferential treatment, and much
of the discussion centred around the problems facing Glasgow.
On the question of repairs to relet property, the Housing Manager
stated that prospective tenants were entitled to receive a
written list of the repairs to be carried out. The complaint about
the counter clerks received a less sympathetic hearing and the
chairman refused the Housing Manager permission to answer questions
on this subject. The delegation was simply given vague assurances
that the situation would improve. The atmosphere changed for the
better when the rates issue was reached. All present agreed that
it was most unreasonable that these should be increased in treatment areas but it was regretted that the Corporation had no
control over the matter as the City Assessor was answerable only
to the central government. Finally, compensation and well
maintained payments were dealt with. Explanations of the procedures were provided and owner-occupiers were advised to apply for
compensation. Although not without delays, people did receive
compensation, but in spite of promises no Gairbraid resident, as
far as is known, ever received a well maintained payment. The
meeting closed after about two hours. Although Gairbraid had
received a lengthy hearing, the delegation came away dissatisfied,
feeling that all the vital decisions had been taken long before-
hand. The meeting had been chaired with extreme partiality and
bias and often the delegation were interrupted and prevented from
making their points. Altogether, it was an incredible performance
if the power wielded by the respective sides is considered.
Against the corporate power of a large city, Gairbraid represented
a tiny area. In fact, on the information supplied by the Housing
Manager, there were then only 240 families left in Gairbraid.

THE BALANCE OF POWER

The lessons learned from the meeting were that the local community
requires to disturb the balance of power before it can hope to
negotiate successfully and it is a truism to add that concessions
are won only in relation to the power or threat of it that is
wielded. The major concession granted to the GHC at the City
Chambers was that residents could demand a written list of repairs
before committing themselves to a house. On this score the
Housing Manager gave firm assurances. However, it appears that he
failed to instruct his staff to behave accordingly. In practice,
Gairbraid residents were unable subsequently to secure a list of
repairs. One woman having presented an official with a list was
told that it was worthless and had it torn up in front of her.
Gaining concessions is all very well but having the power to
ensure that they are instituted is clearly a very different matter.
    Implicit in a consensus approach to community action is the
assumption that all will be well if only channels of communication
can be established. It is as if the authorities are unaware of
the consequences which result from their own policies. The blame
is placed on size and not on the bureaucracy itself, which
suggests that, in spite of good intentions, things have become
unmanageable, causing the system temporarily to leave the rails.
Although there is no evidence to suggest that housing departments
have ever been democratic, it is firmly believed that sanity may
be 'restored' by simply tinkering with the parts and that only
minor adjustments are required. The solution to the country's
housing problems is conceived not in terms of increased house
building and greater power sharing but in hiving off administration to housing associations. The whole Gairbraid experience
demonstrates that these are totally misconceived notions: the
authorities had not the slightest interest in establishing
meaningful communications with the community.
    While no immediate reforms in policy were anticipated as a
consequence of the meeting at the City Chambers, the GHC felt that
it had impressed the authorities sufficiently to expect some
indirect benefits in the near future, particularly, an increased
rate of rehousing from Gairbraid. The committee wished to avoid
simply marking time until the Corporation reacted, if at all,
to the demands put before them. The consensus of opinion was
that the campaign should be extended. After various possibilities had been considered, it was decided to stage a demonstration
outside the Housing Department. Although a degree of hostility
had long been present in the GHC's relationship with the authorities, direct action with open conflict had never taken place.
Despite the impression sometimes given by the Corporation that
the GHC was a hotbed of revolution, the Gairbraid campaign was a
largely restrained affair. Even the demonstration was planned
to take a mild form: leaflets were simply to be distributed at
the Housing Department.
    Clive House rather than the City Chambers was chosen for
several reasons: when rehoused, people deal mainly with officials
rather than councillors and thus Clive House was more readily
identifiable as a focus for protest; officials were less used to

dealing with demonstrations than were councillors; a small demonstration at the City Chambers was in danger of being swamped by
shoppers and thus likely to be less impressive than in the cramped
space around Clive House; the leaflets were intended for people
being rehoused rather than simply passers-by; and finally,
protests at the City Chambers were relatively common while none
were known to have been held at the Housing Department and thus,
being original, a demonstration at the latter was more likely to
attract press publicity. The committee was undecided whether to
hold the demonstration immediately or to postpone it until after
the approaching Christmas and New Year holidays. Some thought
that the protest would have maximum impact if delayed until mid-
January, by which time the authorities could not complain that
they had been given insufficient time to implement local demands.
The GHC felt that the community should be involved before a final
decision was taken and a public meeting was organized to gauge
the extent of local support for the venture.

The public meeting, held on 8 December, was advertised in a
newsletter distributed to every household in the area. It was
chaired by Jimmy Gallagher who, although in the role for the
first time, performed with considerable ability. The two previous
meetings had been chaired by Ken McLachlan and at those crucial
stages he had served Gairbraid extremely well. At the December
public meeting, however, the GHC had come of age and in Jimmy
Gallagher could supply its own skilful chairman. Indeed, he
handled the meeting as if to the manner born. Disappointingly,
only about thirty residents were present, the smallest attendance
so far. Two main issues were discussed during the evening: the
legality of withholding rent from the factors and the proposed
demonstration at Clive House. The first matter was dealt with by
one of the Maryhill councillors who gave firm assurances of his
support in the event of a decision being taken to withhold rent.
The second item on the agenda, the protest at Clive House, was
enthusiastically received. The draft of the leaflet was read
out and one response from the floor was: 'Get them out as soon as
possible, better get down to the print shop tomorrow.' However,
in view of the small attendance, it was decided to postpone the
demonstration until January before which another public meeting
would be held. Later events showed that the committee under-
estimated the degree of local militancy, for it misinterpreted
non-attendance at the public meeting to indicate lack of interest.
Large numbers of those who were not present at the meeting en-
quired about the protest, promised support and were disappointed
to hear that it had been postponed. The experience showed that
degree of local involvement should not be assessed simply by a
head-count at a public meeting.

Although only thirty residents were present, the meeting was
considered highly successful; everyone was able to express their
ideas and participate fully in decision-making. It ended on a
note of great solidarity. With the Maryhill Trade Union Centre
and the Labour Party Rooms in easy walking distance, the GHC was
better off than most for meeting places. Nevertheless, the GHC
suffered from not having a hall available within Gairbraid where
it could hold emergency and small monthly public meetings where

residents could simply drop in. The committee's weekly meetings
in the flat in Burnhouse Street were later to serve this purpose
but it was really too small to accommodate more than twenty people.
Annie Mallon extended an open invitation to all those present to
attend the GHC's weekly meetings. In similar vein, Jimmy Gallagher
closed the discussion by saying:

'You know our stand. We're not going to move 'till we get
a house in this area and we're going to fight to the finish.
I think it would be a good idea if we had a meeting like
this every month. Everybody could get to know each other,
how things were going and if they've got ideas, well, we can
unite them. It would be good to get you all up on a Monday
night, it would be good to get a lot of tenants up there,
especially the ones here.'

The protest at Clive House was in fact not to take place until the
first week in February. Thus about two and a half months were to
elapse between the meeting at the City Chambers and the demonstration. During this time, the Corporation did not meaningfully
concede any of the basic local demands. If the authorities had
shown any readiness to negotiate, it is most probable that the
demonstration would not have taken place. Gairbraid could make
concessions but not about the quality of offers nor about being
left endlessly to rot in inhuman conditions. However, it was
precisely on these questions that the Corporation refused to
concede that the community had any rights at all. Local people
felt that Gairbraid did not initiate conflict but rather, in the
manner of their rehousing, violence was done to them.

WITHHOLDING RENT

Rent strikes are difficult to organize, requiring a considerable
amount of time, energy and resources. The GHC, although wishing
to avoid involvement in a rent strike, was forced to become em-
broiled with the factors. While continuing to accept rent, many
factors ceased to undertake repairs either because the property
was beyond mending, or because any work done would be immediately
vandalized, or because they did not wish to incur additional expenses on short-lived property. Whether justified or not, the
factors' failure to do repairs created considerable hardship for
the remaining tenants and many, as they were entitled to, stopped
paying rent. In order to demonstrate good intentions in the
event of court action, the GHC was advised that the rent due
should be paid into a special bank account. Once rehoused, the
tenant would be able to redeem the full amount which would then
be money saved. As Gairbraid was not a world of cheque books
and bankers' orders, collecting rent in this manner posed
organizational problems. Another complication was that some
factors, quite remarkably under the circumstances, continued to
undertake repairs almost to the very end. Even so, it seemed
unfair that, in appalling conditions, people should have to pay
the same amount as they did before the treatment area resolution
was declared. This situation need never have arisen but for the
gross incompetence of Glasgow Corporation. As 'Glasgow News'

point out, (3) 'the Town Clerk's Department has shown its inability
to prepare a Compulsory Purchase Order in reasonable time'.

Although they had sufficient cause, many people, particularly
the elderly with their memories of past summary evictions, were
afraid to withhold rent. At the December public meeting a local
councillor supported a rent strike, assuring residents that such
action would not jeopardize their position with the Housing
Department. Before houses are allocated tenants need to produce
their rent books, but Clive House, together with senior councillors, agreed that this procedure would be waived for Gairbraid
where rent was being withheld. A few unpleasant incidents subsequently occurred when counter staff demanding rent books threatened
to withdraw offers already made. Although all such misunderstand-
ings were always quickly resolved and no resident suffered as a
consequence, considerable distress was caused. It is yet another
example of the administration's failure to transmit decisions
taken at senior level down to all sections of the staff.

The GHC encouraged tenants to withhold rent but avoided placing
pressure or obligation on anyone to do so. Even among the
committee members unanimity was not demanded and John Smith, for
instance, continued paying rent. Rent strikes in treatment areas,
even on a limited scale, are extremely complicated and should not
be started unless all the possible implications are fully understood. If factors continue to do repairs, it is advisable for
tenants to pay rent, as John Smith found when his factor replaced
window after window, finally fitting an expensive reinforced glass
which the vandals managed to crack but not break. If it were not
for the conscientious efforts of this factor, life would have
become completely intolerable for the Smiths and it was as well
that in their case rent was not withheld.

In the vast majority of cases the factors accepted the situation and made no further demands for payment, but a few took court
action against their tenants for non-payment of rent. On every
occasion, after the GHC had arranged legal representation, the
court ruled in favour of the tenant. One of these cases concerned a tenement where only one toilet, serving forty-four people,
was in functioning order and yet the factor claimed that there
were no outstanding repairs. Arranging legal representation was
exceedingly time-consuming, but without it almost certainly all
the tenants taken to court would have been evicted.

The Small Debt Court in Glasgow deals with rent arrears and in
ninety minutes hears on average between 200 and 300 cases. (4)
The vast majority of these are in dispute with the Corporation.
In the seven years, 1967-73, (5) almost 3,000 council tenants were
evicted and a further 12,000 absconded. It may only take twenty
seconds to issue a decree of eviction but for the family involved
the consequences may last a life-time. The Corporation will not
rehouse until arrears are repaid and even then only in inferior
accommodation. It is unfair to regard all such families as delinquent: for instance, one Gairbraid woman owed money from when her
husband was on strike for a year. The system is hardly designed
to hear appeals on compassionate grounds and the family in
temporary difficulties may find themselves homeless. It would
seem that after a two-year period people should be absolved of

debts incurred in Corporation houses. The alternative to fore-
going these debts is to add to the growing number of homeless
families in the city.

Glasgow's rent arrears problem could be considerably lessened by
a few administrative improvements such as providing tenants with
copies of their lease. These should contain a statement of the
procedures required for vacating as frequently, through ignorance
of the rules, keys are simply handed to a neighbour. As a result,
houses often remain empty for long periods because the Housing
Department is unaware that they are unoccupied. Having failed to
give notice, the ex-tenant is held responsible for the rent during
the period when the house remained empty. When again caught up in
the rehousing process, the family discovers that they are in debt
or in greater debt than they imagined. Such situations need never
arise if people are fully informed about giving notice. As tenants
fall into rent arrears they should not simply be given warning of
notice to quit but should first be allowed the opportunity to explain their circumstances. Further, once an area is designated for
clearance, all those in debt should immediately be informed of the
amount owing and made aware that they are able to repay in instalments. Given an early opportunity to repay debts, many would
manage to do so in the time available before the actual beginning
of rehousing. The belief in Gairbraid was that debts were only
repayable in full and as a result no payments were made at all.
Even once the authorities agreed to accept instalments, there were
occasions when the junior staff at Clive House refused to accept
anything less than the full amount.

Withholding rent was of only secondary importance to the
Gairbraid campaign and rent arrears, either private or Corporation,
affected only a tiny minority of the area's population. Yet,
involvement with these issues uncovered layers of human misery
caused by a combination of mercenary house factors, inadequate
legal protection, and bureaucratic incompetence if not total
indifference.

1972: THE START OF DIRECT ACTION

Under 200 families were left in Gairbraid to usher in the new year.
The hope was that it would be the last Hogmanay celebrated in the
area. The GHC had increased its strength to an active membership
of nine: John Moir, Jimmy Gallagher, Annie Mallon, Isa Hanlon,
Ella Donnelly, Eileen Kelly and John Smith were joined by two new
recruits, Jackie Moir and Tommy Dickson, both of whom were to fill
vital roles in the organization. In addition, Hugh and Eileen
Thompson, although long rehoused, still attended meetings regularly. Georgina Atkinson, one of the committee's founder members,
dropped out because of ill-health but was later, through her work
in one of the local shops, still able to provide valuable assistance.

The first activity organized in January was another public meeting. In order to provide residents with the opportunity of fully
participating in the committee's decision-making, the local
councillors were not invited. However, only about twenty-five

residents turned up. The councillors were, it seems, a major
attraction at the GHC's public meeting. The poor attendance was
again mistakenly interpreted as a sign of falling local interest.
This belief was to influence the GHC's strategy, particularly
that devised for the demonstration at Clive House.

Jimmy Gallagher, as chairman, opened the meeting with a review
of recent rehousing, the efforts made to maintain the area, the
rent strike and the planned demonstration. Harry Liddell of the
Hutchesontown Tenants' Association on the south side of Glasgow,
was the guest speaker. A seasoned and devoted campaigner for the
people of Glasgow, Harry Liddell was then involved with a group
of tenants in a clearance area. Although they had not received
any offers of alternative accommodation, they were threatened with
eviction by the Corporation. The events there, as a foretaste of
what could occur, were of obvious interest to Gairbraid. Harry
Liddell stressed that through organized opposition the evictions
were forestalled and he went on to tell the meeting:

'The success of the thing will revolve around the involvement
of the people. They have got to be prepared to say that they
are going to make a stand. This is vitally important because if they don't say they're going to fight then you really
haven't got a fight.'

Opened to questions, the meeting discussed future tactics in great
detail. Jackie Moir announced that the Corporation was organizing
a public meeting the next day for the residents of a newly declared treatment area. In contrast to the total lack of information provided in Gairbraid it was encouraging that the authorities
were actually initiating contact with residents. The Corporation
seemed to be fulfilling their promise, elicited during the
'Current Account' programme, to provide residents in treatment
areas with information.

Jackie Moir proposed that the leaflet prepared for the Clive
House demonstration could, with a few alterations, be distributed
at the Corporation's meeting. It was, he suggested, an opportunity to realize the threat of organizing many Gairbraids.
Jimmy Gallagher and Isa Hanlon volunteered to help him distribute
the leaflet outside the meeting at the Woodside Halls. All
depended on whether or not the leaflet could be prepared, typed
and duplicated in time. In fact, over 400 were produced, which
would not have been possible but for outside resources. The GHC's
intervention at the Woodside Halls marked a vital stage in the
Gairbraid campaign. Jimmy Gallagher feels that 'it was one of the
turning points ... it really shook them to the roots, they wanted
to keep us quiet.' Jackie Moir believes that:

'The Corporation saw that we were there, stirring it up.
We were showing the people, telling the truth about their
redevelopment schemes. They thought that the sooner they
got rid of us the better. I think this really did accelerate our rehousing. They wanted us off their back.'

The GHC leaflet gave details of Glasgow's housing policy and practice, informed residents of their rights and strongly advised
them, with promised Gairbraid support, to organize in opposition
to the Corporation. Unlike Gairbraid, the meeting was called for
an area which was to be improved rather than demolished. To the

authorities' discomfort, the GHC pointed out that the residents, nevertheless, had a rehousing problem. Even though the property was to be improved, the occupants would have to be at least temporarily rehoused which, going on past performance, was likely to involve periods of between three and four years. Furthermore, as three houses were to be converted into two, a third of the families could not be given the option of moving back into the area. This clearly was not the kind of information that the Corporation wished to disclose. The GHC's intervention meant that the meeting was not a mere public relations exercise. To Jackie Moir, the Corporation 'called these people together to try and palm them off, it was a clear case of whitewash.' Their crude attempts at propaganda leave no doubt as to the accuracy of this conclusion. To demonstrate the benefits of improvement the authorities showed slides of houses before and after being rehabilitated. It was 'farcical', Jackie Moir recalls, as the 'before' slides were shown in black and white and the houses contained old furniture while the 'after' slides were in colour with the 'most modern furniture'. Similarly, the backcourts were shown on the one hand to contain 'old rubbish bins and wash-houses', while on the other 'it was like Hollywood, with park benches, a grass area for the kids, swing parks and neon lights'.

The Corporation called the meeting, Jackie Moir believes, because 'they didn't want the people to get militant or form committees'. As lack of information was the GHC's best initial organizing issue, the authorities had obviously learned from that experience. Initiating contact with a community is a far more sophisticated response than simply ignoring demands and thus could be interpreted as an attempt to pre-empt local militancy rather than an endeavour to inform. In spite of their frequently repeated rhetorical claims about wishing to encourage local participation, judging from their hostile reaction to the GHC leaflet, the Corporation clearly did not desire the spread of Gairbraid-type organizations. The councillors and officials on the platform, far from recommending that those present should take up Gairbraid's offer to help them organize, accused the GHC of troublemaking. Their attitude was entirely divisive, attempting at all times to discredit the GHC. The pamphlet was dismissed as irrelevant in the opening address but was nevertheless constantly referred to during question time. To the chagrin of the authorities, it resulted in many awkward points being raised and clearly, had considerable impact on the meeting.

Although hastily organized, the GHC's intervention at the Woodside Halls had important repercussions. Thereafter, rehousing from Gairbraid appeared to accelerate and more people seemed to be satisfied with the quality of the offers they received. During this period it also became apparent that members of the GHC had established a foothold at the Housing Department. Over several months, beginning in about October, residents were being increasingly granted interviews with a relatively senior official in the house letting section at Clive House (see chapter 9). Some of the committee members felt that in order not to jeopardize what was then still a very fragile relationship with the official concerned, the demonstration at Clive House should again be postponed. It

was further argued that a show of force was then unnecessary as the
leaflets issued at the Woodside Halls were sufficient reminder of
the GHC's ability to take direct action. Adopting the opposite
point of view, others felt that while the rehousing rate had
improved, it was still far from satisfactory. The members were
reminded that the Corporation had so far only made minimal concessions and, as attempts at negotiation had clearly been exhausted,
the GHC had no option but to extend its campaign. It was argued
that the interviews at Clive House were as yet too infrequent and
random to be regarded as a policy change and moreover, the best
means of ensuring that they were continued was by increasing rather
than decreasing pressure. The committee's main dilemma in arriving
at a decision was that, on the one hand, a demonstration might be
unnecessarily provocative while on the other, inactivity was open
to the misinterpretation that the GHC had ceased to function as a
viable force. At stake were some of the new houses being built in
Maryhill, then almost ready for allocation: would a demonstration
jeopardize or enhance Gairbraid's chances of being offered these?
The GHC had no way of knowing. The only certainty was that once
the houses were allocated, nothing further could be done.

At a fully attended committee meeting, the pros and cons of
postponing the demonstration were heatedly argued until finally
it was put to the vote. It was the first occasion on which votes
needed to be cast as hitherto all decisions had been reached by
broad agreement. Both community workers were for postponement,
but against their advice the majority voted to go ahead with the
demonstration as quickly as possible and the date was set for
7 February. It was a significant meeting, irrefutably stamping
the GHC as a mature, democratic organization, where decision-making
was under firm local control. Whatever else was to be achieved in
Gairbraid, the objective of establishing a local organization under
its own leadership was already fully realized. The community
workers' role was quite rightly and clearly perceived as advisory.
It had always been understood that Gairbraid must provide its own
leadership. The wisdom of this philosophy was demonstrated by
later events when the majority decision was proved right and the
professionals wrong. Once having voted, all those in favour of
postponement abided absolutely by the majority decision. Community groups ideally need control over the resources because, in
spite of the vote, the situation could still have arisen where
the community workers, through their control of the duplicating
machine, postponed the demonstration. To have done so, however,
would have been unforgiveable.

The next problem faced was whether or not to apply for police
permission for the demonstration which, even if granted, was
likely to cause delay. It was decided to dispense with the formality and instead to take special precautions not to infringe the
law which, anyway, would have been taken. For these as well as
for pragmatic reasons, it was decided to limit the numbers involved
to about twenty. It did not mean that anyone who wanted to go
would be excluded. On the contrary, all who had already indicated
an interest were contacted. Others, however, were not canvassed.
There were an estimated 180 families still in the area, many of
whom found it impossible to participate because of either young

families, work reasons or because they were too old and frail. A
large turn-out was inconceivable and thus, by announcing in advance
a limited protest, the GHC protected itself against jibes that it
was incapable of mobilizing mass support. The strategy devised
was to demonstrate the GHC's serious intentions and to pose the
possibility of further, more militant, action. The leaflets were
to encourage the formation of organizations elsewhere in the city
and thus, unless pre-empted through rapid rehousing, Gairbraid
threatened both to seek allies and spread opposition. As a sit-in
or occupation of Clive House had been discounted, no activity
suggested itself other than distributing leaflets. A silent vigil
outside Clive House by a mass of people with nothing obvious to do
promised to be cold, boring and not particularly advantageous.
The GHC, making a virtue out of necessity, planned for a small
protest.

Two separate leaflets were prepared. The first, headed 'The
Right to a Decent House in Glasgow', informed people of their
rights when dealing with Clive House and declared 'if everyone
in Glasgow organized, housing policy would have to be changed'.
The second asked: 'Have You been Graded?' As the GHC was no
longer in a position to continue its campaign against the housing
visitor's report, the leaflet was a token of local dissatisfaction
at the Corporation's broken promises to reform. Furthermore,
rights of appeal are purely academic unless people are, in the
first place, made aware of the existence of the grading procedures.
By attacking the grading system, the GHC was striking at the very
heart of housing policy. The administration depends on people
co-operating with the housing visitors and on their being unaware
of grading, let alone appealing against it. If people refused to
comply with the system, it could be made inoperable.

Press releases were sent to twenty newspapers and in response
the 'Evening Citizen' published on its first page a short item
announcing that the GHC were to stage a demonstration against the
(6) 'arbitrary and bureaucratic nature of Glasgow's housing
policy'. Although given this warning, Clive House seemed unprepared. About thirty Gairbraid residents were there though the
press and STV's Scottish News put the figure at forty. Eileen
Thompson made a banner, held aloft throughout, which read 'People
of Glasgow, you have the right to a decent house'. Leaflets
were distributed for about two hours and these were generally well
received, both by people going in and out of Clive House and by
ordinary passers-by. Several enquiries were made, a great deal of
interest was shown and much encouragement given. The protestors
had no direct contact with the officials in Clive House other than
to hand any who appeared copies of the leaflets. Throughout the
demonstration, many of the staff could be seen, glued to the
windows, gazing down on the banner and leaflets in the street below. In spite of Gairbraid's obviously peaceful intentions, the
Corporation felt compelled to summon the police, seven of whom
appeared. After enquiring about the purpose of the protest, they
chatted with the demonstrators. There was no reason for them to
intervene as the GHC had taken care not to obstruct the entrance
to Clive House or foist leaflets on anyone unwilling to accept
them.

Under the headline (7) 'Maryhill tenants in housing battle', the Glasgow 'Evening Times' reported that Gairbraid was 'fighting a last-ditch battle to save their community' and that the GHC had appealed to other tenants' associations to join them. A photograph of the protest appeared in 'The Glasgow Herald' which quoted John Moir: (8) 'why should a community be destroyed?' The newspaper made it clear that Gairbraid was also protesting against the grading system. One demonstrator, who had lived in Burnhouse Street since 1914 and was the last person left in the close - 'water was always coming down on top of him' - was quoted as saying:

'I do not want to leave the area I have known all my life, and I think that it is fair that the Corporation should keep me in the place I know. Our houses are a shambles, and there are three housing schemes in the area that should be used to rehouse us.'

The GHC had received an extremely favourable press and cuttings were displayed in the local shop windows. Both newspapers reported that the protest was to continue and at odd intervals during the next fortnight committee members distributed 1,500 leaflets outside Clive House.

The committee members were extremely satisfied with the demonstration and felt that the decision to go ahead was fully vindicated by the results achieved. The extension of the campaign to include direct action was symbolic of a psychological barrier being breeched. It conclusively demonstrated that the power structure could be challenged and that militant action was, if necessary, an option open to the community. The protest certainly did Gairbraid no harm and the period after was marked by rapid rehousing. No changes in official policy resulted but the committee believe that the authorities were persuaded of the advantages of rehousing the community as quickly as possible. The Corporation resolved their problems in Gairbraid by getting rid of its population. They were left in no doubt that to do otherwise would be to risk the possibility of contending, not only with an increasingly militant Gairbraid, but with several angry communities, organized in co-ordinated opposition to official rehousing policy and practice.

Chapter 9

ORGANIZING FOR REPRESENTATION

For those left in clearance areas waiting to be rehoused, the local postman increasingly assumes importance as life comes to revolve around the hope that tomorrow's post will bring word from the Housing Department. At times, even this life-line was denied as some postmen refused to climb three flights of darkened, debris-littered stairs simply to verify whether or not anyone still lived in the tenement. A resident wishing to hasten the process may appeal to a local councillor and/or to the counter staff at the Housing Department. Councillors often successfully take up individual cases but even if approachable, attainable and willing, are generally regarded as conscientious but over-worked, insufficiently influential and incapable of operating outwith official regulations. Where councillors are seen to be limited, the junior staff of Housing Departments are regarded with even greater suspicion. (1) People in Gairbraid found that visits to Clive House were a frustrating and demoralizing experience. Frequently, people had to wait hours before being called up to the glass-partitioned counter for a brief and often unproductive interview. Even when not actually abusive, the clerks have anyway neither the knowledge nor the authority to be of much use as most of the important decisions are taken by their superiors. As different clerks are usually seen on different occasions, on each, detailed case histories have to be wearily repeated. In short, the ordinary resident wishing to enquire, inform, request or complain, has no real access to authority.

From when an area is earmarked for clearance, until the last family is rehoused, life is continual uncertainty. Where a local authority rehouses thousands each year and where much of it is in relet property whose availability is not always predictable, a degree of uncertainty is probably unavoidable. It is suggested, however, that total and absolute uncertainty is quite unnecessary and inexcusable. The attempt to alleviate uncertainty, particularly in the rate of offers and in the choice of alternatives, was the essential core of the Gairbraid campaign. The Corporation seemed determined to maintain control of all decision-making, that they alone would decide when, where and to whom offers should be made. They intended that people would have to wait, in rapidly

deteriorating and intolerable conditions, until Clive House was
ready to make an offer and then it was for the officials rather
than the applicant to decide which type of house and district was
suitable. The GHC, on the other hand, was determined that people
would not be left to the whim of the Corporation, that residents
would have some influence and control over rehousing. This was
achieved when committee members began accompanying groups of
residents to Clive House to advocate on their behalf with a relatively senior official. It greatly reduced uncertainty, allowing
the residents to take the initiative to determine their own
futures. During the period in which the system was operative,
the GHC avoided becoming over-dependent on the local councillors
who, together with the counter clerks, were largely by-passed.
     From January to March 1972, the GHC concentrated its energies
on organizing these visits to Clive House. During this time it
is estimated that over 100 families were rehoused from Gairbraid
which more than halved the remaining population. Many of those
rehoused included old age pensioners, families in rent arrears,
and families with short tenancies, some of whom were classified
as squatters. By April it was thought that less than a hundred
families still lived in the area, which meant that, by then,
roughly three out of every four houses in Gairbraid were unoccupied compared to a ratio of 1:8 when rehousing commenced about
nine months previously. Although the prime objective of the GHC
was rapid rehousing, it left in its wake serious problems among
which was an alarming acceleration in the decline of Gairbraid's
living conditions as vandals and petty thieves systematically
stripped and destroyed houses almost as soon as they were vacated.
Success also created tactical dilemmas: through continual rehousing, the GHC was being sapped not only of its leadership but
also of its potential support and hence of its power to protect
those remaining who, as a result, increasingly became more and
more vulnerable.

THE COMMITTEE AS ADVOCATE

The GHC achieved representation for the community through gaining
access to authority and that was obtained, over a long period,
almost by chance. It had its beginnings at the first public meeting organized by the GHC in July 1971. The senior housing official
present dealt with complaints by inviting residents to write for
appointments to see him at Clive House. Attempts to do so, however,
proved singularly unsuccessful: letters invariably went un-
answered and interviews were rarely if ever granted. At the
October public meeting the same official was forcibly reminded of
his earlier promise of easy accessibility. He again invited
residents to write for appointments and although he was subsequently
no more available than he had been before, people going to Clive
House gradually began to be granted interviews with one of his
deputees. Isa Hanlon was the first committee member to perceive
the potential of these visits and she started accompanying residents to Clive House. The advantage of seeing this relatively
senior official rather than the clerks was that he, unlike them,

was vested with sufficient authority to make quick decisions.
Hitherto, residents who approached committee members with problems
were usually referred to the councillors. Provided with an opening,
Isa Hanlon began taking residents directly to Clive House. As more
and more people were quickly and satisfactorily rehoused through
this method, word spread amongst the community, swelling the numbers
of those wishing to avail themselves of the opportunity. Other
committee members began accompanying groups of residents until
virtually all became involved. Thus, from rather obscure beginnings, the infrequent visits of one or two residents developed into
a highly organized activity where sometimes every day groups of
ten or more people were interviewed at Clive House.

The procedure followed at the Housing Department was that a
committee member was present during the interview and interceded
on the resident's behalf whenever necessary. There were rare
occasions when residents preferred privacy, which was always res-
pected by the GHC who accordingly withdrew from the interview.
Otherwise the members remained as each resident was in turn called
to present their case. Residents had in the past complained that
from one visit to the next, clerks denied promises made. It seems
that residents were told almost anything simply to be rid of them,
a ploy made easy because residents did not always see the same
clerk. The advantage of the new procedure was that the GHC member
witnessed all that was said. They quickly became expert in house
letting regulations and could quote precedents in support of
individual claims. The official soon became familiar with the
problems facing particular individuals so that on subsequent
interviews, detailed case histories became unnecessary and thus
much time was saved. As the system of interviews developed,
appointments to see the official were made in advance. No longer
did the resident have patiently to await word from Clive House,
he could now bring his case to them.

The advantages were not all with the residents, for the Housing
Department also benefited. Local knowledge was used to provide
information of empty council houses of which the authorities were
not yet aware and these were, thus, able to be let more quickly.
Before coming to Clive House, residents frequently scoured the
areas of their choice in search of empty property and lengthy
lists of these were presented to the official. While not always
able to secure for themselves the accommodation found, these
houses were at least more quickly allocated to others. It also
provided an opportunity for the official point of view to be
explained and often compromises were reached between, on the one
hand individual preferences, and on the other the availability of
houses in particular areas. The staff at Clive House were no
longer stereotyped by the residents as a faceless bureaucracy
but through real contact, the official concerned was seen to be
a caring person with an unenviable job, which under the circumstances, he managed to fulfil with considerable humanity. His
efforts were very much appreciated by the people of Gairbraid.
Through the interviews, arrangements were made to repay Corporation debts about which the residents affected were ill-informed
and often confused. Emergency cases, particularly where fires
and flooding had caused homelessness, could also be dealt with
immediately.

The relative seniority of the official concerned meant that
offers of houses could be made then and there at the interview,
thus increasing the chance of acceptance. Previously, the situation frequently arose where a particular house was rejected by
several families in turn while others in the area, seemingly as
well qualified as them, waited in vain to be offered it.   Instead
of bothering to ascertain if anyone in the area found it acceptable, the clerks attempted to foist the house on people who really
did not want it. Where this occurred, under the system of personal
interviews, people were able to make their desires known quickly
and the house was disposed of to the satisfaction of all concerned.

As far as the GHC was concerned, there were some disadvantages to
the procedures adopted. A house specially requested, if subsequently found unsatisfactory, could not be easily rejected. The
area was also being rapidly depopulated without there being any
changes in policy and although a vast improvement on previous
practice, allocations with some exceptions were still being made
fundamentally within the framework of the existing regulations.
Perhaps most crucially, Gairbraid was dependent on the goodwill
of Clive House, more particularly, on that of one individual.
The GHC attempted to formalize the procedure so that, through
practice, it would come to be regarded as permanent and appear to
be at least semi-official. For instance, lists of the people to
be seen were issued so that the official could save time by having
their files ready and this proposal was accepted as part of the
process. A rota of committee members was established to spread
commitment and to avoid the procedure becoming dependent on the
relationship between the Housing Department and one or two individuals on the GHC. Although not always possible, the committee
also attempted to limit the numbers on each visit so as to
decrease the pressure on the official concerned.

The system devised by the GHC ensured that proper regard was
had for the individual's special circumstances which, in spite of
what is assumed by the existing house letting procedures, change
and do not necessarily remain stable over the usually lengthy
period between when they are noted by the housing visitor and
when rehousing actually occurs. For instance in the interim,
people may revise their list of area preferences, jobs may be
changed, new housing schemes be completed, adolescent children
leave home and babies be born. The possibilities are endless
and almost anything may happen to a family while they wait to be
rehoused. People in Gairbraid found that the existing administrative machinery was inadequate to cope with any sudden changes
in circumstance. In contrast, the GHC created an avenue of
flexible communication with officialdom, allowing the individual
to be heard in the knowledge of the alternatives available and
provided the opportunity for him to question the decision made
about his future. In this way, it enabled large numbers of
people to be quickly and satisfactorily rehoused. The method
seemed to operate smoothly, certainly to the satisfaction of the
Gairbraid residents. The GHC's anxiety was that, at any given
moment, it might be stopped.

THE COMMITTEE AS SOCIAL WORKER

The entire range of housing problems were dealt with at Clive House,
from those who simply wanted to know when their next offer would be
forthcoming to others who were in urgent need of immediate rehousing. At first, residents wishing to be accompanied to Clive
House either approached the committee members in their homes or at
the weekly GHC meetings. However, it was soon recognized that
there were people in the area who, for one reason or another, were
unlikely to seek assistance and the GHC decided to initiate contact
with them. It was anticipated that many of those least able to
cope unless their cases received attention, were likely to be left
in the area until last. These included old people living alone,
families in rent arrears on previous Corporation tenancies,
squatters, and others suffering under particularly poor living
conditions.
    Contact was made with every old age pensioner in the area during
the 1972 miners' strike and emergency coal needed to be provided
for two of them, plus a young family with a six-week old baby. One
old man, Mr A., 86 years of age, had had two serious operations six
years previously and although still extremely active, felt that for
health reasons he should be rehoused as close as possible to his
daughter who lived almost opposite the Wyndford estate. On compassionate grounds alone, he seemed certain to be rehoused there.
Further, he could not have been faulted on the housing visitor's
report, as his home was always absolutely spotless and exceedingly
well kept. The Housing Department, however, decided that as he
had only lived in Gairbraid for five years, he had insufficient
tenancy to qualify for the Wyndford and since there was no other
suitable accommodation in the vicinity, that he would have to be
rehoused at some considerable distance from his daughter. Mr A.'s
problem was that he previously had a Corporation house which he
gave up after his children left home and his wife died. The
house letting regulations, it seems, allow for no exception. All
previous Corporation tenants are equally discriminated against
irrespective of either their reasons for leaving or their present
predicament. The Corporation admitted that they had no complaint
against Mr A. It was also acknowledged that his reasons for
giving up his tenancy were good and sufficient. Nevertheless, in
terms of the regulations, he could not be accommodated in the
Wyndford. His case was referred to the councillors who declined
to pursue the matter. The GHC alone fought his case, which was
raised at every opportunity, and after months of perseverance he
was finally rehoused in the Wyndford. It was a particularly
satisfying victory for the committee members.
    Clive House's rigidity is particularly regrettable as the case
quoted was by no means an isolated instance. The authorities
need to recognize that increasingly more people with previous
Corporation tenancies are bound in the future to be caught up in
their clearance programmes. It is thus crucial that the present
attitude, of regarding all in this category as rent defaulters, be
replaced by a flexible and equitable policy which will take into
account individual circumstances. The argument for urgent change
is strengthened by reference to another example from Gairbraid

where an old couple, Mr and Mrs B., were most unjustly penalized
for their previous Corporation tenancy. Given Glasgow's severe
housing shortage, they had felt morally obliged to vacate their
large Corporation house when their children left home so that a
young family could be given the opportunity of decent accommodation. For this act of generosity they were left until last in
their tenement and were for months terrified by vandals and
drunken youths who congregated outside their house. During this
time Mr B. slept with a hammer under his pillow in case they were
broken into at night. They were 'difficult' to rehouse because
they were neither on the waiting list nor long enough in Gairbraid
to qualify for decent accommodation. Having previously been in a
Corporation house, these were conditions that they could not
possibly fulfil. It was only after the GHC intervened that the
couple received an acceptable offer from Clive House and then
it was not without considerable difficulty. From their experience, it seems that people would be well advised to ignore their
consciences and instead, selfishly, to cling to their Corporation
houses.

The view officially taken is that where people find themselves
in under-occupied property, they should apply for a transfer to a
smaller Corporation house rather than seek privately rented
accommodation. One young woman in Gairbraid, Miss C., was, when
her grandmother died, left alone in a large ground-floor flat
beside playing fields. Feeling insecure, she applied for a transfer but after waiting for almost two years without being granted
one, she moved in sheer desperation to Gairbraid. The fact that
she had unsuccessfully applied for a transfer did not prevent her
being categorized as a short tenancy, and therefore low priority,
resident. In 1972, there were almost 42,000 transfer applicants
in Glasgow of whom only 2,365 were suited by Clive House. (2)
Given the magnitude of Glasgow's housing shortage, an incredible
16,237 of the transfer applicants were in under-occupied property.
Clearly, transferring from one Corporation house to another is not
the simplest or quickest way to change an address. In view of
the massive waiting list, it is grossly unfair of the authorities
to demand that people should rely entirely on transfers and, subsequently, to penalize them for not doing so. The people in
Gairbraid who suffered from their previous Corporation tenancies
were, without exception, extremely vulnerable and but for the
GHC's intervention most, if not all, would have been forced to
accept inferior accommodation.

In addition to advocating on behalf of residents for offers
of alternative accommodation, the GHC was approached for advice
on whether to accept or reject offers already received. While
doubt in these instances was sometimes caused by reservations held
about moving to particular areas, it was mostly a result of
Corporation houses being in various states of disrepair. Again,
the main sufferers were old people who were unable to do any of
the required work themselves. The GHC felt that the decision
about whether or not an offer was suitable could only be taken by
the individual concerned. However, it was made clear that if a
house was accepted, the committee would help fight to ensure that
repairs were completed within a reasonable period, or alternatively,

if rejected, that the individual could rely on the committee's continual support in their endeavour to achieve a more satisfactory offer.

The issue of repairs to Corporation property was brought to a head when a 79-year-old, Mr D., who lived with his middle-aged, mentally defective step-daughter, approached Annie Mallon for assistance. It transpired that they had accepted a house on the understanding that it would be repaired within a relatively short period. After waiting for two months, they felt obliged to move in although only very minor repair work had been done. He con-tacted the committee a month later when he received a notice of eviction from the Corporation for non-payment of the rent due for the time when the house was unoccupied. In order to avoid evict-ion, Mr D. had paid some of the 'arrears' by using the money that social security had given him for wall-paper. The house was not only in a disgraceful state of disrepair, it was gas supplied while Mr D.'s cooking appliances were electric. Thus, for a whole month, they were unable to prepare any hot meals and seemed to have survived almost entirely on fish and chips. A bedroom was damp and an open coal fire seemed to be the only source of heat in the whole place. Once aware of the situation, the GHC immediately contacted the Housing and Social Work Departments. The first withdrew their threat of eviction and forwarded Mr D.'s date of entry so that he was entitled to a refund of the money already paid for the period when the house was unoccupied. A senior official also undertook personally to supervise the repair work. The Social Work Department, the next day, supplied a gas cooker and a mattress. Gairbraid residents, including some youngsters, volunteered to help decorate the house and in no time the walls were papered and linoleum laid. The problem was partly caused by misunderstanding between Mr D. and the Housing Depart-ment but clearly, whatever the reasons, a man of 79 should not have been so neglected.

As more and more residents were rehoused so did the GHC in-creasingly come to deal with the Corporation's failure to do satisfactory repairs. The committee was repeatedly having to re-arrange entry dates because the authorities had failed to complete or, as in many cases, even start the necessary repair work by the time the property was supposed to be occupied. The problem is partly caused by a failure of communication within the Housing Department. Houses are allocated from Clive House, after which responsibility passes to a district office from whence in-structions for repairs are given to a works section. Somewhere along this line, communications obviously break down. The GHC intensified its campaign to ensure that residents had the right to insist upon a written statement of the repairs which the authorities were willing to undertake, together with a completion date, before rather than after they signed accepting a relet house. After all, the Missive of Let that the tenant signs states: (3) 'I accept the house as being in good tenantable condition....' The GHC pressed for a repairs sheet to be especially printed for distribution to each prospective tenant on receipt of an offer of alternative accommodation. The GHC further suggested that a notice, giving full details of the reform, be prominently displayed in each

district office as rights are meaningless unless people are aware
of their existence.

The Maryhill councillors agreed to pursue the matter and, after
some delay, the authorities finally reached a decision. The GHC
was informed that their proposals were irrelevant as houses were
no longer to be offered in poor condition. All of Glasgow rather
than just Gairbraid stood to benefit. Nevertheless, the committee
members were sceptical and not completely satisfied, for the
Housing Department, by rejecting Gairbraid's proposals, had once
again avoided according rights to their prospective tenants. There
was no guarantee that, at some stage in the future, the authorities
would not revert to their former practices. Subsequently, the
houses offered to Gairbraid residents were, on the whole, in good
repair. There were, however, some lapses. For instance, Ella
Donnelly was offered a house which was completely flooded and,
although reported, had according to the neighbours been so for
about a week. Jackie and Jessie Moir, viewing a house by candle-
light, almost stood on a huge and only partly dead rat. The
Corporation had obviously put rat poison in the property but had
not bothered to find out whether it had been effective before
placing the house on offer. Nevertheless, as a result of the
campaign, the condition of houses offered to Gairbraid vastly
improved, especially when compared to what had been received at
the start of the rehousing process.

In November 1971, of the 240 families left in Gairbraid, 24
were in rent arrears on previous Corporation houses. These could
be roughly classified into two categories: those who owed relatively little and/or were themselves able to raise at least a substantial amount of the outstanding debt; and, those who were,
without outside help, unlikely to find the necessary money. The
first group had basically only a housing problem and the GHC
attempted to negotiate with the authorities to ensure that they
were quickly offered alternative accommodation. For the second
group, money from outside sources needed to be raised and for this
purpose, contact was made with the Social Work Department, many,
although not all, in this category having multiple problems.

It is Corporation policy not to rehouse a family until their
previous debt is almost completely repaid. The GHC, by pleading
special hardship, was, in a number of rent arrear cases, able to
negotiate rehousing without debts having to be completely cleared.
An example is Mrs E. who owed £79 to the Corporation. At an early
stage she wrote to Clive House enquiring both whether the arrears
could be paid off in instalments and what minimum weekly rate
was acceptable. In reply to her letter she received only an
acknowledgement and she assumed that she had no chance of rehousing
by the Corporation. However, months later, by which time living
conditions had become critical for the family, Mrs E. appealed
to the GHC for assistance. Her husband was unemployed because of
a kidney complaint and her 9 year-old son was ill with bronchitis.
A total of eight people lived in their tiny room-and-kitchen which
had in recent months become extremely damp. Their water-pipes had
rotted and thus they were continually being flooded, which was
particularly dangerous because of exposed electric wires in the
house. Mrs E. had managed to raise £42 as a first instalment

towards paying off the full £79 owed. Waiting to be interviewed
at Clive House, Mrs E. confided in the committee member present
that she was 'shaking in her shoes'. All depended on the flexibility of the regulations and the discretionary powers of a few
of the senior staff. At first the official insisted that an offer
could only be made after between £65 and £70 had been repaid. In
view of the E.s' dangerous living conditions and after being
assured of their ability to ultimately repay the full amount, he
was persuaded to confer with his more senior colleagues. He
finally returned with an offer in Easterhouse and, although Mrs E.,
for family reasons, had requested Drumchapel, on the other side of
the city, she decided to accept the offer if it turned out to be
even half-reasonable. Hours later, having reached the house, it
was found to be inaccessible as the lock was damaged. The keys
were exchanged for those of another in the same street which was
in a state of total disrepair and was thus rejected. A week later,
the E.s received an offer of a house, in good order, in Drumchapel
and within days, the family moved into it.

Five of the families in the area who were considered to have
the most intractable rent arrear problems were, with their permission, referred to the Social Work Department. Between them, the
families had living at home twenty-one children of whom fifteen
were under 16 years of age. A total of £237 was owed. In four
of the families the man of the house was unemployed, while in the
fifth the husband had deserted. The application to the Social
Work Department was made on 11 February 1972 and their decision,
offering help to only one of the five families, was confirmed on
7 April. The Social Work Department is grossly understaffed and
commands totally inadequate resources in relation to the massive
problems it attempts to tackle. The Department must carefully
weigh its priorities and thus it is difficult to be critical of
their performance in Gairbraid. The GHC, while appreciating that
a scarcity of staff and resources meant that the Department could
not assist all five families, nevertheless felt that decisions
were to an extent influenced by a bias very akin to a 'deserving
poor' attitude. Unlike the unsupported mother, Mrs F., who was
given a grant, all the other families indicated a preference for
the particular areas in which they wished to be rehoused. Though
down, the families were not yet beaten and the GHC, supporting
their claim, felt that even if in receipt of charity, people
should not be dumped anywhere. The Social Work Department gave
the impression, perhaps wrongly interpreted, that people dependent
on outside financial help ought to have been less fussy.

Mrs F., with six children of whom the eldest was then 10 and
the youngest, suffering from spina bifida, 3, was very demoralized
which, under the circumstances, was hardly surprising. It is
difficult to imagine anyone else in the same position coping more
adequately. In spite of all, and her neighbours attest to the
fact, Mrs F. remained throughout an extremely devoted and caring
mother. As she had inherited her Corporation debt of £58 from her
husband, the GHC was able to convince Clive House to rehouse the
family on receipt of only half that amount with the rest to be
paid in instalments. The Social Work Department expressed some
doubt about helping her, when it emerged that Mrs F. was still

seeing her husband, who sometimes stayed for the week-end. Mrs F. was advised by the community worker that while her relationship with her husband was no concern whatsoever of the Social Work Department and that the decision whether or not to continue seeing him was entirely hers, in order to obtain the grant it would be sensible to inform them that she was no longer in contact with her husband. Two sums were finally granted to Mrs F., one of £29 towards her Corporation debt and another of £12 towards a £27 electricity bill. An unofficial condition was, however, added: that once Mrs F. was rehoused the community worker should maintain a case-work type relationship with her, for which he had neither the expertise nor the time. Reluctantly, he agreed that if at all possible this would be adhered to which, regrettably, was not the case. Later, unconfirmed reports suggested that Mrs F. had been evicted from her Corporation house. If so, it is probable that her children would have been taken into care. Money from a variety of sources was subsequently found for the families not helped by the Social Work Department and no further cases of rent arrears were referred to them.

The GHC also helped rehouse many short tenancy families from Gairbraid. Anyone unfortunate or unprophetic enough to move into a house a year before it is declared part of a treatment area, is, according to the regulations, ineligible for rehousing. In general, however, people in this category were able to obtain alternative accommodation from the Corporation. On the other hand, a jaundiced view was taken, by Corporation and residents alike, of people who moved in to Gairbraid after it had been declared a housing treatment area. Most in Gairbraid were extremely antagonistic towards squatters, often with good reason. It was thought that the presence of squatters greatly contributed to the deterioration of the property, making life difficult for everyone else still living there. Squatters were frequently accused of causing disturbances, through drunkenness, all-night parties and brawling and of abusing the communal toilet facilities. The GHC felt that helping these people was beyond its capabilities and an attempt to do so would only succeed in alienating the established community. Yet one of the saddest sights seen in Gairbraid was a bundle of rags, a torn, threadbare blanket and a home-made dart board, left behind in a derelict house by a squatter family after a resident had summoned the police to evict them.

The residents in Gairbraid distinguished one category of squatters from the rest; those who otherwise led normal, respectable lives. These people were not transitory, they moved in with furniture and helped maintain the property. Within relatively short periods such people came to be accepted as part of the community and it was considered proper that the GHC should advocate on their behalf. An example is Mr G. who, having separated from his wife, required hospital treatment for depression and when discharged was homeless. He moved into Gairbraid to live with his sister in October 1971 and remained there when she was rehoused shortly afterwards. He lived with his 11-year-old daughter who chose to be with him rather than with her mother. They managed for several months with neither gas nor electricity and only an open coal fire for cooking and warmth. During this time he

obtained promises of help from both one of the local councillors
and the Social Work Department and had on several occasions been
to Clive House on his own. Mr G. was reluctant to contact the GHC,
feeling that he was not a bona fide resident. However, when his
own initiatives proved unsuccessful, his increasingly intolerable
living conditions prompted him to contact Ella Donnelly and the
GHC immediately took up his case.

Although a squatter, in Mr G.'s favour was the fact that he
had been registered on the house waiting list since 1962. Mr G.
located several empty houses in Maryhill and, accompanied by a
committee member, a list of these was presented to the official
at Clive House. After considerable discussion and argument, the
authorities finally agreed to offer one of the Maryhill houses.
Mr G.'s housing problems were resolved in an afternoon and he and
his daughter moved in the next day. Mr G. remained a keen
supporter of the GHC and helped whenever required.

In addition to advocating on behalf of Gairbraid residents, the
GHC was frequently approached by people from all over Glasgow. It
is estimated that about forty-five people from elsewhere in the
city attended the GHC's weekly meetings to seek advice and assistance. Where these were resident in Maryhill, the local councillors were involved and usually their housing difficulties were
quickly resolved. As news of the GHC spread in the neighbourhood,
so more people began to approach the committee, particularly those
living in and around the Oran Street area. It was there that the
GHC was later to help the local people organize. The GHC's original purpose was to encourage the growth of local organizations
but most of the enquiries were from isolated individuals not in a
position to become involved. Other than advise and inform them
of their rights, the GHC could do little for people from outside
Maryhill. Relying on its reputation, the GHC, however, did write,
on their behalf, to their councillors and this frequently resulted
in rehousing. A councillor forwarded one such letter to the
Housing Manager who abruptly informed the GHC that the affair was
of no concern to Gairbraid. It was the first and only occasion on
which the Housing Department was to initiate a communication with
the GHC.

The GHC thus provided an advocatory and advisory service for
the community. Many people availed themselves of the opportunity
to attend the weekly committee meetings, some simply to be re-
assured and conforted. Where the system created feelings of
isolation and competitiveness, the GHC strengthened solidarity
and unity. For the most vulnerable sections of the population,
committee members assumed roles normally associated with professional community workers. The members found this aspect of their
campaign particularly rewarding. The GHC demonstrated that,
given the resources, working-class communities are perfectly
capable of self-help and of protecting those among them least able
to cope. It is absolutely certain that in every clearance area
there will be a minority of people who, for one reason or another,
cannot manage on their own. It is vital that assistance is
provided before conditions begin to deteriorate rather than afterwards. If families are left in a clearance area until last
because of their inability in the first place to cope, surviving

for months if not years in derelict and nearly deserted property
will surely only serve to exacerbate their original problems.
Local authorities, however, seem unable, if not unwilling, to take
preventive measures, although helping people later rather than
sooner, after their problems are made worse, is ultimately bound
to place even greater demands on already over-stretched budgets.
Logically, once an area is designated for clearance, councillors
together with the Housing, Health and Social Work Departments,
should locate everyone within that area who requires assistance.
In the time usually available, most problems could be dealt with
before the rehousing process actually begins. Without any great
productive loss, Glasgow's housing visitors could, for instance,
be diverted for this purpose from their present endeavours to
grade people.

It is suggested that where already over-burdened Corporation
departments, particularly Social Work, cannot provide such preventive services, local people can and ought to be recruited and
trained specially for this purpose. There will always be people
in clearance areas who need help; the GHC demonstrated that a
community will also possess a wealth of talent and in any area
there are bound to be far more people able and willing to offer
help than those who need it. Particularly where old people are
concerned, local volunteers could provide invaluable assistance.
Old people are often unable to cope physically with the sheer
mechanics of moving: obtaining keys to view a house, handing them
in, signing missives, and arranging for repairs which often require several journeys to various offices located miles apart.
In addition, the old person needs to cope with such details as
contacting gas and electricity boards, furniture removal firms
and with obtaining social security benefits. The committee
members spent much of their time helping people in these ways
and local volunteers could be usefully employed in other areas
to provide similar assistance to their communities. Volunteers,
however, do not provide a solution to the problems inherent in
the rehousing process but could act to ameliorate some of the
worst effects. Ideally, community action resources need to be
provided for each clearance area but failing that, the training
of local volunteers is at leat a step in the right direction.
Gairbraid was able to care for its own community precisely because
it achieved the power to act and thus the GHC believe that a
system of volunteers is no substitute for local organization.
When the GHC was able successfully to negotiate on behalf of
individuals, it was not so much appeals to conscience or persuasive debate which achieved results but rather, demands were met
because of the organizational power wielded by the community.

FINDING THEIR OWN ACCOMMODATION

On figures provided by Glasgow's Housing Management Department,
from the 399 dwellings in Gairbraid, 319 (80 per cent) families
were rehoused by the Corporation, 33 (8 per cent) found their own
accommodation and 47 (12 per cent) dwellings were vacant when rehousing commenced. If only the 352 occupied dwellings are

considered, Glasgow Corporation rehoused almost 91 per cent of the
families living in the area. It is now no longer possible to
know how many of the 33 families who found their own accommodation
did so out of free choice. One family, for instance, emigrated to
Canada, and a wife whose husband died moved in with her parents,
while several others preferred to buy their own houses rather than
rent from the Corporation. On the other hand, an unknown number
found their own accommodation because they were given no reasonable alternative by the Housing Department. One family, because
of intolerable living conditions, abandoned Gairbraid and moved
into their parents' already over-crowded Corporation flat. They
thus forfeited their priority status for being rehoused from a
clearance area and instead joined the 'less urgent' homeless
queue. In another instance, an old age pensioner when offered
a house was refused permission to bring her dog and rather than
leave her pet behind decided to move to another privately rented
room-and-kitchen. Other families who owed money on previous
Corporation tenancies entered the private market because either
they could not afford to repay the debt or, even if paid, felt
that their previous record would ensure that they received only
offers of poor quality housing. However, for each example of a
family in Gairbraid forced to find their own accommodation, there
were several in similar circumstances who, because of the GHC's
support, were rehoused by the local authority. Most of the
families who were forced to leave Gairbraid because of intolerable
living conditions maintained contact with the GHC and the Corporation was persuaded, although not without difficulty, to accept
responsibility for their rehousing. Moreover, the committee's
campaign to have both empty property sealed and the essential
services maintained, ensured that the area did not deteriorate
as rapidly as it might otherwise have done. In another instance,
an old lady who had lived all her life in Gairbraid refused to
accept the fact that she would have to move. She ignored all
communications from the Corporation, who apparently washed their
hands of her until relatively late in the day when the GHC was
able to gain her confidence and ensure that she was properly rehoused. Unlike other clearance areas in Glasgow, very few old
people were among the last to be rehoused from Gairbraid.

   In many cases, the GHC needed to exert considerable pressure
before the Corporation reluctantly agreed to rehouse. The
Gairbraid experience strongly suggests that but for local organization in the area, a great many more than thirty-three families
would have had to find their own accommodation. Information of
the rehousing rate for the whole city is only available up to
1970 where, (4) 'in slum clearance operations in Glasgow the
number of families to be rehoused has been only a little over 60
per cent of the number of houses closed or demolished.' This
figure contrasts dramatically with the 80 to 91 per cent who were
rehoused from Gairbraid. In numbers, a 60 per cent rehousing rate
from Gairbraid, calculated on the basis of the 399 houses demolished, would have meant that the Corporation assumed responsibility for only 239 families, that is, 80 less than were actually
rehoused. If calculated on the basis of the 352 occupied houses,
211 families would have been rehoused, a difference of 108,

compared to the 319 who were rehoused by the Corporation.

Asked to comment on the discrepancy between Gairbraid and previous rehousing rates, Glasgow's Housing Manager dismissed the
60 per cent figure as being based on (5) 'past experience', since
when, under the 1969 housing legislation, the Corporation has been
'dealing with property with a higher rate of occupancy'. He goes
on to suggest that this is only to be expected as in treatment
areas some houses may be above the statutory defined tolerable
standard, but he fails to mention that this explanation cannot
account for the high proportion rehoused from Gairbraid as none
of the houses there were above this standard. It is, however,
feasible to suggest that as the supply of cheap, private accommodation in the city diminishes through clearances, redevelopment
and increased rents, fewer people may, through choice or otherwise,
be able to opt out of the Corporation's rehousing programme. The
Housing Manager refused to provide information on the numbers
rehoused from treatment areas, cleared either concurrently with
or after Gairbraid, on the grounds that it was 'too early for
reaching firm conclusions'. Without this information, which if
available for Gairbraid was surely available for elsewhere, conclusions can only be drawn in comparison with the 1970 data,
unless that is, it is assumed that the information was withheld
because it strengthened the GHC's position.

Given an option, there will always be people who prefer not
to subject themselves to rehousing by Glasgow Corporation but
these, it is suggested, constitute a minority of the '40 per cent'
who in the past found their own accommodation. Do they all
emigrate? It is likely that most of them are unwillingly forced
out of the public housing sector through lack of information, fear,
bureaucratic neglect and/or rigid application of the housing
regulations. From the Gairbraid experience, it seems reasonable
to assume that many in this category are either old age pensioners,
families in rent arrears, unemployed, physically or mentally
handicapped, or unsupported mothers. A large number of dependent
children are also likely to be involved. On these assumptions,
which must seem tenable, an explanation for the relatively large
number of families rehoused from Gairbraid compared to what occurred
previously is that Gairbraid, unlike these other areas, was
organized. The GHC provided the necessary support and wielded
sufficient power to ensure that the Corporation fulfilled its
obligations to those least able to protect their own interests.
It seems a persuasive argument for community action in all of
Glasgow's treatment areas. The alternative could mean large
numbers, in dire need of accommodation, being discarded by the
system.

In 1970 Glasgow Corporation and the Scottish Development
Department jointly published a report which: (6) 'sought to deal
with the programme of housing to meet the needs of the generated
population of Glasgow up to 1981.' The report concludes that,
although there are an estimated 75,000 houses below the tolerable
standard, only 35,000 new or improved houses need to be provided
within the city for those displaced. Thus, Glasgow plans to replace less than 50 per cent of the property below standard which,
as the report notes, may seem inadequate. The arithmetic is,

however, justified by reference to the expected 60 per cent
rehousing rate. As Glasgow's Housing Manager was a party to this
report, which relied heavily on the 60 per cent figure to plan
the city's future housing requirements, his dismissal of it three
years later as merely 'past experience' is, to say the least,
astonishing. Thus, if increased occupancy rather than the GHC
was responsible for the 80 to 91 per cent rehousing rate for
Gairbraid, the Corporation may reasonably expect to rehouse
similar numbers from future treatment areas. In other words, in
their provision of houses for those displaced from clearance areas,
the authorities will need to budget for an expected increase of
between 20 and 31 per cent. In these terms, the 1970 prediction
of a decent house for everyone in the city by 1981 is, at the
planned rate of provision, wildly optimistic. It would seem that
the authorities have a clear duty publicly to disclaim the 1970
report and to announce a revised estimate of the number of houses
required in the city which the Housing Manager has up till now not
done. The alternative, to regard Gairbraid as atypical, would
be to admit the importance of the GHC: Gairbraid clearly differed
from other areas only in that it was organized. It leads to the
extremely unpalatable conclusion that the 60 per cent rehousing
rate was perhaps achieved because a large number of people were
deliberately and even callously forced out of the public housing
sector. The experience of rehousing in Gairbraid strongly
suggests that a fair proportion of the 40 per cent who, at any
rate up to 1970, found their own accommodation, were in urgent need
of decent housing but were too helpless to demand their rights.
The accumulative evidence from Gairbraid and elsewhere in the
city further suggests that in treatment areas, where there is no
local organization, this trend most probably still persists.

Although it may be pleasant if not politically advantageous to
project the imminent solution of Glasgow's housing problems, by
only rehousing 60 per cent of those in clearance areas, the
authorities are, besides causing untold suffering, simply indulg-
ing in statistical fantasies. Uprooting communities and then
forcing the weakest among them to fend for themselves is a means
of not only avoiding the real problems facing the city, it also
greatly exacerbates them. Even in mere financial terms, it is
obviously a short-sighted and ultimately counter-productive
policy. Eventually Glasgow will have to cope with a residue of
families comprised mainly of old people, those in rent arrears
and others who have fled from one treatment area to another.
Admittedly, some of the old people will have died on the way and
some of the children will have been taken into care, but even in
Glasgow there must come a time when there are no more room-and-
kitchens available for refugees from the Corporation's rehousing
programmes. The Housing Department will then have to assume full
responsibility for all the people it has displaced.

THE DILEMMA OF SUCCESS

The committee had no accurate means of ascertaining the current
intentions of the Housing Department. To some extent, this was a

role that the local councillors might have performed but did not,
although their inside knowledge was probably too minimal anyway
to have been of much use. Thus, it was always difficult to decide
if Clive House's current behaviour was due to the GHC's efforts or
not, as it was hardly something that they were likely to publicly
admit. Continual rehousing in the area meant that the committee's
constituency and thus its potential support and power were always
diminishing. In any sphere other than rehousing, a successful
campaign could be expected to correlate highly with a growth in
membership but for the GHC, the greater the success, the fewer the
people left to continue the struggle. In a situation of satisfactory offers, the danger of inactivity is that the Corporation will
assume that further local action is no longer possible. It was,
therefore, crucial that the GHC achieve concessions, particularly
for those most vulnerable in the community, while it still had
the strength to do so. In retrospect, many of the local activists
feel that consistent pressure ought to have been applied. Be this
as it may, it is true to say that in general when there was a
satisfactory flow of decent offers, the GHC did not engage in
militant protest but was most active when these were not forthcoming. From the situation described, it is worth noting that the
GHC's tactics were essentially defensive, being mainly responses
to official policy and practice, rather than the other way round.
The choice was between defending or neglecting what they considered their legitimate rights and, in spite of demonstrations
at Clive House, it was the local community and not the Housing
Department that was under siege.

Throughout the campaign, there was always the threat that the
main activists would be rehoused and although all were committed
to continuing with their membership, once out of the area it is
almost impossible to function in the same way as before. The
crunch for the GHC, when it came, was devastating. Isa Hanlon
moved from Gairbraid in early February and was followed a fortnight later by Annie Mallon. In quick succession thereafter,
John Moir, Tommy Dickson, Eileen Kelly and Ella Donnelly were all
rehoused. At a public meeting held on 1 March, of the ten
committee members present only Jimmy Gallagher, Jackie Moir and
John Smith still lived in Gairbraid. The Thompsons, of course,
had long been rehoused. While most of those who had been rehoused
continued to attend meetings, only Isa Hanlon and Tommy Dickson
lived near enough to continue their former full involvement in
the community. During a period of rapid depopulation it was only
to be expected that at least some of the committee would be
rehoused, but so many in so short a time was considered more than
a mere coincidence. The feeling was that the authorities had
rehoused the leadership to remove them from the area in order to
destroy the organization. John Moir, from his experience at Clive
House, believes this to have been the case as no sooner had he
signed accepting his new house than a senior official appeared,
and knowing all about the Moirs' offer, proceeded to ask 'what
sort of committee have you got - everyone's deserting?' John's
retort was that the authorities had made a mistake and had rehoused the moderate members leaving the militants behind. The
GHC, however, faced a serious crisis of leadership and for a while

it seemed as if Clive House might have succeeded in delivering a
death blow to the organization. At the March public meeting three
new members were recruited but within a week two had been rehoused.
The third, Margaret Hobson, had previously been involved in the
playgroup and she proved an invaluable addition to the GHC, as was
her husband Adam who joined shortly afterwards. The organization
was further strengthened when Davey Bouse, one of the GHC's foun-
ders, renewed his membership, and together with his wife Jeanette
played a prominent part in the coming campaign. Other efforts to
recruit new members, however, were continually foiled by rehousing,
although two other residents did attend committee meetings for
six and eight weeks respectively. Although never key figures,
their presence helped the committee over a difficult period.
With the addition of the Hobsons and Bouses, the committee still
had a core of activists in the area and with the support of the
rehoused members its strength had been maintained.

About fifty residents were present at the March public meeting,
the third chaired by Jimmy Gallagher. In addition to launching
a recruitment drive, its purpose was to place pressure on the
Corporation, to remind them both of the GHC's existence and of
their promised reforms. The meeting was considered a first step
towards re-organization, to prepare for the approaching final
struggle to have the area completely cleared. The GHC viewed the
future with some apprehension as the decline in Gairbraid's
population was fast reaching the point where resistance to the
Corporation would no longer be possible. With between eighty
and ninety families still in the area, the local view was that
the situation had not yet become critical. The authorities,
however, calculated differently and clearly considered that the
GHC was a force already spent. The committee had hardly time to
re-group, let alone revise its strategy, when the status quo was
rudely shattered. Clive House suddenly decided to end their
arrangement with the GHC and in mid-March the interviews with
their officials were discontinued. While an interview was in
progress the official involved was ordered by his senior to stop
seeing Gairbraid residents who, it was said, would have to deal
only with the counter clerks. During the outburst, Jackie Moir,
the committee member present, was offered no explanation and was,
when he tried to intervene, completely ignored. The authorities
made no attempt at prior consultation with the GHC, who were
given neither warning nor reason for the action taken. The GHC
were granted none of the basic courtesies and were clearly not
accorded recognition as an organization representative of their
community. The Corporation's attitude clearly ruled out any
possibility of consensus. It was, in fact, a definite declaration
of war on the community. The organized visits to Clive House had
been stopped in the most abrupt and bureaucratic manner possible,
perhaps on the assumption that since so many had been recently
rehoused, including six committee members, the GHC was no longer
a force to be reckoned with.

Claims later made, that Clive House was unaware of what had
been going on, are not credible. Even in the chaos of Glasgow's
Housing Department the official could not interview groups of
people week after week, during which time significant numbers were

rehoused, without anyone of seniority knowing about it. He must
have had at least the tacit approval of his colleagues. Indeed,
he consulted with them on numerous occasions during interview
sessions. One reason later given for ending the interviews was
that rehousing is purely a private matter between the Department
and the individual concerned which ignores the fact that the
committee's presence was almost always requested by the residents
themselves.

Immediately the interviews were halted a meeting with the
Corporation's Housing Committee and the Housing Manager was requested and after an exchange of eleven letters, not to mention
telephone calls, it was finally convened some eighty-three days
later. The GHC also sent each Glasgow councillor copies of
proposals for reform in housing policy which explained the
procedure that had been followed and suggested that, rather than
discontinue it in Gairbraid, it should be extended to apply to
the entire city with an official assigned to deal with and be
accessible to each treatment area. No reply was received from
any other than the local councillors. Had the authorities agreed
to the proposed meeting within a reasonable length of time and
the position been negotiated, then conflict could have been
avoided. The GHC distributed a newsletter in the community, informing the residents of the changed circumstances and listing
the various alternative courses of action that might be taken.
The letters to the senior councillors and officials were sent
by recorded delivery and after a week without any reply, the
GHC began organizing for direct action.

Chapter 10

PROTEST AT CLIVE HOUSE

Clive House had obviously no intention of resuming the interviews and, given Gairbraid's falling population, there was little chance of the community forcing them to do so. It would have been foolish for the GHC to struggle for what was clearly beyond its capabilities to achieve. Thus, the first task for the GHC was to redefine the issues. Clive House had estimated accurately that in a power struggle the odds were overwhelmingly weighted against the community, but had neglected to consider that a head-on collision was not the only alternative open to the GHC. The interviews were, after all, only a means towards quick and decent rehousing and satisfaction for the residents was not necessarily dependent on the former procedures being reinstated. It was made perfectly clear that the objective, as it had always been, was simply to ensure that the residents were decently rehoused within the shortest possible time. The GHC thus attempted to avoid the situation whereby either the Corporation backed down or the community lost, and thus rehousing rather than the interviews was made the issue.

The ham-fisted behaviour of the senior official involved provided the GHC with an ideal opportunity to attack Clive House for the arbitrary and bureaucratic manner in which the established routine had been discontinued. The Corporation justified their action on the grounds that Gairbraid had previously been given an unfair advantage over residents in other areas. On the other hand, the system had been conclusively demonstrated to operate to the enormous advantage of tenants and officials alike and therefore, the GHC argued, rather than scrap it altogether, the same access to authority enjoyed by Gairbraid should be allowed for all the Corporation's prospective tenants. The GHC campaigned not for preferential treatment but for a major reform applicable to the whole city. In seeking to meet the authorities, rather than simply criticize the Housing Department, the GHC offered positive suggestions for change.

News of the events at Clive House spread gloom through Gairbraid. Rumour was rife and people expressed doubts about the GHC's ability to oppose the Corporation. The GHC had to provide a lead, for failure to act would have created despondency and it was apparent

that the committee would not survive inactivity. To counter
demoralization, the sooner the campaign was mounted the better.
There were already too few people left in the area for the GHC
to organize an impressive demonstration and besides, the urgency
of the crisis demanded more than a mere repeat of the previous
leafletting at Clive House. It was tactically necessary, in a
short, sharp move, to extend the campaign beyond symbolic protest.
The plan devised was simple to execute without being too dependent
on numbers. Gairbraid had been told to see the clerks like everyone else and this is what the GHC proposed to do, not individually
but in mass. The idea was to use the system so as to expose it:
and the intention was to disrupt normal working at Clive House.
To maximize attendance a bus was to be hired to transport residents
to the Housing Department. Once there, a few would remain outside
with banners to distribute leaflets while the majority filed upstairs. Each resident was, as normal procedure required, to queue
so as to hand in their names, requesting an interview with a clerk.
They were then to proceed to the waiting room until called for
interview, at which they were to be accompanied by a committee
member who would insist that in each instance, full case histories
were recorded. Mothers were encouraged to bring young children
to overcome baby-sitting problems and, of course, to add to the
chaos.
    As many of those still left in the area had so far had only
minimal contact with the GHC, any planned action needed to take
account of the possibility that their support might be less
reliable than that previously expressed by those who, precisely
because of their involvement, had since been mostly rehoused. It
was thus considered prudent for the GHC, before it committed
itself to the venture, to ascertain local opinion by individually
visiting each household in the area. The vast majority were
enthusiastically in favour of the demonstration and although some,
because of work reasons, could not lend their support, most
promised to attend. While delaying the protest by about a week,
the door-to-door canvass fully involved the community and as the
day approached there was an air of excitement and expectation in
Gairbraid.

ORAN STREET

It was decided to involve residents from the nearby Oran Street
clearance area. The GHC was already in contact with people from
there who on several previous occasions had approached the committee for assistance. In addition to supplementing numbers, the
inclusion of an Oran Street contingent promised to be of benefit
to both areas. For the GHC, it realized its threat of organizing
beyond Gairbraid and besides was an opportunity to help people in
extreme need of rehousing. The whole area was completely derelict
and those still forced to live there were the last remnants of a
once thriving and proud community. The Corporation had, over
years, neglected and seemingly forgotten about those remaining
who thus had nothing to lose and everything to gain by joining
Gairbraid's demonstration at Clive House. It provided them with

the opportunity, for the first time, to raise their voice in
protest.

Without fear of contradiction, it could be said that the Oran
Street area was the equal of any slum to be found anywhere in
Europe. As the GHC soon discovered, in spite of stereotypes to
the contrary, the majority of residents were perfectly ordinary
and respectable people who were forced, through no fault of their
own, to suffer such intolerable conditions simply because of
Clive House's inability to provide them with decent alternative
accommodation. Details of the residents' plight, compiled by the
GHC, (1) present a horrific picture of endurance and, in the
Britain of the 1970s, of completely unnecessary misery. For
example, Mr and Mrs Z. and their family of two boys and two girls,
aged between 12 and 16 all slept in one room because the other was
rat-infested. They could not use the WC as that too was over-run
with rats. The Z.s had last received an offer of alternative
accommodation from Clive House eleven months previously. Mrs Y.,
the only occupant of her tenement, had been without water for five
months; none of the toilets functioned and there were no lights
on the stair. When their ceiling collapsed on top of them another
Oran Street family, Mrs X. and her six children, moved next-door
to an empty, derelict house where they remained, awaiting an offer,
for six months. Mr and Mrs W. had lived in a top floor room-and-
kitchen in Rolland Street for six years. They had six children,
the eldest being 7. The Corporation failed to seal any of the
empty houses and as a result these were totally vandalized, as
were all the communal toilets, which were rendered unusable. When
it rained water poured in through a gaping hole in the ceiling and
until it dried out all electricity in the house, including the
cooking appliances, were inoperative. Mrs W. had TB and had then
recently undergone a hysterectomy. Their doctor unsuccessfully
tried to have them rehoused. At that stage, the W.s had not
received a single offer from Clive House but later, after the
GHC's intervention, were rehoused.

Oran Street stood as a reminder and warning to Gairbraid of what
might have occurred but for the existence of their own local
organization. Under no conceivable circumstance could Glasgow be
proud of, or begin to justify, the mess that had been created in
Oran Street. By confronting Clive House with conditions there
and exposing them to the glare of press publicity the GHC added
bite to its demonstration. The GHC was largely occupied in
organizing its own community and other than distribute a newsletter
inviting Oran Street to join the protest, little was done to
canvass support there.

THE BUS TO CLIVE HOUSE

The GHC sent press releases to all the local newspapers, and two
days before the demonstration the 'Glasgow Herald' featured the
story. It quoted the Housing Convenor, who had not replied to the
GHC's request for a meeting, as saying: (2) 'I would be willing to
meet these people to discuss their grievances. I have asked for
an enquiry into the situation.' Thus where appeals had failed the

threat of a demonstration achieved agreement for the desired meeting. Also quoted was the Housing Manager who claimed that Clive
House could not deal with 'one intermediary representing a whole
lot of cases'. In a letter later published in the newspaper, (3)
John Moir, on behalf of the GHC, pointed out that this was nonsense
as committee members only ever intervened when requested to do so
by residents who conducted their own interviews. 'Indeed, with the
exception that tenants did not have to face officialdom alone',
John Moir concluded, 'the Gairbraid committee conformed to what the
Housing Manager says is the practice of the department.' Although
losing the element of surprise, the GHC was delighted with its pre-
demonstration publicity. Having been thus warned, Clive House did
not seem in any way prepared for the demonstration and clearly had
great difficulty in coping with it.

A packed bus left Gairbraid, the demonstrators ranging in age
from babies in arms to old age pensioners. It stopped at Oran
Street and where only a handful were expected a further fifteen
waited to squeeze onto the bus. Stragglers from both areas were
brought to Clive House in three car-loads. The brief journey to
the Housing Department helped foster feelings of solidarity and
the committee members used the time to explain and clarify last-
minute details. The demonstrators arrived at Clive House, cheerful
and confident, to be greeted by waiting press reporters. Four
banners were unfolded: 'Organize to Fight for Decent Houses for
All Glasgow', 'Oran Street is a Housing Scandal', 'Gairbraid will
Organize' and finally, Eileen Thompson produced a placard pledging
support for Gairbraid from the Milton Tenants' Association.
Having posed for photographs, the demonstration moved en masse to
the house letting section, leaving a few behind to hold the
banners and distribute leaflets.

Everything functioned according to plan. The queue at the
enquiry desk stretched through the corridor and down the stairs.
The waiting room was suffocatingly full and with babies crying,
children playing, press cameras flashing and everyone reading
the GHC's leaflet the place was in complete turmoil. The clerks
attempted to rush through the interviews, but committee members
insisted that these be properly conducted, with full details being
noted for each case. No resident complained about the clerks who
were neither rude nor abusive. John Moir and Jimmy Gallagher were
frequently called away to deal with newspaper reporters. The
police were summoned but, as on the previous occasion, their
sympathies were clearly with the demonstrators. The house letting
section of Clive House was brought to a standstill for a whole
morning. A bus-load of happy residents departed with the threat
that the demonstration would be repeated if and whenever necessary.
Clive House had been given warning not to underestimate the GHC in
future.

The bus had barely arrived back in Maryhill when an early edition
of the 'Evening Times' (4) appeared, fully reporting the demonstration. The later editions carried a photograph with the caption
'India St Mutiny' (Clive House is situated in India Street). The
headlines, in bold print, were: 'Angry Tenants Besiege City Housing
Officials'. '70 tenants in housing office "siege"' was spread
across a page of the 'Evening Citizen' (5) and included a photograph

of tenants waiting in the house letting section of Clive House.
The demonstration was also prominently featured with photographs
in Glasgow's morning papers. The 'Glasgow Herald' (6) headed
their story 'Tenants Besiege Housing Offices', the 'Daily Record',
(7) 'The Women go to War' and the 'Scottish Daily Express' (8)
announced, 'Families at War over Re-housing'. The demonstration
also appeared in the Edinburgh newspaper 'The Scotsman' (9), and
was mentioned on television during the Scottish news. The numbers
present were variously put at 70, 80 and 100, with the lowest
estimate probably the most accurate.

   The 'Daily Record's' description of the demonstration was:
'While placard-carrying families paraded outside Clive House for
more than three hours, other members of the committee plagued
counter clerks with new housing demands.' The 'Glasgow Herald',
while quoting the Housing Manager - 'we do not have the facilities
to operate the system they suggest' - also reported John Moir's
statement that, 'housing policy should be for the benefit of the
people involved and not for the benefit of the officials'. Similarly, along with the Housing Manager's assertion that houses
were offered in 'a fit state', the 'Evening Citizen' quoted Davey
Bouse saying that he had rejected his offer because it was in 'a
shambles' and that some, particularly old people, were made to
accept houses in 'a deplorable condition'. The paper also
reported the sub-convenor of the Corporation's Housing Committee,
who said that residents 'could be threatened with eviction ... if
they had refused to accept offers of reasonable accommodation'.
The 'Evening Times' repeated the GHC's promise 'to fight with all
means possible any attempted eviction'. It quoted at length from
the GHC leaflet:

   They neither consult us nor inform us that our area is to
   be demolished; housing visitors grade us; they offer inferior
   housing; they promise repairs which take months to be done;
   they leave us in derelict buildings; and finally, they
   threaten us with eviction.

An Oran Street resident was reported as saying: 'We are living in
absolute squalor. I would love to see the Housing Manager live in
my home, to see how he likes it.' The 'Scottish Daily Express'
quoted Jimmy Gallagher declaring that 'things are not moving fast
enough now, the families must get out of these houses'. The
authorities were frequently quoted claiming that they coped adequately with the demonstration while in most of the stories it was
apparent that they had not. There is no doubt that the demonstration was a major embarrassment to the Corporation. Whatever
else accrued from it, the residents certainly enjoyed the
experience. A week later, the 'Scottish Daily Express' (10) had
a feature article on Gairbraid, based on an interview with Jackie
Moir, which stressed the peoples' determination to remain within
Maryhill.

   The GHC was divided on whether or not to continue with the
demonstrations at Clive House. After much discussion, the view
that prevailed was that there were insufficient numbers left to
maintain the momentum and a repeat performance was likely to be
counter-productive. It was decided that a renewed threat of
further direct action, which hinted at an extension of the campaign,

promised to be more effective than an actual protest. In retrospect, however, many of the committee members felt that the GHC was
mistaken and that the demonstrations should have continued.

THE SECOND DELEGATION TO THE
CITY CHAMBERS

At the end of April the GHC organized what was to be its last
large-scale public meeting. Jimmy Gallagher again took the chair
while John Moir delivered a militant opening address. Well over
100 people attended the meeting. The hall in the Trade Union
Centre was packed to capacity as Gairbraid residents were joined
by others from several areas: Oran Street, a group from the
Maryhill Road who wished to have their homes declared a housing
treatment area so that they could be rehoused, and another group
of owner-occupiers from Broompark Drive, Townhead, who were
struggling to save their homes from such a declaration. On the
platform were a Maryhill councillor, a councillor from a neighbouring ward which included part of the Oran Street area and the
prospective Labour candidate for Maryhill in the forthcoming local
election. The Housing Department had been invited to send a
representative but three days before the meeting they requested
further information. Their reply, read out to the meeting, was
greeted with derision: (11) 'In so far as Oran Street is concerned
perhaps you will let me know the matters to be discussed at the
Public Meeting as I have no indication that this area is meantime
affected and requiring special action by my Department.' As later
pointed out in the 'Glasgow News', if unaware of conditions there,
the Housing Manager (12) 'should take a walk up Oran Street, smell
the stench and walk through the filthy puddles. Maybe then he'd
think twice before telling residents to keep quiet and wait.'
        The meeting succeeded as a show of force but it left the GHC
uncertain as to its future course of action. Rapid rehousing
continued in Gairbraid and for the first time in several months
large numbers were also rehoused from Oran Street. The flow of
satisfactory offers was largely attributed, by residents in both
areas, to the protest at Clive House. Oran Street seemed no
longer to be a completely forgotten area. Houses in the newly
built Corporation schemes in Maryhill were about to become available and many Gairbraid residents were given firm assurances of
being offered these in advance of their allocation. Thus, without
actually admitting to the practice, the Housing Department implemented the GHC's long-standing demand to have new property
allocated before completion. For those in this position uncertainty
was not absolutely eliminated as the promises were only unofficial.
Among the committee members, Jimmy Gallagher and Davey Bouse were
assured of new houses in Maryhill. Jackie Moir and later Margaret
Hobson were told that they had received low priority grading and
would thus require to be inspected again by the housing visitors.
As in both cases the second visit was even shorter than the original, recalling the housing visitors seemed a mere formality that
Clive House felt was necessary, presumably for its records, before
being able to offer the Moirs and Hobsons the new houses in

Maryhill. That the authorities were prepared to go to these
lengths indicates both the exaggerated conception held of the GHC's
power and the importance of grading in the house allocations system.

After the bus-run to Clive House, Oran Street residents continued to attend Gairbraid's committee meetings, but to avoid being
swamped and because of a certain degree of hostility towards them
the GHC decided to separate the two communities. Oran Street was
helped to organize its own committee and several well attended
meetings were held there. The residents cleared an empty house
for this purpose and the councillors were invited to attend meetings. Shortly afterwards many of the Oran Street committee were
rehoused and their organization gradually collapsed. There were
too few families left in Oran Street to sustain the group for any
length of time. Gairbraid, because of hostility to Oran Street
and its own declining population, was powerless to help. There
were rumours reported which suggested that some people felt that
the GHC's concern with Oran Street deflected attention away from
Gairbraid. The development of this attitude was almost inevitable because in a situation of chronic housing scarcity, competition for decent accommodation is bound to create bitterness and
despair so that people from other areas are seen not as fellow
sufferers but as threatening, potential rivals. A successful
challenge to Glasgow's rehousing policy and practice depends
largely on co-ordinated action between treatment areas on a city-
wide basis. While the Oran Street experience illustrates the
difficulties involved in achieving such co-operation, these should
not be exaggerated. Organization needs ideally to begin before
rehousing starts while contact between the GHC and Oran Street was
only initiated when conditions had already become desperate in
Gairbraid itself. Furthermore, a large proportion of Gairbraid's
activists, both committee members and supporters, had already been
rehoused and as many of those remaining were non-participants, the
advantages of a joint campaign were less likely to appeal to them
than to many of the former residents. Most crucially, of those
then remaining in Gairbraid probably only a minority expressed
anti-Oran Street feelings. For these reasons, a city-wide campaign,
based on allied organizations in various treatment areas, remains
an attractive and feasible proposition for future community action
in Glasgow.

The flow of offers to Gairbraid meant that the committee's power
of protest continually diminished and with Oran Street no longer a
viable source of support very few options were open to the community. Unless the Corporation provoked Gairbraid by, for instance,
attempting to evict a resident, militancy was clearly ruled out
for the GHC. Strategy was simply defensive, based on maintaining
an appearance of power. Efforts were thus redoubled to achieve
the previously proposed meeting with the Corporation. While agree-
ing to hold it in principle, the authorities did not fix a definite
date because of the approaching local government elections and the
Housing Convenor's absence abroad. Finally, through the efforts
of both the GHC and the local councillors, a meeting in the City
Chambers was arranged for 5 June. The GHC decided to insist upon
an evening meeting. It was argued that, as the members of a
working-class organization could not easily obtain time off work,

a Labour administration particularly should be prepared to hold
meetings after hours. In fact one of the GHC delegates, Jackie
Moir, was then on night shift. From the experience gained at
their first encounter with the Corporation, the GHC considered
that unless approached from a position of strength a meeting with
the authorities was of limited value. Thus the insistance on an
evening meeting was basically a means of bluffing, to give an
appearance of power when it no longer existed. The GHC banked on
the assumption that, because of its past activities, the Corporation would hesitate to again underestimate its strength. When
the authorities did concede to the GHC's request, the members
gained considerable pleasure from the thought that many of Glasgow's
most powerful councillors and officials had gathered in the City
Chambers, after their day's work, to meet, as John Moir put it,
'three ordinary working-class blokes from Maryhill'. A minor
victory perhaps, but it greatly reinforced the delegation's morale
and confidence.

    As final preparations were made for the meeting, eleven
Gairbraid residents, including Jimmy Gallagher and Jackie Moir,
received offers of houses in the new Maryhill 'B' scheme. This
reduced the population to an estimated fifty families; or expressed
differently, about 88 per cent of all dwellings in Gairbraid were
then unoccupied. John Smith, the Bouses and the Hobsons, were the
only committee members still to be rehoused. The GHC was clearly
capable of only defensive action and could no longer take the
initiative. The authorities were bound to be fully aware of
Gairbraid's population statistics and the delegation thus decided
to concentrate on the threat of organizing elsewhere in the city.
John Moir, Jimmy Gallagher and Jackie Moir, all of whom were
already rehoused, represented Gairbraid. Davey Bouse was also
elected but, through a misunderstanding, did not attend the meeting. The GHC did not repeat its previous error of including the
community workers in their delegation and the atmosphere at the
meeting was much improved. Moreover, the GHC could, in terms of
the ability and expertise of the members, provide its own leaders
without any need whatsoever of relying on outside assistance.

    A full sub-committee of senior councillors and officials were
present to meet the Gairbraid delegation. During lengthy discus-
sions, all of Gairbraid's grievances, from the housing visitor's
report to vandalism and interviews at Clive House, were dealt
with. The GHC felt that, under the circumstances, more was
achieved than could have been expected. Determined to avoid a
mere repetition of the first meeting, John Moir recalls: 'We
decided that we had as much right to be there as them.' The
seniority of the councillors and officials who attended, Jimmy
Gallagher points out, 'shows the strength we had'. In John Moir's
words, 'everybody that's anybody in the Corporation was there'.
Jackie Moir believes that the meeting was worthwhile: 'We stressed
the fact that we would still be there as long as there were
tenants left, that they had to rehouse the area before they would
get the committee off their back.' As anticipated, the delegation
was regaled with anecdotes of how, when the councillors were young,
although conditions were even worse, no one complained. The sub-
committee, however, were not allowed to wander off and so avoid

discussion of the pertinent issues. 'The Housing Convenor pointed
out that he was in the same position himself at one time, everybody
had to go through the same thing', but as Jimmy Gallagher remembers,
'we indicated that in 1972, this should not go on any longer, we
were organized into a committee and as far as we were concerned, we
were fighting for the people and we would be fighting right to the
end.' The members stressed that unless the community was quickly
rehoused the GHC intended organizing in other areas and, as Jackie
Moir recalls, the threat seemed to have the desired effect:

> 'They tried to calm us down, to stop us from being more
> militant. I think they were really frightened. When we
> mentioned that we would involve other areas, you could
> see they didn't want this, they told us that this problem
> wouldn't arise'.

All three agree that the meeting was highly successful. In John
Moir's view: 'If it had been a bigger area, think what we could
have done. If a committee like ours can bring the whole of the
Corporation to the City Chambers on a Monday night, the scope is
there for changes to be made.'

The GHC firmly believes that the meeting at the City Chambers
would probably never have taken place but for the demonstration
at Clive House. It clearly strengthened their delegation's bargaining power and the satisfactory rehousing rate that followed
was seen to have occurred as a direct result of the meeting. The
most important outcome, however, was that the sub-committee agreed
to recommend that the GHC's system of interviews, with officials
available for appointments, be implemented for the whole city.
As the recommendation was supported by the most influential
councillors on the Corporation's Housing Committee, its adoption
as official policy seemed a mere formality. The Maryhill councillors suggested that it was only a matter of time, and when the
recommendation was recorded in the Corporation minutes, it clearly
only awaited ratification by the full Housing Committee. It
seemed that, at long last, the GHC had succeeded in achieving a
far-reaching reform in Glasgow's rehousing policy and practice.
If the proposal was implemented in the spirit in which it was
formulated, the right to demand interviews with relatively senior
officials at Clive House promised, by creating easy access to
authority, to alleviate uncertainty and to allow for some local
participation in decision-making.

THE FINAL DESTRUCTION OF
GAIRBRAID

By early July, John Smith and the Bouses were rehoused, leaving
the Hobsons as the only committee members still in the area, and
they were promised a new house in Maryhill when these were next
ready for allocation. A GHC survey showed that thirty-nine
families still lived in Gairbraid while one family, having been
made homeless by fire, awaited rehousing from their parents'
Corporation flat. Of those remaining, including five old age
pensioners, two-thirds were still in Gairbraid through no fault
of their own but rather because of Clive House's inability to

rehouse them. Only six of the remaining families owed money on previous Corporation houses, while a further seven had either extremely short tenancies or were squatters. By then conditions had so deteriorated in Gairbraid that nothing short of an immediate mass exodus was required. The GHC, however, had lost much of its ability to influence the rehousing process. In recognition of its weakness, the GHC concentrated its efforts on ensuring that the local councillors advocated on behalf of the residents. In order to give people the opportunity to press their own cases, meetings were organized almost weekly at which one or other of the Maryhill councillors were present. An extreme disappointment for the committee was the discovery, in the Corporation minutes, that Glasgow Corporation was, on the advice of the Housing Manager, not after all going to institute a system of interviews at Clive House. There was to be no reform. The authorities did not bother to inform the GHC of this change of mind and no explanation was ever offered. The Maryhill councillors were reluctant to pursue the matter and the GHC could not - it had lost its power of protest.

It soon became apparent that clearing the area would be a slow process: by early August there were still thirty-three families left and a month later only a further nine had been rehoused. Of these twenty-four, eleven attended committee meetings, four others were in close contact with the GHC, while the remaining nine showed little interest in the committee. To maintain morale, members continued to visit the families in their homes. At that stage it was decided that the GHC had no further function and it was even thought that its continued existence might be counter-productive. The GHC was by then merely a minor irritant and, in order not to antagonize further either Clive House or the councillors, on whose goodwill the remaining residents were basically dependent, the organization was disbanded. On 18 September, at the sixty-eighth weekly session of the GHC, Jimmy Gallagher, Jackie Moir and Tommy Dickson, as the only members present, unceremoniously decided that unless an emergency arose no further meetings would be held. Although all three maintained contact with the families in Gairbraid until the very end, the GHC never reconvened.

Gairbraid was basically handed over to Joan Shannon, one of the community workers, who maintained a case-working type relationship with the families until the last was rehoused in March 1973. Grants were obtained for families in rent arrears so that they could be rehoused. As many of the men had served in the armed forces, the money was provided by their ex-regiments. The project had to make a loan to one family as no other source of finance was available. Work with old people varied, from hospital visiting where a resident lay dying of cancer, to ensuring that a totally bewildered old lady was decently rehoused. Work with the other families involved ensuring that regular contact was maintained with both Clive House and the councillors. As a power base no longer existed in the community, relationships with authority were essentially consensus orientated. The population slowly dwindled as family after family were satisfactorily rehoused, until by the New Year, only a handful remained and these were soon accommodated.

Gairbraid totally deserted was ugly and eerie. The shattered

buildings bore little resemblance to the place where once over a
thousand people lived. Gairbraid, for all its defects, was then
alive. There is no question that the former residents are better
accommodated in their Corporation houses than they were in their
tenements. Now that they enjoy the basic amenities of modern life,
progress has been made. Gairbraid did not object to rehousing per
se but to official policy and practice and to the outrageous dis-
regard shown throughout the process for human dignity. That a
viable community was dispersed and forever destroyed is an act of
official vandalism far more profound than all the havoc and terror
caused by the waves of teenage gangs that incessantly plagued
Gairbraid. Multiplied for all Glasgow the social cost must be
phenomenal, yet even now the City Fathers, in all their folly,
continue to destroy existing communities. The Corporation seems
to have learnt nothing from the Gairbraid experience, except how
better to handle their rebellious tenants. If the GHC demonstrated
anything, it was that local organization is essential in treatment
areas if local interests are to be safeguarded.

By the end of July 1972, a year after rehousing had begun in
Gairbraid, over 90 per cent of the 352 families in the area had
found alternative accommodation. It took a further eight months
to rehouse the remaining thirty or so families. The last to be
rehoused coped without the GHC but with full-time professional
assistance. The inability to help these people is in a sense a
failure, but unless supported by groups in other treatment areas
there was no way in which the GHC could have prolonged its active
life. Buildings declared dangerous were demolished in Gairbraid
even when people lived in the surrounding tenements. The property,
however, was not finally demolished until March 1974, a whole year
after the last person had left the area. Clearly, the Corporation
was in no hurry to acquire Gairbraid. Oran Street is a prime
example of people left to stagnate for years under intolerable
conditions until the Corporation required possession of the
property. Supported by evidence from clearance areas all over
Glasgow, the members of the GHC believe that a similar fate would
have befallen Gairbraid had it not been for their campaign. Any
time spent in derelict property must seem like an eternity. If
the GHC succeeded in limiting the rehousing process by even a
short period, it was a victory indeed.

Chapter 11

THE COMMITTEE IN RETROSPECT

The GHC had an effective life of about sixteen months, from May
1971 to September 1972. During this time, sixty-eight committee
and seven public meetings were held. Petitions were sent to the
Housing Manager and to the Secretary of State for Scotland, and
Gairbraid was responsible for a trade union resolution condemning
Glasgow's rehousing policy. On two separate occasions the GHC
sent delegations to the City Chambers to meet with senior councillors and officials. The area was featured on a 'Current Account'
television programme and obtained considerable press publicity.
The GHC organized two demonstrations at the Housing Department of
which one involved people from other areas. Ten documents for
external consumption were issued: three to the authorities; three
press releases; and four to the public. Every Gairbraid household also received thirteen newsletters. Numerous meetings took
place with the local Maryhill councillors who, together with
various Corporation departments, were constantly contacted by
letter and telephone. By the end, the GHC had accumulated a
bulging file of correspondence. People from clearance areas
throughout Glasgow approached the GHC for advice and assistance.
The GHC helped residents in neighbouring Oran Street to organize
in opposition to the Corporation and the Gairbraid campaign has
since inspired other groups. Committee members accompanied
residents to the Housing Department, were involved in legal representation, liaison with the police, and advocacy with the Social
Work Department. The GHC organized a pre-school playgroup, bingo
sessions, a mothers' group, a trip to Edinburgh, children's
parties, visits to old age pensioners and various other social
activities.
   The GHC, conducting a diverse and sustained campaign, gained
recognition as a serious organization whose own local leadership
was able to respond to crisis with imagination and flexibility.
It proved adaptable to changing situations, and on a criterion of
sheer survival the GHC must be considered a success. Those who
originally stereotyped the people of Gairbraid as apathetic and
incapable of providing their own leaders were shown to be wrong,
as were the many cynics who predicted that once rehousing started
the organization would collapse. Very often the 'expert advice'

given was based on pure ignorance and prejudice which never considered the possibility that a working-class community could
produce the degree of selfless dedication shown by the members.
Hugh and Eileen Thompson, who remained actively involved months
after being rehoused, are a shining example of the strength of
commitment which made the Gairbraid campaign a reality.

PREFERENTIAL TREATMENT

Gairbraid was demolished only a year after the last resident left.
As John Moir maintains, 'there was no hurry for that area' and but
for the GHC 'we would have still been there'. Irrespective of how
successful the GHC was on any other count, had it been unable to
influence both the quality and flow of offers the community would
have regarded it as a failure. It was in these terms that local
people understood the campaign and indeed, was what the GHC was
all about. In whatever way, outsiders may view the Gairbraid
campaign, for the 'average' resident what really mattered was
where, when and how he was rehoused. The Corporation destroyed
their homes and, through no fault of their own, they were forced
to move. Rightly and reasonably, they wanted for themselves and
their children the best accommodation available.
     Given a limited supply of decent houses, many in authority
claimed that those allocated to Gairbraid should have been more
widely distributed and thus, it is said, Gairbraid's aspirations
were achieved only at the expense of other areas who were unorganized. A local councillor accused the GHC of (1) 'an ugly
parochialism in which Maryhill people are presumed to have a
proprietorial right to any new houses in the area'. While containing a kernel of truth, this view is essentially an argument against
opposition to the status quo, placing a burden on those seeking
accommodation that few if any of Gairbraid's critics would accept
as reasonable for themselves. To expect people to forgo the
chance of a decent house because somewhere in the city an unknown
person may be deprived, is to attribute to them either irresponsi-
bility to their own family, gullibility, stupidity or saintliness.
The system creates extreme competition and it is therefore a dis-
tortion to place the onus for both unfair distribution and the
existing shortage on the residents rather than on the authorities
whose priorities, policies and practices are entirely responsible.
     Gairbraid seemed to awaken a belated concern among the authori-
ties, not in evidence before or after, for the people in other
treatment areas. If the GHC had not existed, people elsewhere
would not have been treated better, Gairbraid would simply have
been treated as badly. In spite of or perhaps even because of
painstakingly formulated regulations, house allocations are
essentially arbitrary. The existence of local groups, by ensuring
that offers correspond to individual preferences, in fact introduce an element of rationality to what is otherwise an unfair
system. All too frequently the situation occurred where individual 'A' who wished to remain in his own area 'X' was shunted
across the city to area 'Y' from where individual 'B' was moved
under protest to area 'X'. Often in Gairbraid offers regarded as

unsatisfactory by some were desired by others and the GHC was able to make representation on the behalf of the latter to ensure that offers matched individual preferences. In such instances the GHC's actions were hardly at the expense of anyone.

The argument of preferential treatment seems to rest on an 'all or none' principle so that where all are unjustly treated either all or none may protest. To accuse the GHC of selfishness is to ignore its record of helping other areas and of consistently attempting to achieve city-wide reform. A justification for the GHC may be found in the belief that, even if powerless to achieve universal reform, it is important that at least some people should receive public housing with dignity, out of free choice and as of right. To behave otherwise is to comply with an unjust system while opposition, even on a small scale, opens it to public debate and perhaps begins a process which inspires others and which ultimately may even change it. By exposing Glasgow's rehousing policy the GHC made people throughout the city, including councillors and officials, more aware of what actually occurs at Clive House. Gairbraid's leaders and to a certain extent many of the non-activists, gained in self-confidence, expertise and knowledge of how the system operates and how best to protect local interests. The experience gained in Gairbraid has since been used and transferred to elsewhere in the city.

All the committee members are, without doubt, convinced that the Gairbraid campaign was extremely worthwhile and highly successful, while to those in authority, as the reference to 'ugly parochialism' suggests, it was both disruptive and distasteful. To others interested in the wider political processes it was merely irrelevant. Clearly the GHC operated at various levels and of those most closely involved, the GHC members, the non-active residents, the politicians, the administrators and the community workers, all view the campaign differently, using a variety of yardsticks. The perspective presented here is that of the committee members and this chapter is largely devoted to their assessment of the events in Gairbraid. Jackie Moir provides a cogent summary of the campaign:

'The committee helped people to get rehoused, they helped people to organize, showed them how to organize, how to fight battles with officialdom. It showed them what you can achieve by standing up for your rights rather than sitting back and waiting for them to come through the door. It has helped a number of old people; it has shown them that there are other people interested in them. It helped not only the area but also a lot of people outside the area. This must be a good thing and we will never really know how successful the committee was - I believe there are a number of people outside the area that may have taken encouragement from the committee.'

THE RIGHT TO A DECENT HOUSE

The members obviously emphasize rehousing in their list of the GHC's achievements, all feeling like Ella Donnelly that 'the

biggest majority got exactly where they wanted'. In Mary Smith's
view, the GHC 'did a good job, getting people houses, getting
them what they fancied, their choice, where they wanted to go -
if it had been left to the Corporation they would have put you
anywhere'. Similarly, Davey Bouse feels that without organization,
'things would have been a lot harder, I don't think we would have
been sitting where we are just now: people got better treatment
because of the committee, that's quite obvious'. Of her own
situation Margaret Hobson says:

> 'When I went to the committee I was blind, I didn't know
> how to go about the first thing and there's us sitting up
> here, a house that we really wanted, that we never thought
> we would get. We have got a decent place for the kids to
> live in and I think there are an awful lot in Gairbraid
> got that.'

Ella Donnelly stresses 'the feeling of togetherness and being able
to fight together, you felt you were achieving something and you
were no longer on your own'. Isa Hanlon believes that the residents 'realized that they didn't have to just take what they were
getting'. The GHC, Eileen Kelly remembers, provided the community
with a sense of security:

> 'no one went up and saw a house and was told "if you don't
> take that you are getting nothing else" and accepted it,
> whereas, if it wasn't for the committee an awful lot would
> have done it, I suppose I would have probably done it myself.'

'I don't think we would have got the houses we've got', Annie
Mallon insists, 'without fighting for them.' All the members
stress organization to explain the committee's success. In
Hugh Thompson's view, it was because 'we were united'. Referring
to rehousing as the 'main goal', Jimmy Gallagher feels that the
GHC also 'got people to realize what an organization is', and that
in their new housing schemes they would now 'realize the necessity
for organization'. Similarly, John Moir believes that the committee 'first of all gave me this house, the house of my choice and
secondly, I realize you must be organized to get anything; I have
always known this, mind, but this has really brought it a hundred
per cent through to me'. Jimmy Gallagher again: 'The biggest
thing the committee achieved was getting people together to have
faith in each other.'

In the beginning, before the organization had established
credibility, some residents, many of whom were old, accepted
offers of inferior accommodation. There were also a handful of
residents who showed no interest or inclination to become involved, and for them the GHC could do little. By the end the
committee had lost its power and thus could not protect the last
remaining in the area. While for a small minority of people the
GHC failed, for the vast majority it was entirely successful,
ensuring that they were better and more quickly rehoused than they
otherwise would have been. The members consider that the GHC's
campaign slogan 'The Right to a Decent House' was successfully
fulfilled.

THE EXPERIENCE OF ORGANIZING

Jimmy Gallagher, being a shop steward, was the only committee
member active in an outside organization, other than those
connected with church affairs. Generally, people in Gairbraid
had little or no experience of organizing or dealing with
councillors and officials. As the campaign progressed from
collecting signatures for petitions to staging demonstrations,
experience and knowledge was gained so that by the end the GHC
possessed a fund of expertise and competence that would have
been a credit to any organization anywhere. Although at first few
had ever spoken in public, organizing meetings soon became old
hat for the GHC. Jimmy Gallagher developed into an extremely
efficient chairman and John Moir delivered his opening speeches
with confidence and composure. Whereas at first people hesitated
to raise points, question time at these meetings became increasingly lively with residents freely contributing from the floor.
    In an area which had been stereotyped as incapable of producing
its own leadership, Gairbraid astounded its critics. The delegation of John Moir, Jimmy Gallagher and Jackie Moir, sent to the
meeting at the City Chambers, perhaps best illustrates the
stature finally possessed by the GHC. John Moir believes that
the Corporation were 'terrified' that organization would spread
to other areas of the city. Referring to the City Chambers he
remembers, 'We were well known in that place and that really
takes a bit of doing, we were as well known as their bloody MPs
that nobody knows .... they were definitely terrified of us'.
Similarly, the Gairbraid campaign provided Hugh Thompson with
'the satisfaction of letting the Corporation know that we wouldn't
be bullied by their paid servants. I wouldn't tolerate flannel
from the town councillors - they are supposed to represent us.'
Georgina Atkinson considers that the GHC 'got people to realize
that they just didn't need to sit back and take what was coming'.
She goes on to add: 'Folk have the right to fight against it and
the people that were in Maryhill realize that now. If there is
anything that they are not satisfied with, they will fight against
it.'
    It is a conventional wisdom to label people in clearance areas
as apathetic where more accurately they have been denied the
opportunity to participate in the democratic process. The GHC
campaign provided many with the knowledge and confidence to cope
with a system which Marxists would say was designed to suppress
their class. Rules and regulations lost their mystique as the
committee members found their way around the intricacies of local
government. For them democracy is now more meaningfully available. Isa Hanlon, for instance, tells of what she gained from
the committee:
    'I think I learnt a lot out of it actually. I had never
    seen a councillor before, they never interested me that
    much. Now, I would fight the bit out with them because
    I wouldn't let them get the better of me. If I was going
    to the councillor for anything, I wouldn't let him shove
    me off with any old trash. I wouldn't take it now whereas
    before I might have said, "he knows, he must be right".

After all, you're voting for that man to do things for
    you.'
Jackie Moir 'learnt a lot about the working man's rights' and
believes that 'it's a matter of having a group behind you, it
must be a committee because there is no other way of doing it'.
He goes on to add:
    'It surprised me how the officials and councillors would
    listen to the working person and do something for him.
    I was always under the impression that you could get no-
    where with the councillors, that they were unapproachable.
    I didn't believe you could go to Clive House, kick up a
    fuss and demand your rights which I now know is the best
    thing to do. I learned on the committee that the working
    man has a right to make himself heard and he will be heard
    and they will listen to him. If I ever had any other
    problems I would be wiser and know what to do about it.'
'The experience did us good', Hugh Thompson says, having since
been involved in a public enquiry, 'now we know all about that
and we will never hesitate to bring legal pressure on the Corporation.'
    In John Smith's view, 'there were a lot of things you never got
told, the only way you got told was when you went to committee
meetings'. Davey Bouse believes that the GHC helped by providing
support and the feeling that there was always 'something behind
you' when dealing with the Corporation. As someone from Oran
Street expressed it to Eileen Kelly after both had been rehoused,
'you were lucky, you had the backing'. Being on the committee
gave Ella Donnelly 'the feeling of togetherness', of knowing that
'you were not on your own'. She advises that getting involved
is 'the best thing because it gives you something to do and
you feel that you are getting somewhere, whereas if you just sit
at home and moan, it just makes you feel frustrated and worried'.
The committee members found their involvement to be personally
rewarding: Annie Mallon feels that the campaign was 'fantastic',
Ella Donnelly 'thoroughly enjoyed it' and John Moir says that 'it
was a great experience for me'. Georgina Atkinson remarks, 'if
we fought for folk and they got houses they wanted, I'm quite
satisfied'. Jackie Moir remembers:
    'To me it was a great experience, going down to Clive House
    with some people and getting them satisfied, getting them
    houses that they wanted, where they wanted. It was a worth-
    while cause seeing people getting rehoused, helping people
    to get rehoused in decent houses and so many people, not
    just one or two people but so many people getting rehoused.'
These sentiments are echoed by Ella Donnelly:
    'I thoroughly enjoyed taking people up to Clive House,
    and actually getting interviews for them. When they
    were successful in getting the house, they came to you
    and said: "Mrs Donnelly I can't thank you enough."
    You're saying "It wasn't me, it was the committee that
    got you it. I'm just a member of the committee, it wasn't
    me personally that did it." It still gives you a great
    feeling of satisfaction that you're doing something,
    actually helping people.'

The GHC provided many of the female members with a release from
purely domestic duties. Of her involvement in the community, Isa
Hanlon observes:

'I enjoyed the atmosphere and working along with other
people, helping old people. I know it sounds daft but
if you're stuck in the house with a lot of weans and
you're out doing something like that, it occupies your
time. I really enjoyed it.'

The GHC's ability to help old people obviously provided consider-
able pleasure. It gave the old people 'a sense of security',
Jeannette Bouse feels, 'to know that somebody was bothering'.
In Adam Hobson's words,

'One of the main achievements of the committee was that
they had a lot to do with the old folk. There were old
folk who didn't know what to do, old folk staying on
their own are frightened and the committee took the time
and perseverence to go and help them and see that they
got houses where they wanted them.'

Of those in rent arrears, Ella Donnelly feels that many 'did not
have much hope', feeling that 'even' the GHC would not be able to
solve their problems but 'the help that they got through the
committee, they would never have got otherwise, they would have
just been left'.

There is a general consensus of opinion among the members that
the GHC generated solidarity and stimulated a spirit of community
in the area. As Betty Gallagher notes:

'People would have started niggling amongst each other.
You know, "why is she getting a house when I've been here
such and such a time?" They would have only been fighting each other instead of the system which created it.
They'd only be fighting each other and that suits the
system. It did not happen in our area because when offers
came out the committee was there for us to go to.'

Margaret Hobson feels that the committee's door-to-door visits
were 'interesting because you met all different types of people'.
Jimmy and Betty Gallagher say that 'it wasn't until the committee
was formed that we began to meet and speak to people'. Georgina
Atkinson thinks that 'people got to know each other a lot better'
and on the question of whether or not more social events would
have achieved greater solidarity in the community she replied: 'I
don't think you could have got them much closer than they were.'
Jeannette Bouse points out that 'what was happening was discussed
every morning by mothers at the playgroup'. As the campaign
progressed, as more and more successes were achieved and
activities diversified, a community, in every sense of the word,
emerged in Gairbraid. When members still had some hope that a
substantial number of the residents would be rehoused together
there was talk of maintaining the committee, and of forming old
folks' and youth clubs in the new areas. In Annie Mallon's words,
'it would have been great'. Jackie Moir feels 'we could have had
a good committee to form a tenants' association'. The Corporation,
while proclaiming the virtues of self-help, dispersed an already
organized community.

'If some of us got rehoused, well at least it would be to the

good, somebody would benefit,' John Moir originally believed, 'but
the record we got must be fantastic although it will never be admitted.' Eileen Thompson is emphatic in her view that 'we achieved
more than I thought we would'. It is evident that the members
feel that they gained a great deal from the campaign, that it was
an outstanding success, worthwhile and enjoyable. Modestly, none
mention the resourcefulness, energy and long hours that their
commitment demanded.

LOCAL PARTICIPATION

Community action aims to stimulate local participation and thus
an assessment of the intervention in Gairbraid must consider the
involvement of the rank and file in addition to that of the relatively few who assumed leadership positions in the community. The
long and sustained campaign conducted in Gairbraid is perhaps in
itself sufficient evidence of massive local support; it does not
seem unreasonable to assume that in community action the one is
always the sine qua non of the other. All those interviewed are
convinced that the GHC was solidly supported by virtually the
entire community.

Although careful records were not kept, it is estimated that,
excluding councillors, community workers, and other outsiders,
attendance at the GHC's sixty-eight committee meetings totalled
577. On average, each was attended by between eight and nine
people of whom six were committee members, two non-active
Gairbraid residents and one, at every second meeting, was from
another clearance area in the city. Twenty residents in all
were considered, by themselves and by others, to be committee
members. Five were active for only short periods and were marginal to the organization. Others, like Jimmy Gallagher who attended
fifty-six of the committee meetings, maintained their commitment
until the last family was rehoused. Of those who joined later,
Jackie Moir and Tommy Dickson attended, respectively, thirty-one
and thirty-two of the last thirty-six meetings. The average
attendance of committee members declined near the end but otherwise was more or less constant. As the campaign developed, more
non-active people, from Gairbraid and elsewhere, attended meetings; there were 143 of them at the last thirty-four meetings
compared to thirty-six at the first thirty-four. At a perhaps
conservative estimate, someone from about one in four of Gairbraid's
families attended at least one committee meeting and the majority
of the last 200 families in the area either attended a meeting,
were accompanied to Clive House or representation was made on their
behalf to both councillors and officials. When public meetings
and the various other GHC activities are considered, it is apparent
that a continual two-way communication existed between the
community and its leadership.

Another indication of local support is obtained from a survey
completed in the area in January 1971, that is, after the television programme but before representation at Clive House was
fully in operation and before any of the demonstrations. It was
not intended to serve as a popularity poll but was designed to

ascertain individual problems and possible ways in which the committee could provide assistance. Attitudes towards the committee were in most instances given spontaneously and these are classified into 'positive', 'negative' and 'indifferent' categories. A relatively large number of people were simply recorded as saying that they had no problems and these are classified as attitude 'not indicated'. The results obtained from 130 questionnaires are shown in Table 1.

TABLE 1

Attitude towards the committee	No.	%
Positive	97	74.6
Negative	8	6.2
Indifferent	5	3.8
Not Indicated	20	15.4
Total	130	100

Those classified as 'positive' either praised the committee, indicated their faith in it, were appreciative of help already received or were themselves willing to take an active part. Examples are: 'I think they are doing marvellously', 'works wonders', 'very helpful', 'doing well', 'we would have got no place without it', 'good to know they are there, I don't feel so afraid', 'I feel sure they will help', 'it was the committee who got me this house when the roof fell in upstairs', 'a mass can do more than an individual', 'you can count on them'. Of those who expressed negative opinions, the most extreme was a young man living alone who accused the committee of being 'a shower of bloody catholics' and two separate instances of old ladies saying they wanted nothing to do with the committee. Of the remaining five who disapproved, one thought that the committee could have been better organized, two that it was 'the Corporation who matter', while another two expressed doubts about the GHC's abilities - 'I don't see them doing much', and 'the committee members have not been able to help themselves, so how can they help others?' Of the five classified as 'indifferent', all said either that they knew 'nothing about the committee' or that they had 'no dealings' with it. In all, only thirteen individuals, 10 per cent of the sample, were either antagonistic or indifferent to the committee. On the other hand, three-quarters expressed approval, many in very enthusiastic terms.

The survey results confirm what the committee members regard as obvious. They, after all, were as much a part of Gairbraid as anyone else and as such did not function in isolation from the rest of the community, having to be both sensitive and responsive to local opinion. In attempting to assess degrees of participation, numbers provide nothing more than a rough guide, realistically regarded by the committee members as an academic obsession with 'head-counting'. Would the community action intervention

in Gairbraid have been more successful if there had been twice
as many active committee members? Twice as successful? In
Georgina Atkinson's opinion, if there had been more members less
would have been achieved: 'There were enough committee members
to decide and if we decided something that wasn't right then the
people were not long in telling you they didn't agree with it.'
In an area the size of Gairbraid there are only a limited number
of leadership roles available at any given time. It is suggested
that beyond this maximum, membership tends to involve little more
than passive observation. On the whole, people sensibly do not
give up their valuable free time unless they are able to contribute significantly to the organization. The problem in organizing
committees like the GHC is not so much recruitment but rather,
creating meaningful roles for the existing membership, particularly in periods between crisis. People do not regularly attend
weekly sessions simply to be involved in a 'talking shop'. Many
of the Gairbraid members did not join earlier because they said
enough people were then already involved. Whenever key activists
were rehoused from Gairbraid they were, almost until the very end,
immediately replaced by new members, while at other times recruitment was more difficult. There was an untapped reservoir of
talent in Gairbraid and many who remained outside the committee
would have been prepared to join had the necessity ever arisen.
A membership count merely provides a superficial picture of a
local organization. Instead its success should be measured by
its ability to reflect and represent local interests. A dynamic
relationship existed between the GHC and the rest of the Gairbraid
population who generally identified with it as their committee.

As a rule, non-attendance at meetings need not necessarily
indicate indifference to the local organization, particularly
where people work overtime, work on night shifts, have baby-
sitting problems or where there are numbers of old and infirm in
the community. In Gairbraid, as conditions deteriorated and
vandalism increased, many people were afraid to leave their homes
unprotected. The GHC members quote examples of keen interest
among those Gairbraid residents who never attended a single
public meeting. Jimmy Gallagher illustrates this point by recalling an instance when a family who had previously had no
contact with the GHC, approached him to say: 'We must thank you
very much for helping us, we know we would never have got this
house unless it was through our committee.' Isa Hanlon believes
that 'the biggest majority of them supported the committee
because you couldn't walk up the street but you were getting
pulled up.' In John Moir's words, 'I was stopped a million times
in the street, with people thanking me, that I had never even
seen before, I used to be stopped going to work, people asking
me things ....' Of some old people who never came to meetings,
John Moir says, 'a few of their relatives said to me, "thanks
very much, my dad's moved", "my mother told me to tell the
committee", and things like that.' Similarly, Georgina Atkinson
thinks that the community 'felt it was their committee, you
couldn't walk up the street but there was somebody, everyone was
interested.' From the vantage point of the local shop that she
worked in, Mrs Atkinson feels that people came in simply to see

'what was happening':

> 'Folk came in and told me if they got offered a house
> or anything like that. They would come in and tell you
> about vandals, the factor stopping doing repairs and
> things. You got a lot of folk coming in. The shop was
> always packed but it wasn't with customers.'

Ella Donnelly, who worked in another local shop, found that people
who could not manage to attend meetings would come in the next day:

> '"What happened at the meeting last night?" I would
> say this or that and the next thing or whatever it was
> we discussed. "Oh that's great." "Do you think we
> will get this or do you think this will happen?"
> These people felt involved.'

Eileen Kelly remembers that after the Monday night committee meetings 'on a Tuesday, you went to the butcher's or somewhere and
someone would come in, "what happened, is there anything new?"'
Jeannette Bouse maintains that the ordinary resident 'might not
have wanted to join but they were very willing to help, you could
chap the door and ask them for help and you very, very seldom got
a refusal'.

Every Gairbraid household received thirteen newsletters, of
which Davey Bouse says 'an awful lot of people just wouldn't come
out of their houses until these things were put in their hands'.
Jimmy Gallagher feels that 'we actually told them everything on
that pamphlet, how to go about progressing their own situation'.
Jackie Moir stresses that the newsletters gave the community 'an
assurance, at least once a month that there was still someone
concerned about their problems .... They knew if they did run
into trouble, the committee was there.' Eileen Thompson considers that they were

> 'one of the most important things, because people felt a
> part of it when they got a newsletter. It was an instant
> source of communication, therefore, people were always up
> to date, they knew exactly what was going on. I think
> that was fantastic, it was the only way to do it.'

By the time newsletters were discontinued, the remaining residents
were being visited at least once a week by committee members.

Annie Mallon firmly holds that the ordinary resident 'learnt
a lot' during the campaign, for instance, about 'Corporation
policy that they never knew before'. The GHC operated on the
general principle that the more pressure placed on the authorities
the better. Thus, in addition to advocating on behalf of
individuals, people were always encouraged to pursue their own
cases and members readily passed on all the knowledge and expertise
they had gained on how best to approach the authorities. The most
important function of the GHC, Margaret Hobson considers, was:

> 'letting people know how they stood and letting them
> know how to go about things. There were a lot of people
> who went down to Clive House at first and took a lot of
> cheek. They really did and they got offered right bangers;
> houses that were worse than they were staying in. To me
> the committee's best achievement was that people got this
> across through the committee and they knew that they could
> go down to Clive House, what their chances were before they

went, how to go about it, and to hang on and wait for what
they wanted.'
In the beginning, Annie Mallon remembers, 'people were scared to
go near Clive House, they just came away broken hearted'. After
the first flood of poor offers, Eileen Thompson feels that people
'thought if we don't stick together this is all we are going to
get'. Betty Gallagher insists that but for the GHC people 'would
never have rejected as many houses as they did even though they
were in bad condition', and she adds:

'People lost the fear they had to start with. When they
got the one offer and were told to look for other accommodation, they were terrified because we met them in the streets
and we had to advise them. We used to say, "Don't listen to
them, they must offer you a house, they won't be putting you
out".'

The residents, John Moir feels, 'have realized that you get nothing
unless you are organized'. Eileen Thompson thinks that they will
now be 'more inclined to join a tenants' organization where they
probably wouldn't have bothered before'. Georgina Atkinson
observes that 'there was never anything like that up in Maryhill,
tenants' association or anything', and continuing, adds that now
'there are an awful lot of them that would like to try and form
a committee.' Margaret Hobson points to the example of one former
resident who, although previously inactive, 'has got involved in
the tenants' association because she knew that the Gairbraid
committee had achieved a lot'.

It appears that while many former Gairbraid residents have
joined tenants' associations in their new areas, only a few have
so far become actively involved. Hugh and Eileen Thompson are,
since leaving Gairbraid, probably the most active of all the
committee members. Eileen attributes this involvement to
Gairbraid:

'We have discovered we've got a talent for mixing it with
the Corporation. We have been mixing it ever since. It
made you aware of the community as a whole so now we have
rolled right into the community here. If that hadn't
happened, we probably wouldn't have been involved in the
tenants' association here and therefore, I would not have
been involved in an advice centre either.'

The Hobsons and Bouses are involved in the new tenants' association
in their area and Jackie Moir and Jimmy Gallagher in theirs. On
the whole, however, ex-GHC members have not become actively involved in their new communities. Perhaps after the excitement of
crisis organizing in Gairbraid, the everyday concerns and formality of tenants' associations may seem dull and boring.

ATTITUDES TO THE LABOUR PARTY

Maryhill is solidly working-class and its political representatives
are traditionally members of the Labour Party. The campaign in
Gairbraid was a clash between a working-class community and a
Labour-dominated local authority. Although housing is intrinsi-
cally bound up with politics, the GHC was not overtly political,

and representing neither Party nor ideology, it conducted a purely
localized campaign. The committee was open to all Gairbraid
residents, indeed, to any Glaswegian in dispute with Clive House.
No one was ever disqualified for their beliefs and the members are
proud of the fact that the GHC was non-religious, non-racial and
non-political. While the residents were mostly disinterested in
the wider political implications of their struggle, the campaign
could not but reflect on Glasgow's rehousing policy and practice
for which, as it happened, Labour were responsible. The Gairbraid
activists emerged from their campaign aware of the power of
community groups, knowledgeable in the workings of local government, cynical of the political processes and, in varying degrees,
disillusioned with the Labour Party. For most of the community,
contact with the Labour Party was restricted to the Maryhill
councillors on whose performances Labour was judged. Their unenviable task was to gain local acceptance of a policy which
operates to the disadvantage of the majority of Glasgow's prospective tenants. As the councillors mostly chose to occupy the
middle ground between the community and the power structure, even
on those occasions where their support was unequivocal, the GHC
invariably regarded their motives with suspicion. The gulf
between Gairbraid and its political representatives was bound to
affect attitudes towards the Labour Party.

All but three of the eighteen Gairbraid residents interviewed
were Labour supporters, the exceptions being two Scottish Nationa-
lists and a Tory non-voter. By the end of the campaign, six of
the fifteen Labourites considered no longer voting at all. Even
among those who continue to support the Labour Party, few seem
to do so with any enthusiasm. 'They say that Labour does a lot
for working-class people, well, in Gairbraid they proved that
they were not bothering their face,' declares Isa Hanlon who still
votes Labour because 'most working-class people do'. Ella
Donnelly remains loyal because Labour is the 'best out of a bad
lot', while Jimmy Gallagher, although still a staunch supporter,
feels that 'it does not matter if there's a Labour or Tory
Council'.

While attitudes towards the councillors differ quite considerably, all are convinced that their contributions were at best
limited. In Jackie Moir's view 'they were helpful in a mild way
but we don't owe a great deal of our success to the councillors'.
While stressing that it is a 'thankless job', John Moir states
that 'if I hear one councillor, I have heard them all'. Ella
Donnelly believes that, although helpful, 'without the committee
the councillors were absolutely useless'. Similarly, Adam Hobson
feels that 'you had to push them a wee bit to try and get somewhere because if you just let them go their own way, I don't
think that you would have got any satisfaction'. Annie Mallon
recalls that until the GHC was formed 'the only time I ever saw
a councillor was, what do you call him, outside the gate on election day'. John Smith excuses a councillor by saying 'he didn't
know much about our problems because he was only voted in about a
couple of months before'. Margaret Hobson believes that there
were 'an awful lot of folk disappointed in their councillors',
while Ella Donnelly 'felt sorry' for one of them who she believes

'really tried but the job was too big for him'. The councillors
often complained about being excluded from the GHC's decision-
making, but when asked, all the committee members felt that under
the circumstances greater co-operation was neither possible nor
even desirable. 'We did everything we could', Jackie Moir
believes, 'but they really didn't want to be involved'. Betty
Gallagher feels that 'on certain issues we forced their hand, they
had to move or they'd get a showing up'. John Moir maintains
that 'we were doing part of the work for them, if the councillors
had been half as interested as we were, we could have done a lot
more'.
     Conflict arose through differences in role perception: the
councillors wished to represent the community as leaders and
spokesmen, while the GHC, not wishing to surrender control over
its own affairs, expected their political representatives to use
their position and power to advance the local cause. All
decision-making, the GHC believed, was the prerogative of the
local community which obviously limited the councillors' functions.
The councillors' demand for leadership was considered quite un-
tenable as very often they did not support the GHC's programme.
At its formation, as a matter of principle, the GHC excluded
councillors from decision-making, and as the campaign progressed
an assessment of the existing power structure in Glasgow suggested
that there was no reason to revise this policy. Many of the
members came to believe that power tends basically to rest with
officialdom rather than with the elected representatives. Eileen
Kelly, for instance, says: 'I don't think the councillors had as
much influence, not even a quarter of what we thought they had
and I feel that the committee accomplished more than the councillors did.' Betty Gallagher believes that 'they're limited, they
can only be involved so much and then they have to restrain
themselves'. John Moir thinks that the council is 'a shambles':
     'An honest man wouldn't take that job, three weeks would be
     his limit. He could not, to be honest with himself, sit
     there and listen to that drivel. He would need to pack in
     or be right rebellious and then he would be on his own and
     he probably wouldn't get anywhere anyway.'
Jeannette Bouse thinks that councillors 'don't like stepping out
of line too far, and that their basic attitude to Gairbraid was
'I'll humour them'. Hugh Thompson criticizes the councillors,
saying that they simply 'stuck to the rules', while Jackie Moir
feels that they merely regarded Gairbraid as 'a nuisance'.
When pressing for the house he was eventually offered Adam Hobson
was told by a councillor that 'there was no hope for me, yet he
was the one who was supposed to be fighting the case to get us it'.
     Failing to obtain their unqualified support, the role that the
GHC defined for the local councillors was advocacy on behalf of
individuals. The councillors resented this, as to them housing
is more a matter of politics, policy and planning than it is of
dealing with individual cases, and as a consequence a great deal
of mutual antagonism arose. It is little wonder that perspectives
and priorities differed so widely; it is difficult for people
who actually live in dilapidated room-and-kitchens to forego their
sense of personal urgency in order to appreciate another's vision

of the city in future decades. This conflict in attitude and life-experience is, as Hindess observes, a general phenomenon, typical of a local Labour Party and its working-class constituents which provides considerable 'scope for misunderstanding' (2).

The GHC had no contact at all with the local Member of Parliament, and although he had represented Maryhill for many years he seemed better known in Gairbraid by name than by sight. For example, displayed in the Maryhill Labour Rooms was a picture of the one local councillor not involved with the GHC, and for months the playgroup mothers mistakenly thought it was of the MP. Hiring their premises was the GHC's sole contact with the Maryhill Labour Party and no encouragement, not the slightest, was ever received from them. Before the GHC was formed Jimmy Gallagher attempted unsuccessfully to become a member of the local Labour Party but 'you didn't get much assistance from the people there, they weren't giving you any incentive to join'. Alone among the committee members Jimmy Gallagher feels that the GHC might have been more effective had it attempted to operate within the Labour Party - 'to push them to do things'. Whether the GHC would have been tolerated inside the Labour Party is debateable and certainly, the local branch made no attempt to recruit any of the local activists. The Maryhill Labour Party, although claiming to represent working-class interests in the area, was, if not actually hostile, totally indifferent to Gairbraid. In Glasgow and apparently in many other places too, the problems associated with rehousing have seemingly ceased to be the concern of the local ward Labour Party. Hindess, writing of (3) 'the present weakness of the Labour organization in working class areas of cities', suggests that the working class no longer attempt to obtain control over housing policy through the local Labour Party but instead form tenants' associations and community organizations.

The City of Glasgow stands as an indictment of its Labour Party. The decaying tenements of the inner city and outwards the new drab uniformity of its massive housing estates are together, in different ways, stark reminders of Labour's failure to alter significantly the balance of power in favour of the mass of its working-class population. The events in Gairbraid suggest that if Labour once viewed rehousing from a local perspective, it has long since lost all interest. In whatever way Gairbraid is perceived, the struggle was undeniably directed against the city's Labour administration. If it is allowed that Gairbraid's was a just cause, it becomes impossible to exempt Labour, whose majority was unassailable, from severe criticism. Local government as a democratic institution is quite meaningless unless the majority group have control over both policy and administration.

Gairbraid stands as an indictment of Labour perhaps most fundamentally because it failed to recognize the GHC as a genuine expression of working-class aspirations. By ignoring its own potential grassroots support, the party seemed to divorce itself from its natural base, promising future sterility. The Gairbraid campaign was an expression of local talent and potential, which Labour, in so far as it reacted, attempted to thwart rather than to encourage. A local party which can afford to ignore, virtually on its own door step, the talents of a Jimmy Gallagher, John Moir,

Eileen Thompson or a Jackie Moir to mention but a few, is either
in the extremely improbable position of having more such members
than it can cope with, or else has become so moribund that anyone
with energy and independence is considered a threat. The fact of
the matter is that in the first place organization in Gairbraid
should not have been left to outside community action but more
properly should have been the responsibility of the labour movement. The solution to Britain's housing problem awaits the
emergence of a mass, genuinely socialist, working-class party.
     Gairbraid's enforced isolation from the mainstream of the labour
movement ensured that the GHC's attack on housing policy remained
largely devoid of ideological content. It meant that once
Gairbraid itself was cleared the campaign would be discontinued;
with no permanent structures available, it could not but be otherwise. It is suggested that had the labour movement identified
with Gairbraid, offered an umbrella of support, genuine concern
and had attempted to advise rather than control, then it would
have gained for itself the gratitude of the Gairbraid people.
Had such an organization been able to utilize the knowledge and
expertise of the GHC, then most of the members would have been
only too willing to continue working for the benefit of people in
areas elsewhere in the city. The labour movement by ignoring
Gairbraid not only lost the GHC leadership, it also missed the
opportunity to earn the support of all the other residents.
Politically, the Labour Party purports to represent working-class
interests; in the field of rehousing at least, it appears to have
abdicated all responsibility. Gairbraid certainly felt abandoned
by the Labour Party. In that many of the members still vote for
the party, it is entirely in spite of rather than because of
Labour's role in Gairbraid.

THE COMMUNITY WORKER'S ROLE

In all probability Gairbraid would not have organized but for outside intervention in the area. The emergence of a local leadership
is a complex process, dependent upon the personalities and issues
involved, existing social relationships, chance and not least of
all, the influence of the community workers. It is usually a
mistake for outsiders to attempt to initiate a local organization
simply by calling a public meeting in the belief that leaders will
come forward. It is as likely as not to result in the formation
of a non-representative group with the one middle-class resident
being elected as chairman. The natural selection of leaders must
of course be encouraged but chance alone will not necessarily
produce the best leadership and it is here, at the beginning, that
the community worker's role is vital. The professionals in
Gairbraid were accorded high status by virtue only of being middle-
class in a solidly working-class area. Thus, in discussing local
problems, the mere act of frequently visiting some rather than
other individuals while encouraging them to participate also served
to single them out as potential leaders. It is not simply a matter
of status transference nor manipulation, but without encouragement
some people hesitate to become involved. Not all want to be

leaders, while others lack self-confidence and have to be convinced that the effort will be worthwhile. It is no small thing
for a resident to embark upon a campaign against a powerful local
authority, sacrificing much of his spare time, where in the end
the only consequence might be to jeopardize his own chances of
rehousing. The outsider does not impose a leadership on the
community but rather, his function is to ensure that the most able
and widely acceptable people are prepared to accept activist roles.
To be landed with the wrong committee can be disastrous and even
though it is neither possible nor desirable that the outsider
should control all the influencing factors, the organization formed
is ultimately his responsibility. It is an organizational failure
when committees do not get off the ground - the working class, as
Gairbraid yet again demonstrated, can provide its own capable
leadership and people are seldom apathetic without reason.
       The community workers stimulated, encouraged and sometimes sus-
tained the GHC. The physical resources provided, such as a meeting
place, a telephone, typing and duplicating facilities, made
organizing that much easier. The middle class seeking to protect
its interests has easy access to the seats of power; it knows the
rules; information and expertise are readily available to it; it
can, through its social mobility, quickly and effectively participate in the democratic process. In these terms, the working class
is clearly disadvantaged, it can muster few if any resources, its
grievances are not accepted as legitimate, it does not even speak
the same language as the power structure. The community worker
is not there to act as an intermediary between local people and
the authorities, nor is he to pose as the 'expert'. His role is
to ensure that the community acquires the skill and confidence to
conduct its own campaign and to make available resources otherwise
not normally to be found in the area. People do not only need
'expert' advice, they need to know how and where to find it. The
community worker's role is to equalize the contest. In Gairbraid,
the community workers' range of contacts with housing specialists,
lawyers and others was important and in the case of the television
people was crucial.
       The community worker is in a sense general secretary to the
organization, influential but with no voting or negotiating rights,
a 'paid' servant who ideally should be employed by the community.
Where residents are continually leaving a clearance area, the outsider provides continuity as the local leadership constantly
changes. During crises, local activists very often spend every
evening and all week-end organizing in the community. The professional, being full-time, needs whenever possible to undertake the
necessary but time-consuming and boring tasks which might otherwise
be neglected or be too demanding of the local activists. Being an
outsider, the community worker also has a diplomatic function
within the community, to smooth over personality clashes which
inevitably occur whenever groups of people come together. The
unity of the organization must at all times be maintained and
individual loyalties must not be allowed to interfere. Being
paid, the professional has the time to devote considerable thought
to the various possibilities available and to the contingencies
that might occur. He is thus an 'ideas man' who must anticipate

crisis; temporary set-backs cause despondency and become permanent defeats unless the group is able quickly and effectively to take counter-action. For instance, when interviews at Clive House were stopped a delay could easily have destroyed the GHC but instead was turned to the community's advantage.

The aim in Gairbraid was to work through the GHC, the main two-way line of communication being professionals to the leaders to the community. The GHC disproved the myth of professional expert-ise when on several occasions, they were right and the community workers wrong. Perhaps the best example is when, against outside advice, they decided to go ahead with the first demonstration at Clive House. Whatever is owed to the community workers, one thing at least is certain, they owe a great deal to the community. Many theoretical conceptions about community action were revised with the help of local ideas. For instance, it was assumed that had Gairbraid been organized sooner, say a year rather than three months before rehousing began, more might have been achieved. Thus, instead of being faced with a fait accompli, the community might have been able to insist on being rehoused together and fewer people would have felt obliged to accept the first, inferior offers that they received. Clearly, an area where there is strong social cohesion is in a better position to react immediately and challenge local authority decisions than are areas which are disorganized. Various social activities, such as an adventure playground or an old folks' club, could have been organized before rehousing became an issue. Would these really have helped the community in its later struggle? The committee members think not; without exception they are convinced that organization in Gairbraid was started at roughly the most appropriate time. Their view fundamentally challenges what has virtually become a conventional wisdom in community work, that socially orientated group activity, as a means to an end, will develop into organizations capable of meeting crisis situations when these arise. The most persuasive argument against this strategy is that the leadership who emerge around social issues are likely to be different to those who come to the fore during a crisis.

Tenants' associations are themselves by no means immune to bureaucratic behaviour, and in crisis situations control by people with conventional ideas will, if not entirely pre-empt a more radical response, cause conflict and division within the community during a time when unity is absolutely essential. The strategy of organizing in anticipation of a crisis seems to be based on a static conception of leadership: that in any given community, the same leadership will emerge irrespective of the issue. The lessons from Gairbraid suggest that this is a misguided notion: there were in fact a great many people in the area with leadership potential. Depending on the issue, any number of different indi-viduals might have been active. There is nothing to suggest that someone who runs a youth club, for instance, will also have the inclination or, more crucially, the ability, to confront the Corporation over their housing policy. Extreme caution needs to be exercised before organizing around relatively minor and non-contentious issues in the belief that this will develop into community action, for the consequences could in fact be negative.

On reflection, the local activists rather than the academic
theorists were proved right in Gairbraid; organization prior to
the GHC would probably have deflected from, rather than aided,
the later campaign.

It is pointless attempting to apportion praise; it suffices
to say that without the active participation of the local community the campaign in Gairbraid would have been impossible.

COMMUNITY ACTION IN CLEARANCE
AREAS

Glasgow's Director of Planning, commenting on the adverse effects
of large-scale migration from the City, writes that those who
leave (4) 'are generally people who are economically and biologi-
cally active and of higher than average capability and ambition'.
The implication, for which no evidence exists, is that those who
remain are none of these things. It stereotypes Glasgow's population, particularly of the inner city, as mostly feckless and
apathetic and is used to justify the glaring lack of participatory
democracy available to the ordinary working-class citizen. The
residents of·clearance areas are denied the opportunity of involvement in decision-making about their own futures because they
are deemed incapable and, moreoever, disinterested in so doing.
While it is predictable that such attitudes will be expressed by
the authorities, it is disheartening to find that Shelter, in
Maryhill, after much good work in the area, should come to the
same conclusions. Their housing advice centre, opened in December
1971 on the Maryhill Road about a mile from Gairbraid, had 'local
organization' as one of its objectives. The failure to achieve
this aim is explained by: (5)

    the type of area in which we are working; i.e. a clearance
    area with great uncertainty as to the future, with ward
    committees and tenants' associations dedicated to the more
    established ongoing community and perhaps not so involved
    with individuals who are in a less stable position. This
    is no criticism of their efforts but involvement by local
    activists is necessary in order to remedy situations which
    are causing the plight of individuals in this area.

If being unaware, virtually on their own door-step, of the GHC,
is an indication of general unfamiliarity with the area, it is
hardly surprising that Shelter failed to stimulate a local organization. Basically, their attempt failed because advocacy on behalf
of individuals, as practised by the Shelter organizers, creates
dependency rather than initiative; local groups seldom emerge from
welfare rights campaigns. The Shelter report assumes that local
activism is a synonym for tenants' association and clearly dis-
counts the possibility that people in clearance areas may also
provide their own articulate leaders.

The message from Gairbraid is clear: the potential for local
leadership and organization in clearance areas is enormous. If
Shelter, let alone the Corporation, is unaware of this surely
obvious fact, what about the people never directly involved in
the rehousing process? There can be no doubt of the ability,

dedication and commitment possessed by the members of the GHC nor for that matter, of the qualities shown by the ordinary resident through whose continued support only, was a sustained campaign made possible. Gairbraid was not unique, and given the resources its successes could be repeated in any one of the country's many clearance areas. Millions of people in Britain are forced to suffer poor housing conditions and have, as their only means of escape, to subject themselves to an often scandalously bureaucratic process of rehousing by their local authority. The telling of the Gairbraid story, if it manages to dispel a single stereotype, if it encourages further community action and, above all, if it inspires any resident in any clearance area anywhere to organize and demand his rights, will have been worthwhile.

Chapter 12

REFORM THROUGH COMMUNITY ACTION

There are very few instances during the life of the Gairbraid
treatment area from which Glasgow Corporation might be said to
emerge with any credit. Even ignoring relatively minor irritants
such as the non-availability of keys to view houses under offer,
the GHC's list of grievances covers the entire rehousing process.
Gairbraid had reason to object strongly to the following main
aspects of Glasgow's policy and practice:

    the lack of information and consultation;
    the timing of the treatment programme;
    the housing visitor's report;
    the quality of offers of alternative accommodation;
    the disrepair of relet houses;
    the behaviour of the clerks at Clive House;
    the inaccessibility of authority;
    prolonged rehousing and the lengthy period of waiting for
    offers;
    the inflexibility of the regulations;
    the neglect of old people;
    the failure to maintain essential services;
    the inefficient boarding-up of empty property;
    inadequate police protection against vandalism;
    delays in receiving compensation;
    the non-receipt of well maintained payments.

The list of complaints is virtually endless. The issues central
to the GHC campaign remain unresolved. Glasgow has not reformed,
on the contrary, Clive House is (1) 'to initiate a more rigid
means of dealing with waiting list applicants who refused to
accept offers in areas for which they would qualify'. A survey
(2) conducted between May and June 1974 in the Oatlands treatment area shows experiences there to be depressingly similar to
those of Gairbraid. Old people, some of whom had between forty
and sixty years' tenancy, were equally neglected, receiving fewer
offers than other residents. Offers too were determined by
grading rather than by choice: while only one resident indicated
a preference for the Castlemilk estate, out of the sixty-two
offers reported, twenty were for that area. While the Corporation
made 'no attempt' to board up empty flats, Oatlands was plagued by

vandalism - one lady left alone in a tenement 'polished the brass on all the doors in the close so that vandals would not think that the flats were empty'. The Oatlands survey could have been written about Gairbraid two years previously and Oatlands could have provided the scenario for the later Robson Street treatment area: (3) out of 283 offers received there only thirty-nine were acceptable. Gairbraid, Oatlands and Robson Street were all organized: what of the majority of Glasgow's treatment areas where there is no organization?

RESISTANCE TO CHANGE

To many in Gairbraid, official policy often seemed heartless, self-defeating and inexplicable. However, rehousing in Glasgow cannot simply be dismissed in these terms. Reference to bureaucracy provides only a partial explanation, ignoring the functional aspects of existing policy. Rehousing must be viewed in the overall context of the city's housing problems. Cullingworth and Watson found that (4) 25 per cent of Corporation houses in Glasgow were either below or just above the tolerable standard. A third of all Glasgow's Corporation houses were built between the wars and a small percentage are pre-1919. All things being equal, people tend to prefer new to old council houses but even the new, if considered badly situated, are not necessarily prized. In 1972, at the height of the Gairbraid campaign, Clive House allocated (5) 12,111 houses of which 3,028 were new, that is, of every four families accommodated only one received a new house.

The Housing Department must first solve the problem, at least to its own satisfaction, of whom from the mass of families in need it will next rehouse. These must then be fitted to the houses that are available for allocation, most of which will be neither new nor generally desirable. Essentially, a local authority must bully, threaten, misinform and force people into accepting houses which they do not want and which they would not choose for themselves. This, together with the general housing shortage, is the dilemma facing Glasgow Corporation and, in a nutshell, is the issue that dictates all of Glasgow's rehousing policy and practice. It is what the Gairbraid campaign was all about; four into one won't go.

It appears that Glasgow now tells people in clearance areas how they are to be affected which, compared to Gairbraid, is a welcome change in practice. However, information is still not provided about the timing of the treatment programme, when it will begin, how long it will take and most crucially, what choice of house and district will be available. Telling people about the decisions taken about them, if nothing else, is good public relations. Beyond that, however, a really well informed public may not easily be persuaded to accept inferior housing, and thus local authorities seldom provide their prospective tenants with the sort of information normally given to private home buyers. While acknowledging the problems involved, Cullingworth feels (6) that 'local authorities have to try to surmount these difficulties in order to provide the information which people have the right to expect and the advice which they need'.

As conditions were not desperate, rehousing from Gairbraid could have waited until other local clearances were completed. Most people usually wish to be rehoused in their neighbourhood, but instead of regulating rehousing according to the number of vacancies locally available, the Corporation simultaneously cleared several adjoining areas which, in a sense, artificially created a situation of shortage. This enabled them to justify poor quality offers and delays in rehousing. Where the offer of a decent house to one man brings joy to him and disappointment to his neighbours, solidarity of purpose amongst tenants may become fragile. It is obviously the kind of competitive situation that any local authority, eager to avoid organized opposition, would welcome if not deliberately create. Above all else, scarcity enabled the authorities to convince people of the necessity of accepting second best. In an area where demand greatly exceeds supply, people will often try to increase their chance of an early move by opting for less popular areas, and thus inferior houses in these relatively low amenity districts are filled. If people were fully consulted and able to meaningfully participate in decision-making and influence the timing of their rehousing, then the Corporation's difficulty in letting unwanted houses would undoubtedly increase. If rehousing in Gairbraid had been delayed until other clearances in the vicinity had been completed, and others not started until Gairbraid had been cleared, fewer houses outside Maryhill would have been accepted. The fact that people were not consulted, at the same time as it limited individual choice, also acted to increase greatly the Corporation's power and control.

While the GHC was formed too late to influence the timing of the Gairbraid clearance, a major campaign was mounted against the housing visitor's form. There can be no doubt that the people of Gairbraid were better housed than they would have been had the GHC not existed. That is, for Gairbraid, the grading system was in large measure made inoperative. Although the Corporation was forced to alter the wording of the housing visitor's report, in terms of permanent, meaningful reform the GHC was no more successful in changing the grading system than it was in achieving consultation.

As a means of accurate assessment, the grading system can have little value. It is without any semblance of scientific validity or reliability and in these terms, as a means of classification, it is essentially nonsense. However, to attack its validity may miss the point for it may not be meant to function as an accurate measure at all. What ever else it fails to do, the grading system gives the Housing Department authority and power and provides it with an instrument of control. A tenant cannot be told that he is being offered a house because of a draw out of a hat. Allocations need authority and the aura of expertise that surrounds a formal system. The requirement is not accuracy nor even fairness which, under the circumstances, are anyway near impossible to achieve, but rather its purpose is to increase the possibility of acquiescence. Above all else, the Housing Department needs docility and acceptance of its decisions which need at least to appear reasonably consistent and impartial. The grading system

performs these functions. It provides an inherently chaotic
system with a rationale, order and a feeling of finality - if one
offer matches personal grading so will the next and, therefore, to
refuse the first may seem pointless.

In the above terms, grading is not a lunatic measure that in
the face of all the available evidence, the Corporation, for some
inexplicable, bureaucratic reason, insists on retaining. On the
contrary, the grading system is the very essence of housing policy.
In addition to being both relatively easy and inexpensive to
administer - no specially trained staff are required - it ensures
that the Corporation firmly controls all house allocation decisions.
It fills unwanted houses. The meaningless changes to the visitor's
report can thus be understood. Short of Clive House grinding to a
halt, there was never any real possibility of the changes being
otherwise. So too, the reluctance to grant the principle of rehousing communities en bloc may be explained. To do so on any
large scale would involve scrapping the grading system.

Every reform proposed by the GHC which appeared even slightly
to alter the balance of power in favour of the community was
either ignored or neutralized through meaningless changes. Discontent was silenced by promises of reform never fulfilled.
Throughout, the Corporation assiduously avoided according any
rights to the individual. For instance, complaints about the
clerks at Clive House resulted not in any administrative changes
but in a staff reshuffle. In spite of firm promises by the
Housing Manager, prospective tenants are still not able to
present lists of repairs required to relet property. Although
confirmed in the Corporation minutes, senior officials have not
been assigned to each treatment area in the city. The proposals,
by making the authorities both accessible and accountable, demanded not minor administrative changes but a transfer of power.
It is suggested that once real participation was seen as a
possible consequence, the reform was immediately axed.

DIVIDE AND RULE

'If we look more closely into the machinery of capitalist democracy', wrote Lenin, (7) '...we shall see restriction after
restriction upon (genuine) democracy, ...in their sum total these
restrictions exclude and squeeze out the poor from politics, from
active participation in democracy.' The rehousing process throughout Britain is characteristically undemocratic. The organized
labour movement, because it has concerned itself with industrial
as distinct from community problems, has left the individual
caught up in rehousing largely to his own devices. Blackburn
could well add clearance areas to his list when he writes: (8)
'If the labour movement is to defend itself effectively then it
must learn how to take up the cause of its most vulnerable and
exploited sectors, such as immigrants and women workers.' Betty
Gallagher asks: 'Do you think the trade union movement is aware
of the conditions that some people are living in or maybe, they
just don't care?' She goes on to point out: 'You're modernized
in your work and you haven't even got an inside toilet in your

home, you haven't even got hot running water.'

Rehousing is 'tolerated' because the isolated individual has little choice but to accept existing administrative procedures. If he refuses what the authorities have decided for him, he does so at his own peril, without the assurance that it will be worthwhile or that he will ultimately succeed. He faces threats, if not actual eviction or alternatively will simply be left until last in what rapidly becomes intolerable conditions. He can but wage a war of nerves. In a battle between the individual and the institutions, it will most certainly be the former who expends the nervous energy, for it is he and not the institution who stands to gain or lose.

The individual awaits the offer of accommodation with no certainty of when or where this will be. If he rejects an offer he does not know when the next will arrive or whether it will be an improvement. Glasgow's house letting regulations are hardly a charter of tenant rights: (9) 'If an applicant refuses any offer for reasons which in the opinion of the Housing Manager are not good and sufficient, consideration of the application may be suspended for a period of up to one year.' This clause exemplifies the discretionary power of the local authority, determining who will receive what house, where, and deciding for the individual what is 'good and sufficient'. Such decisions are without obligation to justify or explain and are unhindered by rights of appeal. It amounts to almost absolute control of the supply and allocation of houses and establishes a relationship between local authority and tenant of superiority-inferiority, of power and dependence.

Basically, people have to wait and endure while the Corporation decides about their future. Power is vested with the local authority and the well-being of the family caught up in the rehousing process depends almost entirely on chance and the whim of officialdom. It is thus essentially a humiliating experience, and the feeling of helplessness is more profoundly so than the mere lack of toilet facilities. The rehousing process cannot but undermine the confidence, position and authority of parents whose lack of power to alter the situation must be apparent to even the youngest of school children. Parents can only counsel patience as their children complain and rebel against intolerable living conditions. Thus, at an early age, the child is made aware that in the order of things, he, his family and his class, occupy a subordinate position in society from which, even in the provision of housing, little compassion may be expected. It is perhaps small wonder that many of the young turn to vandalism.

If the Gairbraid experience is at all typical, and there is no reason to believe otherwise, then rehousing policy bears responsibility, at least indirectly, for a significant number of the fires in the city. (10) Children started fires in Gairbraid, sometimes with near-tragic consequences, merely to see fire engines in action. Though the problem of vandalism is seldom considered within the context of housing policy, prolonged rehousing is certainly a contributory factor.

The system is unjust and is seen to be unjust. It is tolerated, at least partially, because it has the power to reward. The

individual enters the rehousing process in the hope that he will
be among those favoured. He is not likely to complain about the
lack of participatory democracy if he is offered the house of his
choice. Housing Departments are able to function successfully
because they deal with individuals and not communities. No matter
how capricious a system, those whom it rewards will tend neither
to challenge nor to question it and thus, for organized opposition,
solidarity of purpose is difficult to achieve and easily broken.
As long as it is a decent house that is wanted, and it is unreasonable to expect initial opposition to rehousing policy on any other
basis, the advantage remains with the local authority. Simply, a
suitable offer cannot be refused merely because a neighbour has not
been given the same. Protest based on individual aspirations and
not on principle or ideology is obviously vulnerable.

Glasgow, in common with other local authorities, rehouses its
tenants one by one over a lengthy period of time. (11) Through
continual rehousing, an organized local group will increasingly
be weakened by depopulation, with loss to its leadership and
support. Inevitably, numbers will decline to a point after which
opposition will no longer be viable and the defeat will have to
be admitted. The GHC was able to extend its activities because
members agreed to remain active after being rehoused which postponed but did not avoid final impotence. Such situations are
unavoidable unless people are prepared to fight for rehousing en
bloc which is only likely to occur in traditional, well established
communities such as the Edinburgh mining village of Newcraighall.
However, the loss in leadership and power could be countered if
several clearance areas organized in co-ordinated action against
the local authority.

Housing policy is designed to divide and rule, dealing with
individuals rather than with communities. The advantage of maintaining existing communities are obvious and are acknowledged by
most local authorities including Glasgow. Nevertheless, rehousing
communities en bloc is rarely attempted, perhaps because this
involves a real transfer of power to the local community. While
an individual may be forced to accept an unwanted relet, a
community is less likely to be as easily coerced. The local
authority often dare not, by creating a single community interest,
dispel the belief that 'every man is for himself'.

REHOUSING THROUGH FEAR

Housing Departments cannot easily accommodate criticism - insist-
ence on even the most elementary of rights is usually perceived as
'trouble-making'. To achieve docility, a housing department must
have the ability to penalize malcontents, and control over the
flow of offers gives it its force of sanction. In deciding whether
to accept or reject an offer, the individual faces the implicit
and often loudly articulated threat that to refuse may mean being
left until last before being rehoused. It could involve months
and even years of living under intolerable and dangerous conditions, especially in tenements where even one empty flat may
signify ruin for the whole building. It is a life of coping with

one crisis after another, of living with rising damp and dry rot,
of learning to manage without running water, functioning toilets
or electricity, of never being able to leave the house unattended.
Clearance areas invariably become centres of attraction for
vandalism and petty theft. Houses are frequently flooded, ceilings
collapse and backcourts become cesspools, strewn with muck and
rubbish where mice and rats abound.

It hardly needs to be demonstrated that under such conditions
people are liable to accept houses they would otherwise reject.
However, this limitation on freedom of choice restricts not only
those last in the area, it also affects the first out, for the
fear of being left tarnishes the whole process from beginning to
end. Rehousing has been going on long enough for everyone to
know at least something of what is involved. In Glasgow, it is a
part of working-class culture.

It is unnecessary to argue that delays in rehousing are deliberately engineered so as to create fear. It is sufficient merely to
point to the fact that rehousing in Glasgow takes on average two
years to complete, near the end of which time conditions are quite
intolerable. These conditions arise as a consequence of policy of
which the authorities are fully aware and do nothing to ameliorate.
In Gairbraid, the fear of being left until last influenced the
acceptance of offers long before conditions had actually deteriorated - people knew that sooner or later the area would decline.
In these terms, prolonged rehousing leading to intolerable living
conditions is not an unfortunate but unavoidable aftermath of
policy. On the contrary, it is what enables policy to work.

To shorten the time between when the first and last tenant
leaves would certainly create administrative difficulties. Among
other things, co-ordination, planning and greater efficiency is
required, which in itself may go some way in explaining the local
authority's reluctance to do anything about it. Changes, however,
do not seem beyond the realm of human endeavour. The effort and
expense involved seem little price to pay when compared to what
exists, particularly in Scotland where the predominance of
tenement property ensures that the consequence of prolonged rehousing will be drastic. However, to do so would remove the
'big stick' from housing policy. Remove the element of fear and
control is weakened. It would deprive the administration of its
teeth as the force of sanction is vital to the implementation of
present policy: it is fear that cements the process, creating
acquiescence. As long as rehousing policy exists in its present
form, the end result, of people suffering in unbearable conditions, will remain and cannot be changed without radically altering
the whole process.

IMPLICATIONS

During its campaign, the GHC generated considerable publicity,
adversely reflecting on Glasgow's rehousing policy and practice.
In response, the authorities acknowledged deficiencies in most
aspects of the rehousing process and although reforms were
promised, only marginal changes were ever achieved. In quality

and situation, the available supply of accommodation in Glasgow does not even remotely meet the growing demand for decent houses. The Corporation is resistant to change because it faces an impossible task. If policy did not exist in its present form, for the Housing Department to function, it would have to be invented. It is undemocratic because it must be. The authorities have little room in which to manoeuvre and basically only marginal reform is possible. This is not to say that there cannot be concessions to individuals or even groups, as Gairbraid illustrates. However, these are regarded as special cases which do not alter basic policy. Thus these exceptions to the rules do not alter the assumption that, as the system now stands, reform is impossible.

Different aspects of policy taken singularly may appear to be irrational and even self-defeating, but seen together as mutually supportive parts of an integral system each becomes comprehensible. This argues strongly against piecemeal reform. No part may be radically altered without also disturbing the entire process and seriously undermining the principles governing policy. On these grounds, the relatively few changes achieved by the GHC may be understood. In Gairbraid, local priorities were continually forced to change as different aspects of policy were applied in the area. Pressure could not be maintained on any one grievance long enough to ensure that promised reforms were instituted. Thus, community action in Gairbraid was forced by the demands of the situation to seek piecemeal reform where only total change was possible.

What of the future? Various pundits (12) of the Glasgow scene predict the imminent solution of the city's housing shortage. As a concomitant, it could be argued that as demand for houses decreases so will policy become liberalized. However, the easing of demand is unlikely in itself to produce reform. Meaningful local participation will more probably be achieved through pressure from the grass roots than from policy decisions made at the top. Moreover, given present national and local government priorities, neither in Glasgow nor anywhere else in Britain is housing shortage likely to be overcome in the foreseeable future. Community action needs to concentrate on what exists rather than on what some administrators or academics think might happen. From the bleak standpoint of present-day reality in Glasgow visions of a future where no new public housing needs to be built seem foolishly premature and quite utopian.

Community action, with limited resources and which is geographically localized within a relatively small area, cannot be expected significantly to dent the prevailing power structure. It simply attempts to 'chip away' at existing inequalities in the hope that the cumulative effect may eventually lead to some real reforms. It is a strategy of change through nuisance value which, if persistently applied, may in the end produce some positive results but only where the system is able easily to accommodate change. Housing reform is extremely unlikely to be achieved in this manner. If community action is to pursue social reform in housing it will need to mobilize a great deal more power than it has so far been able to do.

This is not to deprecate the achievements of community action in

organizing small areas around single issues, but merely to say
that the implications of such successes are necessarily limited.
The need for co-ordination in community action is recognized by
the Gulbenkian Community Work Group (13) who call for the establishment of area and national resource centres. What was required
in Gairbraid for bureaucratic control to be seriously threatened
was organization in several clearance areas spread throughout the
city allied in co-ordinated action. If rehousing policy cannot
be reformed, it needs to be totally changed, but real change will
only take place through the power of mass organization able to
force a radical overhaul of policy. It may be that a head-on
collision is necessary whereby the local authority is forced to
admit that it cannot cope and that it will no longer continue to
function as the vehicle through which impossible government policies are administered. Housing must become a major priority in
this country and a massive infusion of interest-free government
funds is required.

Community action needs to ensure not only that a great many
more houses are built but also that a meaningful measure of
local control is exercised over the rehousing process. Community
action, as it is presently financed, sponsored by either local
authorities, central government, charitable trusts or the univer-
sities, is without the resources of freedom of action necessary
to mount a challenge on the scale required. Bryant (14) sees
the solution ultimately in terms of 'a radical realignment in
the politics and organization of the British Labour Movement' and
suggests that support needs to be gained from the trade unions.
To do so, community action must first accept its inherently political function and abandon its pretensions of being a non-
ideological third alternative to the established political order
or the far Left. Community action, if it is to contribute
meaningfully to social change, must attempt to forge for itself
a place, independent if possible, (15) within the mainstream of
working-class politics.

The Gairbraid campaign demonstrated the viability of community
action, showing the potential for leadership existing in a hitherto unorganized working-class community. It exposed the inequalities of Glasgow's rehousing policy and practice. Throughout this
book reforms have been suggested which if implemented could
considerably improve every stage of the rehousing process. However, unless accompanied by meaningful local participation, in the
long term, these would not in themselves greatly alter the situation. Bureaucracy has a talent for adapting to new circumstances
to ensure that little or nothing fundamental is changed. Democracy
is illusionary when exercised solely from above. The majority of
people in Gairbraid were rehoused with a certain amount of choice
and dignity. This was achieved not through reform, for little
was changed, but through the organized power of the community.
An 'ideal' rehousing policy was deliberately not presented here
as this would have simply been yet another blueprint imposed from
the outside. Moreover, it would have missed the whole point of
the Gairbraid campaign: the system cannot be improved. A more
enlightened and efficient bureaucracy is not the answer, but
power to the people.

NOTES

CHAPTER 1 HOUSING: SHORTAGE, DEMAND AND BUREAUCRACY

1 Ministry of Housing and Local Government, 'Council Housing, Purposes, Procedures and Priorities' (The Cullingworth Report), HMSO, 1969, p.24.
2 The 'Guardian', 23 October 1974.
3 'Evening Times', 13 September 1971.
4 Allaun, Frank, 'No Place Like Home', London, Andre Deutsch, 1972, p.193.
5 Barratt Brown, Michael, The Worker's Pound, 'Bulletin of the Institute of Workers' Control', no.10, 1973, p.36.
6 'Shelter Report on Slum Clearance', London, Shelter, 1974.
7 Butt, John, Working-class Housing in Glasgow, 1851-1914, in Chapman, S.D. (ed.), 'The History of Working-class Housing', Newton Abbot, David & Charles, 1971, pp.57-8.
8 'Report of the Glasgow Housing Programme Working Party, 1970', The Corporation of the City of Glasgow and Scottish Development Department, p.18.
9 Williams, Eric, 'Capitalism and Slavery', London, Andre Deutsch, 1967, p.64.
10 Brennan, T., 'Reshaping a City', Glasgow, The House of Grant, 1959, p.19.
11 Butt, op.cit., p.57.
12 Ibid., p.58.
13 Johnston, Thomas, 'The History of the Working Classes in Scotland', Glasgow, Forward Publishing (no date), p.291.
14 Engels, Frederick, 'The Condition of the Working Class in England in 1844', London, Allen & Unwin, 1968, p.37.
15 Ibid., p.38.
16 Hobsbawm, E.J., 'Industry and Empire', Harmondsworth, Penguin, 1969, p.305.
17 Johnston, op.cit., p.281.
18 Ibid., pp.294-5.
19 Ibid., p.284.
20 Cullingworth, J.B., 'Housing and Local Government', London, Allen & Unwin, 1966, p.15.
21 Butt, op.cit., p.61.

22 Ibid., p.85.
23 Ibid., p.85.
24 Hobsbawm, op.cit., p.307.
25 Chapman, op.cit., pp.11-12.
26 Butt, op.cit., p.82.
27 Hobsbawm, op.cit., p.308.
28 Ibid., p.308.
29 Moorhouse, Bert, Wilson, Mary and Chamberlain, Chris,
    Rent Strikes - Direct Action and the Working Class, in
    Miliband, Ralph and Saville, John (eds), 'The Socialist
    Register 1972', London, Merlin Press, p.135.
30 Milton, Nan, 'John Maclean', London, Pluto Press, 1973, p.89.
31 Gallacher, William, 'Revolt on the Clyde', London,
    Lawrence & Wishart, 1936, p.52.
32 'The Times', 18 May 1973.
33 Adam, Corinna, Cleaning up in Glasgow, 'New Statesman',
    7 May 1971, p.617.
34 Mansley, R.D., 'Areas of Need in Glasgow', The Corporation
    of Glasgow, 1972.
35 Report of the Glasgow Housing Working Party, 1970,
    op.cit., p.8.
36 Cullingworth, J.B. and Watson, C.J., 'Housing in Clydeside
    1970', Edinburgh, HMSO, 1971, p.58.
37 'Annual Report 1972', Corporation of Glasgow, Housing
    Management Department, pp.12-13, 15, and 'Annual Report 1971',
    p.16.
38 Jephcott, Pearl, 'Homes in High Flats', Edinburgh,
    Oliver & Boyd, 1971, p.145.
39 'Scottish Miner', no.188, February 1972.
40 Jephcott, op.cit., p.15.
41 'Annual Report 1972', op.cit., pp.10-11.
42 'The Times', 18 May 1973.
43 Quoted by Dennis, Norman, 'People and Planning', London,
    Faber & Faber, 1970, p.341.
44 Noble, Graham, In Defence of Easterhouse, 'New Society',
    20 August 1970, p.328.
45 Dennis, op.cit., p.334.
46 Mansley, op.cit., p.10.
47 Hindess, Barry, 'The Decline of Working Class Politics',
    London, Paladin, 1971, p.53.
48 Mansley, op.cit., p.6.
49 Gans, Herbert, J., 'People and Plans', Harmondsworth,
    Penguin, 1972, pp.188-216.

CHAPTER 2   FROM YOUTH WORK TO COMMUNITY ACTION

1 Coates, Ken, and Silburn, Richard, 'Poverty: The Forgotten
   Englishmen', Harmondsworth, Penguin, 1970, p.233.
2 Alinsky, Saul, 'Reveille For Radicals', New York,
   Vintage, 1969, p.58.
3 Morse, Mary, 'The Unattached', Harmondsworth, Penguin,
   1968, p.223.
4 Smith, C.S., Farrant, M.R. and Marchant, R.J., 'The Wincroft

Youth Project', London, Tavistock, 1972, pp.245-6.
5 Marris, Peter and Rein, Martin, 'Dilemmas of Social Reform',
   London, Routledge & Kegan Paul, 1967, pp.89-90.
6 Worsley, Peter, et al., 'Introducing Sociology',
   Harmondsworth, Penguin, 1970, p.374.
7 Ibid., p.383.
8 Ibid., p.376.
9 'Another Chance for Cities, Snap 69/72', London,
   Shelter, 1972, p.6.
10 Ibid., p.143.
11 Alinsky, Saul, 'Rules for Radicals', New York, Vintage,
   1972, p.119.
12 Coates and Silburn, op.cit., pp.223-4.
13 Bryant, Richard, Community Action, 'British Journal of
   Social Work', vol.2, no.2, 1972, p.206.
14 Holman, Robert, 'Power for the Powerless: The Role of
   Community Action', London, Community and Race Relations
   Unit of the British Council of Churches, 1972, p.5.
15 Gulbenkian Foundation, 'Current Issues in Community Work',
   London, Routledge & Kegan Paul, 1973, p.40.
16 Alinsky (1969), op.cit., p.55.
17 Liddell, Harry and Bryant, Richard, A Local View of Community
   Work, in Jones, David and Mayo, Marjorie (eds), 'Community
   Work One', London, Routledge & Kegan Paul, 1974, p.97.
18 Alinsky (1972), op.cit., p.104.
19 Dennis, Norman, 'People and Planning', London, Faber & Faber,
   1970, p.346.
20 Alinsky (1972), op.cit., p.105.
21 Bryant, op.cit., p.207.
22 Alinsky (1972), op.cit., p.106.
23 Alinsky (1969), op.cit., p.64.
24 Ibid., p.65.
25 Bryant, op.cit., p.209.
26 Ibid., p.209.
27 Marris and Rein, op.cit., p.198.
28 Gans, Herbert, 'People and Plans', Harmondsworth,
   Penguin, 1972, p.326.
29 One of the most active committee members declined to be
   interviewed and thus he does not appear as prominently
   as his very considerable contribution would warrant.

CHAPTER 3   REHOUSING AS AN ISSUE

1 'Sunday Mail', 3 February 1974.
2 Sinclair, Upton, 'The Jungle', Harmondsworth, Penguin, 1965.
3 Young, M. and Willmott, P., 'Family and Kinship in East
   London', Harmondsworth, Penguin, 1969, p.41.
4 The Scottish Development Department, in a letter to the GHC
   dated 16 December 1971, confirmed that the Gairbraid control
   of occupation order was not in the form prescribed in the
   Housing (Forms) (Scotland) Regulations 1969. As no
   prosecution for breach of the order was ever brought, the
   legal implications of this discrepancy were never tested.

CHAPTER 4 FORMING THE GAIRBRAID HOUSING COMMITTEE

1 'Annual Report 1971', Housing Management Department, Corporation of the City of Glasgow, p.7.
2 'Annual Report 1972', ibid., p.7.
3 As things turned out, the Gallaghers did eventually receive the house and district of their choice, while as a result of constant Gairbraid pressure the clerk in question about whom many complained was removed from the counter at Clive House.

CHAPTER 6 THE START OF REHOUSING

1 Dennis, Norman, Half-beating City Hall: the Duke Street Story, 'New Society', 4 October 1973, p.7.
2 For the GHC's purposes, detailed statistical information of rehousing from the area was quite unnecessary. While such records would have greatly assisted in the writing of this book, the time, effort and resources required to keep track constantly of the number of offers received and of movement out of the area could not be justified in terms of local priorities. Once the area was cleared, the Housing Department was asked for details of the monthly rate of rehousing from Gairbraid which, however, they were unable to supply.
3 For example, one young couple with a year-old baby were unable to have their water supply re-connected for over a fortnight. Such experiences still widely persist in Glasgow. The 'Sunday Mail' (25 January 1974) featured the story of a young woman with a three-month-old baby who was without access to running water or toilet facilities. She had twice 'pleaded' to have her water restored, supporting her claim with a letter from her doctor expressing concern about the child's health. A month later she was still without water. Clive House had no explanation of why she, the only tenant left in the building, had not been rehoused. The columnist commented, 'I could fill this page week in week out with scandals like hers.'
4 The power of local groups to compel co-operation from their councillors is illustrated by the action taken by the residents of the Oatlands treatment area in Glasgow when their councillors refused, without explanation, to attend a public meeting. They organized a petition complaining about their councillors and amidst publicity sent copies to Harold Wilson, the local MP, the leader of Glasgow's Labour Group, and the Secretaries of the Scottish Labour Party and the local ward party ('The View', December 1973).
5 The 'Guardian', 17 April 1974.

CHAPTER 7 A WEEK OF ACTION

1 Alinsky, Saul, 'Rules for Radicals', New York, Vintage, 1972, p.128.
2 Ibid., p.129.

3 The resolution was contained in a letter addressed to City Labour Party Delegates. It read:

'Arising from an approach to Branch Committee by members of this Union, Branch Committee have agreed to forward the following resolutions to our delegates of the City Labour Party in order that they may be raised at the earliest opportunity. The evidence of malpractice within the area specified (The Gairbraid Treatment Area) would, Branch Committee consider, apply to other areas of Glasgow under the Corporation Housing Department.

Branch Committee are of the opinion that a Labour administration should be free of any suggestion of bureaucratic practices. The charges are as follows:

(1) Refusal to rehouse people within the area although suitable housing is available.

(2) Insistance that low grade houses in unsuitable areas are continually offered.

(3) Threats of eviction arising from refusals of inferior housing.

(4) Failure of the Corporation to maintain the property in a reasonable condition, in order to force intolerable conditions upon the tenants.

(5) Deliberately misleading statements and insulting behaviour by the staff of the Housing Department.

In the light of the seriousness of these charges, Branch Committee ask the delegates to move the following resolution:

That, the Labour Group and City Labour Party immediately fully investigate these charges and take all necessary action to end such malpractices.'

4 The people of Newcraighall eventually won their struggle when Edinburgh Corporation agreed to rehouse them in new property in the village.

5 'Current Account', BBC Scotland, 15 October 1971. This and all subsequent quotations referring to the television are taken from this programme featuring Gairbraid and Newcraighall.

6 'Scottish Daily Express', 12 October 1971.

7 The 'Glasgow Herald', 12 October 1971.

8 The 'Scotsman', 16 October 1971.

9 'Glasgow News', 25 October 1971; 'Shelter' (Scottish Campaign for the Homeless), December 1971; '7 Days', 23 February 1972; The 'Word' (Glasgow), 10-23 March 1972; 'Focus' (Edinburgh), no.10, October 1972.

10 The 'Glasgow Herald', 29 October 1971.

11 Norman, Peter, A Derelict Policy, 'Official Architecture and Planning', January 1972, p.32.

12 Damer, Sean and Madigan, Ruth, The Housing Investigator, 'New Society', 25 July 1974, p.227.

13 Ministry of Housing and Local Government, 'Council Housing, Purposes, Procedures and Priorities', (The Cullingworth Report), HMSO, 1969, p.31.

14 Ungerson, Clare, 'Moving Home', London, Occasional Papers on Social Administration, no.44, Bell & Sons, 1971, p.15.

15 'Annual Report 1972', Corporation of Glasgow, Housing Management Department, p.56.

16 'Glasgow News', 6-19 December 1971.
17 Damer and Madigan, op.cit., p.226.
18 Norman, op.cit., p.32.
19 Bell, E.M., 'Octavia Hill', London, Constable, 1942, p.178.
20 Cullingworth, op.cit., p.32.
21 Ibid., p.33.
22 Ibid., p.33.
23 Ibid., p.31.
24 Bell, op.cit., pp.177-8.
25 The 'Guardian', 23 June 1973.
26 Damer and Madigan, op.cit., p.227.
27 Cullingworth, op.cit., p.30.
28 Damer and Madigan, op.cit., p.227.
29 Cullingworth, op.cit., p.33.
30 Unemployment in Scotland in September 1971 was 6.2 per cent
    compared to the national average of 3.9 per cent. 'Evening
    Times', 23 September 1971.
31 'Glasgow News', 6-19 December 1971.
32 Letter to the GHC dated 10 December 1971.
33 The 'View', December 1974.
34 'Shelter Report on Slum Clearance', London, Shelter, 1974,
    p.11.
35 '7 Days', 23 February 1972.
36 'Sunday Mail', 9 January 1972.
37 'Daily Record', 18 April 1972.

CHAPTER 8 THE THREAT OF MANY GAIRBRAIDS

1 'Joint Working Party Report on Community Problems', appointed
   by the Corporation of the City of Glasgow and the Secretary of
   State for Scotland, set up on 8 December 1967, p.8. Glasgow's
   Housing Manager is a party to the report.
2 'Annual Report 1972', Corporation of Glasgow, Housing
   Management Department, p.6.
3 'Glasgow News', 25 October 1971.
4 The 'View', December 1974.
5 The 'View', October 1974.
6 'Evening Citizen', 2 February 1972.
7 'Evening Times', 7 February 1972.
8 The 'Glasgow Herald', 8 February 1972.

CHAPTER 9 ORGANIZING FOR REPRESENTATION

1 A survey of attitudes undertaken in Gairbraid in January
   1972 which sampled 145 families, roughly 65 per cent of
   the population, shows that only a minority considered that
   either councillors or the Housing Department were helpful.
   The results obtained are shown in the table on the next
   page.

| | Councillors | | Housing Department | |
	No.	%	No.	%
Helpful	34	23.4	26	17.9
Unhelpful	19	13.1	71	49.0
Mixed feelings	10	6.9	6	4.1
No contact	69	47.6	29	20.0
No response	13	9.0	13	9.0
Total	145	100.0	145	100.0

Thus, of the residents sampled, less than one in four thought that the councillors were helpful while less than one in five thought this of the Housing Department. While almost half the population had negative feelings towards Clive House, relatively few were actually antagonistic towards the councillors. Although rehousing had been in progress in Gairbraid for about six months, almost half the population had not yet found it worthwhile to contact the councillors. Interpreting the results, the attitude mostly expressed towards the councillors was indifference and towards the Housing Department, hostility.

2 'Annual Report 1972', Corporation of Glasgow, Housing Management Department, pp. 16-17.

3 Ibid., p.61.

4 'Report of the Glasgow Housing Programme Working Party, 1970', The Corporation of Glasgow and Scottish Development Department, p.17.

5 Letter from the Housing Manager, Corporation of Glasgow, 6 August 1973.

6 'Report of the Glasgow Housing Programme Working Party, 1970', op.cit., p.18.

CHAPTER 10 PROTEST AT CLIVE HOUSE

1 In slightly different form the case studies here, having been compiled by the GHC, were printed in 'Glasgow News', 19-25 May 1972.

2 The 'Glasgow Herald', 10 April 1972.

3 The 'Glasgow Herald', 13 April 1972.

4 'Evening Times', 12 April 1972.

5 'Evening Citizen', 12 April 1972.

6 'The Glasgow Herald', 13 April 1972.

7 'Daily Record', 13 April 1972.

8 'Scottish Daily Express', 13 April 1972.

9 The 'Scotsman', 13 April 1972.

10 'Scottish Daily Express', 20 April 1972.

11 Letter to the GHC, from the Housing Manager, the Corporation

of Glasgow, 21 April 1972.
12 'Glasgow News', 15-29 May 1972.

CHAPTER 11   THE COMMITTEE IN RETROSPECT

1 'Glasgow News', 5-18 June 1972.
2 Hindess, Barry, 'The Decline of Working Class Politics',
   London, Paladin, 1971, p.76.
3 Ibid., pp.77-8.
4 Mansley, R.D., 'Areas of Need in Glasgow', The Corporation of
   Glasgow, 1972, p.9.
5 SHAC, Glasgow, 'Report', Edinburgh, Shelter, Scottish
   Campaign for the Homeless, (no date).

CHAPTER 12   REFORM THROUGH COMMUNITY ACTION

1 The 'View', December 1974.
2 Cooper, Gerald, 'A Report on a Survey Conducted in the Oatlands
   Housing Treatment Area', 8 May-21 June 1974, unpublished.
3 The 'View', November 1974.
4 Cullingworth, J.B. and Watson, C.J., 'Housing in Clydeside
   1970', Edinburgh, HMSO, 1971, p.60.
5 'Annual Report 1972', Corporation of Glasgow, Housing
   Management Department, p.13.
6 Ministry of Housing and Local Government, 'Council Housing:
   Purposes, Procedures and Priorities' (The Cullingworth
   Report), HMSO, 1969, p.26.
7 Quoted by Horowitz, David, 'Imperialism and Revolution',
   Harmondsworth, Penguin, 1973, p.346.
8 Blackburn, Robin, Labour and the Marxist Left, 'New Statesman',
   14 September 1973, p.346.
9 Housing Letting Regulations, quoted in 'Annual Report 1972',
   op.cit., p.57.
10 After the fire at St George's Cross in November 1972 in which
   two people died and thirty-one were injured, the Convenor of
   Glasgow's Police and Fire Committee suggested that steps
   should be taken to have all derelict buildings demolished.
   The 'Glasgow Herald', 20 November 1972.
11 In its favour, Glasgow generally does not shunt families from
   one clearance area to another.
12 Mansley, R.D., 'Areas of Need in Glasgow', The Corporation of
   Glasgow, 1972. Also Norman, Peter, A Derelict Policy,
   'Official Architecture and Planning', January 1972.
13 The Gulbenkian Foundation, 'Current Issues in Community Work',
   London, Routledge & Kegan Paul, 1973, pp.134-6.
14 Bryant, Richard, Community Action, 'British Journal of Social
   Work', vol.2, no.2, 1972, p.214.
15 Jordan, for instance, expresses the fear that Claimants' Unions
   could be absorbed by the labour movement and that its activists
   'could very easily be rendered safe and innocuous by these much
   more powerful forces'. Jordan, Bill, 'Paupers', Routledge &
   Kegan Paul, London, 1973, p.72.